Ancient Rome

**Recent Titles in
Historical Facts and Fictions**

The Victorian World: Facts and Fictions
Ginger S. Frost

The Vikings: Facts and Fictions
Kirsten Wolf and Tristan Mueller-Vollmer

American Civil War: Facts and Fictions
James R. Hedtke

The Middle Ages: Facts and Fictions
Winston Black

The History of Christianity: Facts and Fictions
Dyron B. Daughrity

The History of Buddhism: Facts and Fictions
Geoffrey C. Goble

Ancient Egypt: Facts and Fictions
Stephen E. Thompson

Ancient Rome

Facts and Fictions

Monica M. Bontty

Historical Facts and Fictions

BLOOMSBURY ACADEMIC
NEW YORK • LONDON • OXFORD • NEW DELHI • SYDNEY

BLOOMSBURY ACADEMIC
Bloomsbury Publishing Inc
1385 Broadway, New York, NY 10018, USA
50 Bedford Square, London, WC1B 3DP, UK
29 Earlsfort Terrace, Dublin 2, Ireland

BLOOMSBURY, BLOOMSBURY ACADEMIC and the Diana logo
are trademarks of Bloomsbury Publishing Plc

First published in the United States of America by ABC-CLIO 2020
Paperback edition published by Bloomsbury Academic 2024

Copyright © Bloomsbury Publishing Inc, 2024

Cover photo: Vintage colour lithograph from 1881 after the painting
by Gerome of Gladiators in the ancient Roman Arena. (duncan1890/iStockphoto)

All rights reserved. No part of this publication may be reproduced or
transmitted in any form or by any means, electronic or mechanical,
including photocopying, recording, or any information storage or retrieval
system, without prior permission in writing from the publishers.

Bloomsbury Publishing Inc does not have any control over, or responsibility for,
any third-party websites referred to or in this book. All internet addresses given
in this book were correct at the time of going to press. The author and publisher
regret any inconvenience caused if addresses have changed or sites have
ceased to exist, but can accept no responsibility for any such changes.

Library of Congress Cataloging-in-Publication Data
Names: Bontty, Monica M., author.
Title: Ancient Rome : facts and fictions / Monica M. Bontty.
Description: Santa Barbara, California : ABC-CLIO, An Imprint of ABC-CLIO, LLC, 2020. |
Series: Historical facts and fictions |
Includes bibliographical references and index.
Identifiers: LCCN 2019043277 (print) | LCCN 2019043278 (ebook) |
ISBN 9781440855627 (hardcover) | ISBN 9781440855634 (ebook)
Subjects: LCSH: Rome—History.
Classification: LCC DG211 .B66 2020 (print) | LCC DG211 (ebook) | DDC 937—dc23
LC record available at https://lccn.loc.gov/2019043277
LC ebook record available at https://lccn.loc.gov/2019043278

ISBN: HB: 978-1-4408-5562-7
PB: 979-8-7651-2493-2
ePDF: 978-1-4408-5563-4
eBook: 979-8-2160-4790-2

Series: Historical Facts and Fictions

To find out more about our authors and books visit www.bloomsbury.com
and sign up for our newsletters.

Contents

Preface ... vii
Introduction ... ix

1. The Romans Destroyed Carthage and Plowed Salt into the Soil ... 1
2. Cato the Elder Hated Greek and Punic Culture ... 27
3. Caesar's Last Words Were "Et Tu, Brute" ... 49
4. Livia Murdered Augustus's Heirs to Make Tiberius Emperor ... 73
5. Caligula Made His Horse, Incitatus, a Consul ... 97
6. Nero Fiddled While Rome Burned ... 121
7. Romans Vomited in Vomitoria ... 143
8. The City of Rome Was Very Hygienic ... 165
9. Not All Gladiators Were Slaves ... 189

Ancient Sources ... 213
Secondary Sources ... 225
Index ... 235

Preface

Rome sweet Rome. Fifteen hundred years after the end of the Western Empire, books, movies, and television are still infatuated with emperors, gladiators, and tales of intrigue. Why? For one, the United States based its system of government on the Romans, who overthrew their king and created a republic. Furthermore, historians, archaeologists, and philologists have devoted innumerable books and articles to narratives and examinations of their endeavors. Some scholars have focused on the more sensational activities of the Romans, for example, militarism, oppression, slavery, scandalous emperors, out-of-control empresses, gladiatorial contests, excess, and so on. Others have noted the more positive aspects of the Roman Empire, such as aqueducts, baths, and roads that enabled them to communicate throughout a region that stretched from Scotland to the Middle East.

Given the allure of the Romans and the vast amount of attention they have been given by scholars and avocational historians alike, it should come as no surprise that, over time, many misunderstandings have circulated about ancient Rome. Despite websites and articles that point out errors, these misperceptions continue, especially in media productions and sensational documentaries. Such rumors persist because they make the Romans sound fascinating.

This book addresses these tall tales. Some people realize that not all of Rome's emperors were crazy or perverted, yet readers might be surprised to learn that the emperor Nero was actually quite popular or that Livia was a beloved empress and not the evil stepmother 2.0. Many think that gladiators were slaves who fought to the death in the arena. Others fall for the cliché that early Christians were martyred in the Colosseum or that Nero fiddled while Rome burned.

The nine chapters of *Ancient Rome: Facts and Fictions* debunk the most commonly held falsehoods on the ancient Romans. Each chapter is divided into three concise parts. The first is a brief overview of what people believe about the topic, followed by a section detailing how the misunderstanding was popularized. The final part presents evidence exposing the falsehood. The primary documents responsible for the misunderstandings are included after segment two. Sources that clarify the fabrications are located following the third section. This book is written so that you can begin reading wherever you wish. If Nero is your thing, you can start there.

I have many individuals to thank for this book. First, I wish to thank my professors at UCLA for motivating me to learn about the ancient world. Special thanks to the late Professor John Callender, Professor Antonio Loprieno, Professor Elizabeth Carter, and Professor Ronald Mellor. I also thank my sisters, Patricia Harling and Julia Bischoff, for their support. Norma Gurba assisted with primary documents. I am indebted to Dr. Peggy Bowers for many helpful discussions and suggestions. I am obliged to George Butler for giving me the opportunity to write this book. This book is dedicated to the memory of my parents, who introduced me to sword-and-sandal (gladiatorial) movies as a child.

Introduction

Most of Hollywood's movies set in ancient Rome, including contemporary works, are directly based on nineteenth-century historical novels, toga plays, and paintings. Even *Gladiator* (2000) includes essential features such as imperialism, oppression, brutality, and a crazy emperor. Despite articles and websites to the contrary, some still believe the wild confusions on ancient Rome.

The narrative about ancient Rome is replete with stories of crazy, debauched emperors famous for their waste and their enjoyment of killing Christians in the arena. Pop-cultural treatments on ancient Rome generally concentrate on the late Republic and early Empire, partially because the ancient Romans condemned Jesus of Nazareth to crucifixion. However, the Romans did not call their vast expanse an empire. It is a modern concept derived from the Latin verb "*imperare*," meaning to command or rule. Our English word "emperor" comes from the Latin "*imperator*" through the Old French "*empereur*."

Rome's reputation has had its ups and downs throughout the centuries. Narratives of its corruption and decadence began with the early Christian writers and have continued to the present. For example, movies based in the early imperial period depict conquest, oppression, and enslavement of people. Perverted or insane emperors persecuting innocent Christians is another popular trope. Ancient Roman armies were indeed ruthless to anyone who opposed them. Between 509 and 146 BCE, Rome conquered Italy and added parts of North Africa, Iberia, and the eastern Mediterranean. This quick expansion, importation of large numbers of slaves, and foreign influence led to a series of civil wars that eventually resulted in the establishment of one-man rule. Between 40 BCE and 117 CE, Rome conquered vast swathes of land, including Britannia and parts of Germania. Trajan defeated the Dacians and expanded the empire to its largest extent.

Romanization allowed the successful integration of various populations, especially in Western Europe. The Latin language and Roman culture spread, leading to the embrace of many Roman institutions such as aqueducts, public baths, arenas, and gladiatorial contests. Even after the transition of the western empire into early medieval Europe, Roman institutions such as representative democracy, the Roman Catholic Church, and Romance languages are powerful reminders of the enduring memory of Rome.

Despite all of its achievements, the image of ancient Rome has suffered. Roman senators and equestrians wrote about Roman history. Biographers embellished tales of the emperors because the Senate lost all of its power with the establishment of the imperial system. Authors slandered previous emperors in order to make the new emperor happy. These wacky tales should be taken with a grain of salt.

Early Church writers claim that Christians experienced persecution, suffering, and martyrdom during gladiatorial bouts in Rome during the first three centuries of the common era. A main source was the *Accounts of the Martyrdom of Perpetua and Felicity*, a diary written by a young woman killed in the arena along with others at the birthday celebration of Geta, the son of the emperor Septimius Severus in 203 CE, which presents an unflattering portrait of the Romans. Eusebius's graphic depiction of the deaths of Christians in Gaul, *Church History*, vol. 5, as well as Tertullian's comment in his *Apology*, "they [Romans] believed that Christians are the cause of every public disaster and calamity," are to blame for the misperception that early Christians were victims of persecution and punished with death.

It goes without saying that these graphic descriptions present the Romans as persecutors of Christians for refusing emperor worship. Stories of grisly, violent deaths were supposed to provide inspiration to the faithful and have highly influenced the misperceptions about ancient Rome.

Petrarch's revived interest in Cicero's letters started the Renaissance in Italy. Petrarch (1304–1374) inspired others, such as Poggio Bracciolini, a scholar devoted to classics, to search for and recover many rotting Latin manuscripts throughout Europe. Rome's reputation was rehabilitated and viewed as a model to imitate.

Flavio Biondo's (1392–1463) greatest work, *Decades of History from the Deterioration of the Roman Empire* (1489), suggested the notion of historical "decline." His *Rome in Triumph* (1459) presented ancient Rome as the prototype for contemporary political improvements and brought about respect for ancient Rome.

Germans were highly influenced by claims of "purity" in Tacitus's *Germania* (98). German humanists of the sixteenth century exploited this image and contrasted it with the corrupt Romans. Tacitus's work was adopted by Nazi leaders, who used it to advance their notions of superiority and race. This negative image of the empire remained popular in Germany until the end of World War II.

During Tudor times Rome was the archetype of civil unrest. William Shakespeare's *Julius Caesar* (1599) and *Antony and Cleopatra* (1607) were set in the civil wars that ended the Roman Republic. His works have remained popular ever since. Shakespeare used Sir Thomas North's *Plutarch* (1579) as a source for several plays. Shakespeare's portrayal of Caesar's death has resulted in the spread of the misconception that the Ides of March was a bad day, and that Caesar spoke as he was being killed. Most people don't realize that Caesar's final utterance in *Julius Caesar* was borrowed from Shakespeare's earlier play, *Henry VI*, pt. 3 (1591), as well as *Caesar Interfectus* (1582) by Richard Edes. At that time, no history of Rome written in English existed. However, Shakespeare's audience would have been acquainted with the persons and events in the plays in part because England was part of the Roman Empire from 43 CE to 408 CE. Moreover, the political uncertainty in *Julius Caesar* was similar to the political and social upheavals of the time. Many feared that a civil war similar to those in Rome might occur after the death of Queen Elizabeth I.

Two additional works from the eighteenth century influenced Victorian perceptions of the Romans. Rome was seen as an analog to the British Empire. Despite a negative image, there was much to emulate from the Romans. Scholars hoped to learn from Rome's mistakes to avoid a "decline and fall."

In 1734 Charles Montesquieu wrote *Reflections on the Causes of the Grandeur and Decline of the Romans*. This work inspired Sir Edward Gibbon's six-volume *The History of the Decline and Fall of the Roman Empire*, written between 1776 and 1788. Gibbon's work covers Roman history from 98 to the end of the Byzantine Empire in 1453. He decried Roman imperialism and considered Rome to be a repressive and immoral empire.

During the seventeenth and eighteenth centuries, the Grand Tour was an excursion that concluded the education of wealthy young men (and a few women). The culmination of the trip was Rome. However, its purpose was not to educate but rather to demonstrate ownership of Classical culture and therefore Western civilization. Neo-Classicism resulted from the educated and wealthy Victorians who made the trek. In addition to published accounts, guidebooks to Rome and Johann Joachim Winckelmann's *History of the Art of Antiquity* (1764) generated more interest in the classics. It promoted the belief that modern society would become great through learning from the ancients. At the same time, interest in ancient Rome increased in Britain as a result of the discovery of significant Roman buildings and artifacts. This led to a more positive view of ancient Rome. Comparisons between imperial Britain and Rome were common.

Nonetheless, literature of the late nineteenth century led to negative stereotypes. England considered itself the heir of ancient Rome because it had become an empire. Historical novels set in ancient Rome became popular. One such book, Edward Bulwer-Lytton's *The Last Days of Pompeii* (1834), inspired by Karl Bryullov's painting, *The Last Day of Pompeii* (1830–1833), which depicts the deadly volcanic eruption that destroyed the city, was republished more than a dozen times. Lytton's Rome is in moral and social decline, with its graphic images of feasting and sexual deviances. In it, Roman pagans are corrupt and inferior to the courageous, moral Christians. Subsequent novels revolved around the "triumph of Christianity." Contemporary religious strife provided the backdrop to imagine the type of Rome that early Christians experienced.

For instance, during the early nineteenth century, a resurgent Roman Catholicism caused a religious uproar. At the time, several government measures supported the minority Catholic Church, and some Anglican scholars from Oxford expressed dissent from their colleagues. In response, the Oxford Movement, led by John Henry Newman, wanted closer ties with the Catholic Church. This led to his conversion to Catholicism. Newman's personal battle with persecution and intolerance found expression in the historical novel *Callista*, which drew parallels between ancient Rome and contemporary Britain. The story is set in the period of Christian persecution under the emperor Decius, but its themes also reflect Newman's struggles as a convert as well as the religious dissonance between Catholic and Anglican dogmas.

Other British examinations of Rome struck similar chords. For example, George John Whyte-Melville's *The Gladiator: A Tale of Rome and Judea* (1863) depicts the Roman Empire as a model to emulate for its rise but to avoid for its collapse. More importantly, Thomas Babington MacCauley composed a series of narrative poems on the heroes of ancient Rome that were included in *The Lays of Ancient Rome*, published in 1842. In the first poem, Horatius and two companions are willing to die to defend the bridge and protect Rome from Lars Porsena and the Etruscans. Similarly, the Battle of Lake Regillus celebrates the Roman victory over the Latin League. *The Lays of Ancient Rome* was republished many times and was used as a school text to introduce schoolchildren to ancient Rome for more than one hundred years.

The most influential novel was Lew Wallace's *Ben-Hur: A Tale of the Christ* (1880). Here, Rome is the epitome of dark, evil powers that terrorize virtuous Christians. Likewise, in Frederic William Farrar's *Darkness and Dawn: Scenes in the Day of Nero* (1891), Nero's court is marked with decadence and sexual license. Women murder husbands, have no morals, and are unable to love.

Quo Vadis? A Narrative of the Time of Nero, by Henryk Sienkiewicz (English translation, 1896), also describes the excess at Nero's palace and a Roman general's conversion to Christianity for the love of a young Christian woman named Lygia. As in many of these novels, historical persons come into contact with early Christians. Christianity triumphs despite persecution by the evil emperor Nero. Sienkiewicz won the Nobel Prize in 1905 for outstanding writing.

These themes from historical novels and plays greatly affected the image of ancient Rome. It was powerful and impressive, but it was also home to unlimited brutality, indulgence, lavishness, and immorality.

Roman-themed plays of Shakespeare's works were also common in the 1880s and 1890s. Earlier plays include John Howard Payne's *Brutus* (1818) along with John Sheridan Knowles's *Caius Gracchus* (1815) and *Virginius: A Tragedy* (1820). Later toga plays stressed Christianity as a remedy to the wastefulness and lascivious conduct of the elite and to the dangers of unrestrained power, as well as exemplifying the proper place for women in society.

Claudian (1883), another famous play, was written by Henry Herman and W. G. Wills and featured Wilson Barrett, a famous English actor with crowd appeal. Themes included decadence and the possibility of moral renewal. The successful adaptation of Lew Wallace's *Ben-Hur* in 1899 resulted in the translation of many other historical novels to the theater. The stage version echoed many of the topics and circumstances of the novel.

A popular version of *Quo Vadis?* was adapted to stage in 1900, and an opera was produced in 1909. A similar plot to *Quo Vadis?* is found in Wilson Barrett's *The Sign of the Cross* (1895), a historical tragedy. Nero is enamored with a young woman and converts to Christianity, while his wife Poppaea falls for a Roman noble, Marcus. Both of them die in the arena.

Another theatrical genre, toga plays, were clever adaptations of literature that relayed basic themes and elements from historical novels. They, too, were moral pieces that nineteenth-century Britain used to deal with societal problems. Toga plays claimed accuracy based on the use of archaeology. They were believed to be didactic and to provide a realistic rendering of the clothing and manners of ancient Rome. These performances were responsible for the transmission of many misunderstandings about Rome. Even today, most people learn Roman history from cinematic reproductions.

Early films sought to repeat the success of toga plays in a more realistic manner. For example, Lew Wallace's *Ben-Hur* was made into a fifteen-minute short in 1907. The 1927 film *Ben-Hur* was an adaptation of the historical novel and the earlier silent production. *The Sign of the Cross* (1925) became an epic film produced and directed by Cecil B. DeMille and based on Barrett's 1895 historical novel set during the time of Nero. The 1914 silent drama was also based on the book. Nero appeared in many movies as the poster boy for decadence and sexual excess in the Roman world. Nero, and by extension Rome, are thus thought to be defined by unrestricted power and immorality. Unhampered authority leads to corruption and oppression. In this film genre, Christians, Jews, and slaves are mistreated outsiders.

Notwithstanding misconceptions and myths in popular culture and media, films set in ancient Rome are still popular. While some might criticize movies, docudramas, or books as inaccurate images of the ancient world, these productions will continue to play a role in the depiction of historical events. They are great ways to get people interested in history, and they are also a way of making the past accessible.

1

The Romans Destroyed Carthage and Plowed Salt into the Soil

What People Think Happened

Ancient Carthage dominated the Mediterranean during the first millennium BCE and was Rome's enemy in the Punic Wars (264–146 BCE). The Romans believed Carthage had to be permanently destroyed, so in 146 BCE (so people think), the site of Carthage was sown with salt to make it uninhabitable.

After Rome won the First Punic War (264–241 BCE), thereby acquiring Sicily, Carthage was forced to pay a large indemnity. Thanks to Hannibal's family, though, Carthage rebounded to form a new empire in Spain. Hannibal supposedly swore an oath of hatred upon Rome. Eventually, the two states fought the Second Punic War (218–202 BCE). Hannibal marched across the Alps with his war elephants, terrorizing Italy for fifteen years. Although Hannibal was recalled to Carthage in 203 BCE to defend his city, the Carthaginians lost the war in 202 BCE. Rome thus acquired Spain and forced Carthage once again to pay huge indemnities. As the story goes, Hannibal nearly brought Rome to its knees to the point that long after his demise his memory still wreaked havoc on the Romans who would say, "Hannibal is at the gates" (*Cic.Orat.*1.5, *Livy.Ab.Urbe. Cond.*26.14.12) in times of danger.

Why did Carthage receive such harsh treatment from Rome? Cato the Elder despised and distrusted Carthage because of his experiences in the Second Punic War. He led a senatorial delegation sent to monitor Carthage and was alarmed about the Carthaginian economic recovery. Upon his return to Rome, he spoke of the need to destroy Carthage. He dramatically revealed a Libyan fig from his toga, and "as the senators admired its size and beauty, [he] said that the country where it grew was only three days' sail from Rome. And in one thing he was even more savage, namely in adding to his vote on any question whatsoever these words: 'In my opinion Carthage must be destroyed.'" (*Plut.Vit.Cat.Mai.*27.1). Cato did not live to see the city defeated, but his fears led to the Third Punic War (149–146 BCE). Carthage resisted for the first two years, but in 146 BCE Scipio Africanus the Younger (also called Scipio Aemilianus) began his attack. He performed a ceremony and asked the Carthaginian deities to abandon Carthage and to accept a new home in Rome (*Macrob.Sat.*3.9.7–8). Scipio then was free to destroy the godless Carthage.

Diodorus's books, now lost, claim the city was razed to the ground (*Diod.Sic.*32.14.1) or that Carthaginians were completely annihilated (*Diod.Sic.*32.26.2). Velleius Paterculus claimed Rome "could not hope for security so long as the name of Carthage remained as of a city still standing" (*Vell.Pat.*1.12). He also said Scipio "destroyed to its foundations the city which was hateful to the Roman name." Sallust said, "Carthage, the rival of Rome's sway, had been perished root and branch" (*Sall.Cat.*1.10.1). Propertius (*Prop.*3.9.41), Horace (*Hor.Carm.*1.16.21), and Seneca (*Sen.Clem.*1.26.4) reported a city's symbolic razing with a plow as a mark of total destruction.

Other authors hinted at hallowing or rededication. Appian mentioned that "Augustus... built the present Carthage, not on the site of the old one, but very near it, in order to avoid the ancient curse" (*App.Pun.*28), while Cicero said the land was "consecrated" (*Cic.Agr.*1.5). Plutarch revealed how reports of bad omens were enough to provide religious justification for putting an end to the ill-fated colony (*Plut.Vit.C.Gracch.*10–11).

Roman sources declared that Carthage was obliterated, and the site was cursed. Over time, the story of its demise has passed into myth.

How the Story Became Popular

A popular version of the story states that the Romans salted the land to prevent anything from growing. This account arose in the nineteenth century without documentation from any sources. Instead, the narrative of the "sowing of salt" is a corruption that originated from the well-known rituals of city destruction in the ancient Near East.

Ancient historians say Carthage was cursed, completely demolished, and that people were banned from living there. Such sources influenced writers of the early modern period. L. Echard wrote an early work on the Roman Republic in 1694 in which he said that the commissioners ordered, "none of Carthage should be left, and that it should not be rebuilt, they denounced heavy curses on any that should offer to do it" (*Roman History,* London 1717, 233), while C. Rollin, in *Histoire Romaine* (1738–1748), reported on the destruction of Carthage and the prohibition against settlement. Mommsen, in *History of Rome*, vol. 3 (1888, 55), said, "put an end in legal form to the existence of the city and curse the soil and site forever, that neither house nor cornfield might ever reappear on the spot." Scholars of the late eighteenth century mentioned the plowing story and historians subsequently repeated it verbatim until the early nineteenth century. Stevens noted that the story was modeled on the ancient rite of symbolically founding or destroying a city. Because no ancient text mentions Carthage, over time the legend became even more provocative.

The earliest appearance of the myth is in a highly praised reference book by George Ripley and Charles Anderson Dana, *New American Cyclopedia: A Popular Dictionary of General Knowledge* (1863, 39), which reads: "[A] second Scipio, the son of Paulus Aemilius, the conqueror of Perseus, adopted by the son of the conqueror of Hannibal, took the city by storm, and destroyed it, razing it to the ground, passing the ploughshare over the site, and sowing salt in the furrows, the emblem of barrenness and annihilation."

In 1930, B. L. Hallward, a classicist and headmaster and later first vice-chancellor at the University of Nottingham, published a chapter on Carthage in the *Cambridge Ancient History* Vol. 8 (1930, 484) that had a massive impact on subsequent authors of the twentieth century. He wrote, "Buildings and walls were razed to the ground; the plough passed over the site, and salt was sown in the furrows made."

Hallward may have been influenced by the vivid depiction of Carthage as described by L. Bertrand ("Les villes africaines," in *Revue des Deux Mondes*, Vol. 5, No. 28, 1905, 661):

> I have never seen Carthage except in dust and wind: I do not regret it too much! This hostile and livid atmosphere is one that suits the land where this city of violence, cruelty and lust was. Carthage is no more than a vast necropolis, buried under a uniform shroud of plains and hills without character. The ruins themselves perished. It looks like the curse of Scipio-Aemilianus is still weighing on her. In these places, where salt has been sown and the plow passed, pronouncing terrible imprecations, the human work can no longer repel: the ground, dug like a sepulcher, would collapse under the burden of a city new!

Subsequently, many historians have repeated the story as fact, with slight variations. Several ancient texts inspired the misunderstandings of the salting myth. For example, in the Hebrew Bible, Judges 9:45 reads, "And Abimelech fought against the city all that day; he took the city and killed the people that were in it; and he razed the city and sowed it with salt."

Plowing and salting stories are found in Hittite and Assyrian texts. In the ancient Near East, it was a common ritual that consecrated a demolished city and cursed anyone who might rebuild it. For example, the proto-Hittite king Anitta of Nesa (an ancient city in Anatolia) destroyed the capital of King Piyusti at the site of the future Hittite capital in 2000 BCE. "I took it at night by storm. In its place, I sowed weeds."

Similarly, the Assyrian King Adad-nirari I (1307–1275 BCE) destroyed and burned the city of Taidu and strewed *kudimmus* (a type of plant that emitted salt or lye and was placed over ruins to symbolically pronounce the site as barren) over it (*CAD*.8:493). The city of Arinna was destroyed by Shalmaneser I (1265–1235 BCE) and strewn with *kudimmus* (*ARI*.1.258).

Plowing and salting stories occur in medieval Italian chronicles. Attila the Hun allegedly destroyed and salted Padua in 452 CE. After vanquishing Milan, Friedrich Barbarossa supposedly plowed and salted the city in 1162. Pope Boniface VIII demolished Palestrina in 1299 and said, "I subjected it to the plough, following the example of Carthage of old in Africa. We also made salt in it, and commanded that it be sown over, so that it should have neither the condition, nor name, nor title of a city." Other medieval plowing and salting stories include the Siege of Jerusalem in 1370.

Actually, however, the many sources discussing the scattering of a variety of plants and minerals over the site of a destroyed city were describing an action that was intended to fertilize the site, *not* to make it uninhabitable. In the ancient world, salt was used as a fertilizer. For example, Boniface's plowing and sowing was meant to make Palestrina fertile: "and we also made salt in it, and commanded that it be sown over" (Pope Boniface VIII, *Papal Bull*). Theophrastus (c. 371–287 BCE) mentions that "salinity is also suited to some vegetables" (*Theophras.Caus.Pl*.3.17.8).

Pliny the Elder's *Natural History* has a section devoted to the uses of salt, one of which was as a fertilizer: "and many (plants) are better entrusted to salted earth, as they are safer from being harmed by animals breeding there" (*Plin.HN*.17.29).

The New Testament (*Luke* 14:34–35) also mentions salt as a means of fertilizer: "'Salt is good; but if salt has lost its taste, how will its saltiness be restored? It is of no use either for the soil or for the manure heap. It is thrown away." Furthermore, in Matthew 5:13, Jesus says, "You are the salt of the earth, but if salt has lost its taste, how shall its saltiness be restored? It is no longer good for anything except to be thrown out and trampled under people's feet." Here Jesus is referring to its use as a fertilizer.

Carthage is best known for its destruction by Rome. Although Scipio Aemilianus besieged, sacked, and burned the city to the ground and sold its survivors into slavery, sowing the fields with salt is a modern myth inspired by ancient Near Eastern texts and Biblical verses.

PRIMARY DOCUMENTS

The sowing of Carthage with salt has been portrayed historically as an act of savage brutality perpetrated by Scipio Aemilianus after the defeat of the city. Many Roman authors reported the destruction of the city, yet no surviving primary documents support the plowing-and-salting story.

For instance, Polybius was an eyewitness to the city's destruction. His account is clear that the city was in ruins, but not that the city had vanished.

When the Carthaginian commander thus threw himself as a suppliant at Scipio's knees, the proconsul with a glance at those present said, "See what Fortune is, gentlemen! What an example she makes of irrational men! This is the Hasdrubal who, but the other day disdained the large favors which I offered him and said that the most glorious funeral pyre was one's country and its burning ruins. Now he comes with suppliant wreaths, beseeching us for bare life and resting all his hopes on us. Who would not learn from such a spectacle that a mere man should never say or do anything presumptuous?" Then some of the deserters came to the edge of the roof and begged the front ranks of the assailants to hold their hands for a little; and, once Scipio had ordered a halt, they began abusing Hasdrubal, some for his perjury, declaring that he had sworn again and again on the altars that he would never abandon them, and others for his cowardice and utter baseness: and they did this in the most unsparing language, and with the bitterest terms of abuse. And just at this moment Hasdrubal's wife, seeing him seated in front of the enemy with Scipio, advanced in front of the deserters, dressed in noble and dignified attire herself, but holding in her hands, on either side, her two boys dressed only in short tunics and shielded under her own robes. First, she addressed Hasdrubal by his name, and when he said nothing but remained with his head bowed to the ground, she began by calling on the name of the gods, and next thanked Scipio warmly because, as far as he could secure it, both she and her children were saved. And then, pausing for a short time, she asked Hasdrubal how he had had the heart to secure this favor from the Roman general for himself alone . . . and, leaving his fellow-citizens who trusted in him in the most miserable plight, had gone over secretly to the enemy? And how he had the assurance to be sitting there holding suppliant boughs, in the face of the very men to whom he had frequently said that the day would never come in which the sun would see Hasdrubal alive and his native city in flames. (*Polyb*.39.4)

Livy recounts the end of Carthage but does not say anything about a ritual.

When Hasdrubal surrendered to Scipio during the final stage of the siege, his wife, who had—only a few days before—been unable to convince her husband to escape to the victor, threw herself from the citadel into the flames of the burning city with her two children. (*Livy.Ab.Urbe.Cond.Per.*51)

In Appian's account of Scipio's destruction of Carthage, the city is not declared cursed.

The next day there were sacrifices and solemn processions to the gods by tribes, also games and spectacles of various kinds. The Senate sent ten of the noblest of their own number as deputies to arrange the affairs of Africa in conjunction with Scipio, to the advantage of Rome. They decreed that if anything was still left of Carthage, Scipio should obliterate it and that nobody should be allowed to live there. Direful threats were leveled against any who should disobey and chiefly against the rebuilding of Byrsa or Megara, but it was not forbidden to go upon the ground.

The towns that had allied themselves with the enemy it was decided to destroy, to the last one. To those who had aided the Romans there was an allotment of lands won by the sword, and first of all to the Uticans was given the territory of Carthage itself, extending as far as Hippo. Upon all the rest a tribute was imposed, both a land tax and a personal tax, upon men and women alike. It was decreed that a praetor should be sent from Rome yearly to govern the country.

After these arrangements had been carried out by the deputies, they returned to Rome. Scipio did all that they directed, and he instituted sacrifices and games to the gods for the victory. When all was finished, he sailed for home and was awarded the most glorious triumph that had ever been known, splendid with gold and gorged with statues and votive offerings that the Carthaginians had gathered from all parts of the world through all time, the fruit of their countless victories. It was at this time also that the third Macedonian triumph occurred for the capture of Andriscus, surnamed Pseudophilippus, and the first Grecian one, for Mummius. This was about the 160th Olympiad. (*App.Pun.*27.135)

Velleius Paterculus informed his readers that Rome was freed from the fear of Carthage after Scipio demolished the city. In doing so, he emphasized that the destruction of the city paved the way for the decline of Rome.

The war against Carthage begun by the consuls two years previously he now waged with greater vigor and destroyed to its foundations the city which was hateful to the Roman name, more because of jealousy of its power than because of any offense at that time. He made Carthage a monument to his valor—a city which had been a monument to his father's clemency. Carthage, after standing for six hundred and seventy-two years, was destroyed in the consulship of Gnaeus Cornelius Lentulus and Lucius Mummius, one hundred and seventy-three years from the present date. This was the end of Carthage, the rival of the power of Rome, whom our ancestors began in the consulship of Claudius and Fulvius two hundred and ninety-two years before you entered upon your consulship, Marcus Vinicius. Thus, for one hundred and twenty years there existed between these two people either war, or preparations for war or a treacherous peace. Even after Rome had conquered the world she could not hope for security as long as the name of Carthage remained as a city still standing: to such an extent does hatred begotten of conflict outlast the fear which caused it; it is not laid aside, even when the foe is vanquished does the object of it cease to be hated until it has to be. (*Vell.Pat.*1.12.5)

Another contradiction to the common narrative is that the ruins of Carthage may have been visible for centuries. For example, the uncle of Julius Caesar, Gaius Marius (157 BCE–86 BCE), once visited the site. He was rejected by the governor, Publius Sextilius. Cassius Dionysius's version of Mago of Carthage's farming manual was dedicated to Sextilius when he was a praetor. (See below: Varr.Rust.*1.10)*

At this news Marius was a little refreshed, and made bold to push on from the island to the neighborhood of Carthage.

The Roman governor of Africa at this time was Sextilius, a man who had received neither good or ill at the hands of Marius, but who, as it was expected, pity alone would move to give him aid. Hardly, however, had Marius landed with a few companions, when an official met him, stood directly in front of him, and said: "Sextilius the governor forbids thee, Marius, to set foot in Africa; and if thou disobeyest, he declares that he will uphold the decree of the Senate and treat thee as an enemy of Rome." When he heard this, Marius was rendered speechless by grief and indignation, and for a long time kept quiet, looking sternly at the official. Then, when asked what he had to say, and what answer he would make to the governor, he answered with a deep groan: "Tell him, then, that thou hast seen Caius Marius, a fugitive, seated amid the ruins of Carthage." And it was not inaptly that he compared the fate of that city with his own reversal of fortune. (*Plut.Vit.Mar.*40.3–4)

St. Augustine of Hippo notes that the city was totally extinguished. He does not mention a curse but agrees that the removal of Rome's great rival opened the door to Rome's moral decline.

But when the last Punic war had terminated in the utter destruction of Rome's rival, which quickly succumbed to the other Scipio, who thus earned for himself the surname of Africanus, then the Roman republic was overwhelmed with such a host of ills, which sprang from the corrupt manners induced by prosperity and security, that the sudden overthrow of Carthage is seen to have injured Rome more seriously than her long-continued hostility. (*August.De.civ.D.*3.21)

Macrobius, who lived in the early fifth century, hundreds of years after the destruction of the city, is the only source that mentions a curse on Carthage. However, there is no mention of Scipio. Rather, it summons the protective deity from the city of Carthage by promising temples and worship in Rome. Then the curse asks the Roman spirits of the underworld to help destroy Carthage, its army, and the surrounding territory while protecting the Roman military.

If there is a god, if there is a goddess of these people who defends this city of Carthage, and you most high, I pray that you desert the people and the Carthaginian state, that you leave the sacred places, temples, and city. (*Macrob.Sat.*3.9.7)

Orosius wrote that the devastation was so bad that the city was reduced to dust.

The wife of Hasdrubal, acting as would a man in grief and a woman in rage, threw herself and her two sons into the middle of the fire. Thus, the last queen of Carthage came to her end by the same death as that which in ages past had claimed the first queen. The city burned for seventeen consecutive days, furnishing the conquerors with a pitiable spectacle to illustrate the fickleness of human fortune. Thus, Carthage was destroyed, and her entire stone wall reduced to dust seven hundred years after her foundation. With the exception of a few leading men, every one of the captives was sold into slavery. The Third Punic War now came to an end in the fourth year after it had begun. (*Oros.*4.23.5–7)

Thus, the plowing story has no basis in fact and is probably an extension of a Roman ceremony that was used to ritually destroy cities. The ritual destruction of cities is frequently found in Roman literature, but none mentions Carthage by name. Seneca provides one such example.

The cruelty even of private men has sometimes been revenged by their slaves in spite of the certainty that they will be crucified: whole kingdoms and nations when oppressed by tyrants or threatened by them, have attempted their destruction. Sometimes their own guards have risen in revolt, and have used against their master all the deceit, disloyalty, and ferocity which they have learned from him. What, indeed, can he expect from those whom he has taught to be wicked? A bad man will not long be obedient, and will not do only as much evil as he is ordered. But even if the tyrant may be cruel with safety, how miserable his kingdom must be: it must look like a city taken by storm, like some frightful scene of general panic. Everywhere sorrow, anxiety, disorder; men dread even their own pleasures; they cannot even dine with one another in safety when they have to keep watch over their tongues even when in their cups, nor can they safely attend the public shows when informers are ready to find grounds for their impeachment in their behavior there. Although the spectacles be provided at an enormous expense, with royal magnificence and with world-famous artists, yet who cares for amusement when he is in prison? Ye gods! what a miserable life it is to slaughter and to rage, to delight in the clanking of chains, and to cut off one's countrymen's heads, to cause blood to flow freely wherever one goes, to terrify people, and make them flee away out of one's sight! It is what would happen if bears or lions were our masters, if serpents and all the most venomous creatures were given power over us. Even these animals, devoid of reason as they are, and accused by us of cruel ferocity, spare their own kind, and wild beasts themselves respect their own likeness: but the fury of tyrants does not even stop short at their own relations, and they treat friends and strangers alike, only becoming more violent the more they indulge their passions. By insensible degrees he proceeds from the slaughter of individuals to the ruin of nations, and thinks it a sign of power to set roofs on fire and to plough up the sites of ancient cities: he considers it unworthy of an emperor to order only one or two people to be put to death, and thinks that his cruelty is unduly restrained if whole troops of wretches are not sent to execution together. True happiness, on the other hand, consists in saving many men's lives, in calling them back from the very gates of death, and in being so merciful as to deserve a civic crown. No decoration is more worthy or more becoming to a prince's rank than that crown "for saving the lives of fellow citizens" not trophies torn from a vanquished enemy, not chariots wet with their savage owner's blood, not spoils captured in war. This power which saves men's lives by crowds and by nations, is godlike: the power of extensive and indiscriminate massacre is the power of downfall and conflagration. (*Sen. Clem.* 1.26.4)

Horace also mentions the symbolic destruction of a city in Book 1 of his Odes. His four books are imitations of short lyrical Greek poems. The Odes were adapted to social life in Rome and focused on love, friendship, morality. The topic of this poem is an apology to a woman whom Horace insulted.

O lovelier than the lovely dame
That bore you, sentence as you please
Those scurrile verses, be it flame
Your vengeance craves, or Hadrian seas.
Not Cybele, nor he that haunts
Rich Pytho, worse the brain confounds,
Not Bacchus, nor the Corybants
Clash their loud gongs with fiercer sounds
Than savage wrath; nor sword nor spear
Appals it, no, nor ocean's frown,
Nor ravening fire, nor Jupiter
In hideous ruin crashing down.
Prometheus, forced, they say, to add
To his prime clay some favorite part
From every kind, took lion mad,
And lodged its gall in man's poor heart
'Twas wrath that laid Thyestes low;

Tis wrath that oft destruction calls
On cities and invites the foe
To drive his plough o'er ruin'd walls.
(*Hor.Carm.*1.16)

*Despite the common motif of ritual plowing, which was well-known to the Romans, there is no evidence that the city of Carthage was plowed. Nonetheless, many modern writers and historians repeated the assertion that the city of Carthage had been plowed under. L. Echard reports, "Commissioners ordered that none of Carthage should be left and that it should not be rebuilt. They denounced heavy curses on any that should offer to do it" (*Roman History, London, 1713, 233*).*

The New American Cyclopedia *article on Carthage added salt as a detail to the plowing story. Its source was B. Hallward's 1930 chapter on Carthage in the* Cambridge Ancient History, *which reported that "the plough passed over the site, and salt was sown in furrows made." The salt sowing at Carthage also hearkens to rituals of city destruction in the ancient Near East. For example, a number of parallels exist in biblical, Hittite, and Assyrian texts: the best known is from Judges 9:45: "And Abimelech fought against the city all that day; he took the city and killed the people that were in it; and he razed the city and sowed it with salt."*

Salting and sowing was an ancient tradition, as indicated by Anitta, son of Pithana, King of Kussara (1720 BCE), who boasts that he sowed the site with seeds. The city was taken by storm:

The city of Hattusas [tablet broken] contrived. And I abandoned it. But afterwards, when it suffered famine, my goddess Halmasuwiz handed it over to me. And in the night, I took it by force; and in its place, I sowed weeds. Whoever becomes king after me and settles Hattusas again, may the storm-god of Heaven smite him! (*Kim.Sloc.Proc.Anitt.*)

The Assyrian King Adad-nirari (1307–1275 BCE) tells of his defeat of an enemy city. Later, the city was rebuilt. The kudimmu *was placed over ruins to pronounce the place as barren. It is used here in a symbolic act and not to make the site uninhabitable.*

I captured by conquest the city of Taidu, his [Wasashatta's] royal city, the cities of Amasaku, Kahat, Shuru, Nabala, Hurra, Shuduhu and Washshukanu. I took and brought to my city, Ashur, the possessions of those cities, the accumulated wealth of his fathers and the treasures of the palace.

I conquered, burnt and destroyed the city of Taidu and strewed *kudimmus* over it. (*ARI*.1.60)

Agricultural manuals overflow with citations on the use of salt to enrich the soil. Virgil explains the use of it as manure in the next section.

But who for milk hath longing, must himself
Carry lucerne and lotus-leaves enow
With salt herbs to the cote, whence more they love
The streams, more stretch their udders, and give back
A subtle taste of saltness in the milk.
Many there be who from their mothers keep
The new-born kids, and straightway bind their mouths
With iron-tipped muzzles. What they milk at dawn,
Or in the daylight hours, at night they press;
What darkling or at sunset, this ere morn
They bear away in baskets—for to town
The shepherd hies him—or with dash of salt
Just sprinkle, and lay by for winter use. (*Verg*.3.394)

Pliny the Elder demonstrates the benefits of using salt in agriculture.

Cato has treated so well of the precautions that are necessary in cultivating the olive, that we cannot do better than employ his own words on the subject. "Let the slips of olive," says he, "which you are about to plant in the hole, be three feet long, and be very careful in your treatment of them, so as not to injure the bark when you are smoothing or cutting them. Those that you are going to plant in the nursery, should be a foot in length; and you should plant them the following way: let the spot be turned up with the mattock, and the soil be well loosened. When you put the cutting in the ground, press it down with the foot only. If there is any difficulty in making it descend, drive it down with a mallet or the handle of the dibble, but be careful not to break the bark in doing so. Take care, too, not to make a hole first with the dibble, for the slip will have the better chance of surviving the other way. When the slip is three years old, due care must be taken to observe the direction in which each side of the bark is situate. If you are planting in holes or furrows, you must put in the cuttings by threes, but be careful to keep them separate. Above ground, however, they should not be more than four fingers distant from one another, and each of them must have a bud or eye above ground. In taking up the olive for transplanting, you must use the greatest caution, and see that there is as much earth left about the roots as possible. When you have covered the roots well up, tread down the earth with the foot, so that nothing may injure the plant." (*Plin.HN.*17.29)

Pliny notes that cows who graze on meadows composted with salt produce more dairy products: "Herds of cattle being covetous of a salt pasture, give a great deal more milk; and the same is much more agreeable in the making of cheese, than where there is no such saline ground" (Plin.HN.*31.7*).

Salt was commonly used during the lifetime of Jesus of Nazareth. Jesus is referring to salt as a fertilizer instead of a seasoning in the much-misunderstood figure of speech from the New Testament Gospels. The agricultural understanding makes more sense: "Salt is a good thing. But if the salt loses its salty taste, then you can't make it salty again. It is worth nothing. You can't even use it for soil or for plant food. People throw it away. You people that hear me, listen!" (Luke *14:34–35*).

What Really Happened

After Rome defeated Carthage in the Second Punic War in 202 BCE, Carthage was demilitarized and left as a regional power following the loss of its territories. Carthage's swift recovery and early repayment of war debt, however, was cause for Roman unease. Therefore, Rome looked for any pretense to go to war with Carthage, and out of sheer spite, it eventually did. Brave Carthaginians held out for more than two years before their city was sacked and utterly devasted, its population sold into slavery. Carthaginian history was erased, and it became a Roman province.

The Romans feared and hated Carthage because of the humiliating defeats at Lake Trasimene (217 BCE) and Cannae (216 BCE) during the Second Punic War. Hannibal was particularly despised because he brought Rome to its knees. Thus, after winning the Second Punic War, Rome imposed harsh terms on its rival. Throughout negotiations, the Senate dealt with great hostility toward the Carthaginians. Disarmed and stripped of all its territories in Africa, Carthage also surrendered its war elephants, and its navy was reduced to just ten ships. Carthage was required to pay Rome the sum of 10,000 talents over fifty years (*Livy. Ab.Urbe.Cond.*30.37). The Romans cruelly burned Carthage's warships in the presence of the Carthaginian envoys, the sight of which "caused as much grief to the people as if Carthage itself were burning" (*Livy.Ab. Urbe.Cond.*30.43). The Romans imposed these heavy fines upon the

Carthaginians in order to humiliate and weaken them by, in effect, making it supposedly impossible to afford a large mercenary army. The inability to wage war without Rome's permission was yet another means of disgrace.

Despite Rome's worst intentions, however, the heavy war payments did not incapacitate Carthage at all. As very successful merchants and traders, Carthage paid off the last installment of the reparations (which the Romans refused to accept) forty years early (*Livy.Ab.Urbe.Cond.*36.4). Rome's heavy military restrictions had the opposite of their intended effect. Because Carthage no longer had to fund an army, it invested in agriculture, as suggested by the large amounts of grains supplied to Rome and its army in Macedonia, as well as in the war with Antiochus (*Livy.Ab.Urbe.Cond.*31.19.2; 36.4.5–9).

Carthage also redirected its energies by reinvesting in a magnificent new port. "The harbors had communication with each other, and a common entrance from the sea seventy feet wide, which could be closed with iron chains. The first port was for merchant vessels, and here were collected all kinds of ships' tackle. Within the second port was an island, which together with the port itself, was enclosed by high embankments. These embankments were full of shipyards which had a capacity for 220 vessels" (*App.Pun.*20.96).

Carthage's economic resurgence and harbor renovations set off a red flag. The early repayment of the war debt in addition to vivid memories of the terror of Hannibal prompted the Romans to be highly suspicious.

Roman sources are full of negative depictions of Carthaginians. The origin of Hannibal's supposed hatred of Rome is one example. According to Polybius, Hamilcar held Hannibal over a fire and forced him to make an oath that he would never be friends with Rome (*Polyb.*3.11.7). Livy claimed that Hannibal's father "led the boy up to the altar and made him touch the offerings and bind himself with an oath so that soon as he should be able he would be the declared enemy of the Roman people" (*Livy.Ab.Urbe.Cond.*21.1). His other version of the same event is similar to that of Polybius: Hannibal declared, "My father Hamilcar, Antiochus, led me, still a little boy, to the altar when he was sacrificing and bound me by an oath never to be a friend to the Roman people" (*Livy.Ab.Urbe.Cond.*35.19). Silius Italicus (28–c.110) wrote a Latin epic poem titled "The Punica" in seventeen books. He used Livy as his primary source. Silius presents Hannibal as hell-bent on revenge: "When I come to age I shall pursue the Romans with fire and sword and enact again the doom of Troy" (*Sil.Pun.*1.115–118).

Even ordinary Carthaginians were cast as dishonest and untrustworthy. Livy wrote that the Romans were warned to "be on their guard against the treachery of the Carthaginians" (*Livy.Ab.Urbe.Cond.*43.3). In literature, it was the same. For example, a Carthaginian trader had a dishonest reputation in a work of Greek Comedy, which was the source of the negative stereotypes of Carthaginians found in Plautus's play *Poenulus*. Dating to 194 BCE, it contains lines in Carthaginian Punic spoken by the character Hanno, the typical Carthaginian merchant who will deal in anything just to make money. Even the title "little Carthaginian" is unfavorable. Plautus's audience was familiar with Carthage as Rome's twice-defeated rival. Throughout the play, Hanno, the Carthaginian merchant, is subject to ridicule and anti-Carthaginian insults.

The prologue warned Romans how deceitful and dishonest Carthaginians were: "He knows all languages, too; but, though he knows them, he pretends not to know them. What need is there of talking? He is a Carthaginian all over" (*Pl.Poen.Prologue.*0).

The Carthaginian character was the constant subject of negative stereotypes that were quite common to Roman onlookers. In the following scene, Hanno embraces his daughters but is mistaken for the patron of a prostitute. Subsequently, a soldier accuses him of being lecherous.

"You skinnea pilchard, you defamed image of Serapis, you half apron, you sheepskin jacket, you pot of stinking salt; more crammed, too, to boot, with leeks and garlic than the Roman rowers" (*Pl.Poen.*5.5).

The general message of *Poenulus* was that Carthaginians were dishonest, manipulative, and inferior. Like Plautus, the majority of Roman authors depicted Carthaginians in a negative light.

Cato, playing on existing stereotypes, presented Carthage as worthy of destruction, declaring the Carthaginians as enemies: "Who are the people who have broken the treaty?" (*Cato.Orig.Frag.*78–9).

Carthage haters such as Cato the Elder brought on the Third Punic War. When Cato discovered the degree of prosperity at Carthage, he convinced the Senate that Carthage was a threat to Rome. He used existing stereotypes and claimed that Rome would suffer, in order to persuade his fellow senators that Carthage was a threat. He was not above using dramatics—he once presented figs to his fellow senators in order to emphasize Carthage's prosperity, its proximity to Rome, and therefore its danger. All of its riches could belong to Rome if Carthage were destroyed.

Masinissa of Numidia knew that Rome would act accordingly if Carthage crossed into his territory, so he annexed land. The Carthaginians complained bitterly to Rome, but to no avail. The Romans consistently favored Masinissa over the dishonest Carthaginians. Livy reported that a son of Masinissa warned the Senate "to be on their guard against the bad faith of the Carthaginians: they had formed the design of fitting out a great fleet, ostensibly to assist the Romans against the Macedonians. When this fleet was equipped and manned they [the Carthaginians] would have it in their power whom they would choose as an enemy or an ally" (*Livy.Ab. Urbe.Cond.*43.3).

Rome's choice in favoring Numidia demonstrates that the Senate had already made up its mind to go to war with Carthage. Rome eventually acted upon this notion in 149 BCE.

The Senate acted only in its own interests. The early repayment of the war reparations also meant the loss of a very profitable source of money. Carthage was an attractive target for Rome because of its mercantile and agricultural wealth.

The Carthaginians tried to avoid war by negotiating with the Romans. In 149 BCE, as a token of good faith, they agreed to an unconditional surrender and handed over 300 noble children as hostages. Carthage also complied with the Roman request to hand over weapons in exchange for peace.

However, the Senate had already decided on the war. Appian reported that the Senate had been eager for war and that the senators voted to declare war against Carthage (*App.Pun.*15.75).

Carthage was told that it could live free and under its own laws, but there was a catch to this independence. Carthage had to move ten miles away from the sea and build a new city. For the Carthaginians, this meant the destruction of their way of life and, consequently, a cultural death sentence. The Carthaginians were the descendants of Phoenician traders from the port of Tyre, and they made their fortune from the sea. Moving inland would also imply abandoning Carthaginian shrines and gods, an outrageous demand.

Carthage had no choice but to fight. It declared war on Rome. Slaves were given their freedom, and Hasdrubal, the grandson of Masinissa, was named as general.

Manius Mamilius initially led the Roman army with little success. Carthaginians had quickly transformed temples and unoccupied space into workshops where men and women worked around the clock producing 100 shields, 300 swords, 1,000 catapults, and 500 javelins and spears daily (*App.Pun.*19.93).

The tenacity of the Carthaginians frustrated the Romans for more than two years. Finally, the Romans chose the adopted grandson of Scipio Africanus, Scipio Aemilianus, to take over the campaign. He dammed the harbor and breached the city walls. The Romans fought their way through the narrow streets and slaughtered anyone in their path. One by one they cleared houses. Scipio ordered fires to be set in alleys. With the city in flames, women, old men, and children died from fire or fell from collapsing buildings. The wife of Hasdrubal, disgusted that he had surrendered, was among the victims. She threw herself and her two sons into the inferno in full view of the Romans. General Hasdrubal was put on display in Rome during Scipio's triumph and lived out the rest of his life there.

Most of the population was dead. The remaining 50,000 were trapped in the city, which burned for days. Scipio ordered the troops to destroy buildings and to sack the city. Polybius said that Scipio became emotional at the sight of the city in ruins. He wept when he saw the city of Carthage totally devastated, realizing that what happened at Ilium would happen to Rome:

> Scipio, beholding this city, which had flourished 700 years from its foundation and had ruled over so many lands, islands, and seas, rich with arms and fleets, elephants and money, equal to the mightiest monarchies but far surpassing them in bravery and high spirit (since without ships or arms, and in the face of famine, it had sustained continuous war for three years), now come to its end in total destruction—Scipio, beholding this spectacle, is said to have shed tears and publicly lamented the fortune of the enemy.
>
> After meditating by himself a long time and reflecting on the rise and fall of cities, nations, and empires, as well as of individuals, upon the fate of Troy, that once proud city, upon that of the Assyrians, the Medes, and the Persians, greatest of all, and later the splendid Macedonian Empire, either voluntarily or otherwise the words of the poet escaped his lips:
>
> "The day shall come in which our sacred Troy and Priam, and the people over whom spear-bearing Priam rules, shall perish all." (*Hom.Il.*6.448–449)
>
> Being asked by Polybius in familiar conversation (for Polybius had been his tutor) what he meant by using these words, he said that he did not hesitate frankly to name his own country, for whose fate he feared when he considered the mutability of human affairs. And Polybius wrote this down just as he heard it. (*App.Pun.*27.132)

Back in Rome, citizens cheered when they learned of Carthage's demise. After a siege of three years, Carthage was reduced to ashes in 146 BCE. Rome was now master of the world.

After the capture of the city, the Senate ordered all twenty-eight volumes of Mago's agricultural treatise to be translated into Latin. Rome was the last empire standing. Carthage's rival, Utica, was made the capital of the region. Carthage was resettled by Augustus and became one of the major cities of the empire. During the Christian period, it was home to many church leaders. It was destroyed once again for the final time at the Battle of Carthage in 698 CE.

The salt myth was finally laid to rest in a series of articles by R. T. Ridley, B. H. Warmington, P. Visonà, and S. T. Stevens in the late 1980s.

PRIMARY DOCUMENTS

Polybius and Livy describe how as a child, Hannibal swore an oath of eternal hatred against the city of Rome. After his father dipped his hand in blood, Hannibal pledged on an altar to go to war.

Hannibal then defended himself at great length, but without success, until at last he made the following statement: "When my father was about to go on his Iberian expedition I was nine years old: and as he was offering the sacrifice to Zeus I stood near the altar. The sacrifice successfully performed, my father poured the libation and went through the usual ritual. He then bade all the other worshippers stand a little back, and calling me to him asked me affectionately whether I wished to go with him on his expedition. Upon my eagerly assenting, and begging with boyish enthusiasm to be allowed to go, he took me by the right hand and led me up to the altar, and bade me lay my hand upon the victim and swear that I would never be friends with Rome So long, then, Antiochus, as your policy is one of hostility to Rome, you may feel quite secure of having in me a most thoroughgoing supporter. But if ever you make terms or friendship with her, then you need not wait for any slander to make you distrust me and be on your guard against me; for there is nothing in my power that I would not do against her." (Polyb.*3.11.7*)

The boy Hannibal, nine years old, was coaxing his father to take him with him, and his father led him up to the altar and made him swear with his hand laid on the victim that as soon as he possibly could he would show himself the enemy of Rome. The loss of Sicily and Sardinia vexed the proud spirit of the man, for he felt that the cession of Sicily had been made hastily in a spirit of despair, and that Sardinia had been filched by the Romans during the troubles in Africa, who, not content with seizing it, had imposed an indemnity as well. (*Livy.Ab. Urbe.Cond.*21.3)

However, it was Rome that destroyed Carthage out of revenge for all the damage done by Hannibal. Cato and many in the Senate also desired to exploit the economic and agricultural wealth of the Carthaginians.

The intervening country in which it was necessary for them to march was divided into gardens and plantations of every kind, since many streams of water were led in small channels and irrigated every part. There were also country houses one after another, constructed in luxurious fashion and covered with stucco, which gave evidence of the wealth of the people who possessed them. The farm buildings were filled with everything that was needful for enjoyment, seeing that the inhabitants in a long period of peace had stored up an abundant variety of products. Part of the land was planted with vines, and part yielded olives and was also planted thickly with other varieties of fruit bearing trees. On each side herds of cattle and flocks of sheep pastured on the plain, and the neighboring meadows were filled with grazing horses. In general, there was a manifold prosperity in the region, since the leading Carthaginians had laid their private estates and with their wealth had beautified them for their enjoyment. (*Diod. Sic.* 20.8.3–4)

Rome hated Carthage but loved Mago of Carthage. Rome sought to acquire Carthaginian practices because of their agricultural expertise. For instance, the Romans translated all twenty-eight books of Carthaginian farmer Mago's highly esteemed manual into Latin. Varro rated him as the pinnacle of farming techniques.

Those who have written various separate treatises in Greek—one on one subject, another on another—are more than fifty in number. The following are those whom you can call to your aid when you wish to consider any point: Hiero of Sicily and Attalus Philometor; of the philosophers, Democritus the naturalist, Xenophon the Socratic, Aristotle and Theophrastus the Peripatetics, Archytas the Pythagorean, and likewise Amphilochus of Athens, Anaxipolis of Thasos, Apollodorus of Lemnos, Aristophanes of Mallos, Antigonus of Cyme, Agathocles of Chios, Apollonius of Pergamum, Aristandrus of Athens, Bacchius of Miletus, Bion of Soli, Chaerestus and Chaereas of Athens, Diodorus of Priene, Dion of Colophon, Diophanes of Nicaea, Epigenes of Rhodes, Euagon of Thasos, the two Euphronii, one of Athens and the other of Amphipolis, Hegesias of Maronea, the two Menanders, one of Priene and the other of Heraclea, Nicesius of Maronea, and Pythion of Rhodes. Among other writers, whose birthplace I have not learned, are: Androtion, Aeschrion, Aristomenes, Athenagoras, Crates, Dadis, Dionysius, Euphiton, Euphorion, Eubulus, Lysimachus, Mnaseas, Menestratus, Plentiphanes, Persis, Theophilus. All these whom I have named are prose writers; others have treated the same subjects in verse, as Hesiod of Ascra and Menecrates of Ephesus. All these are surpassed in reputation by Mago of Carthage, who gathered into twenty-eight books, written in the Punic tongue, the subjects they had dealt with separately. (*Varro.Rust.*1.7–10)

After losing the Second Punic War and its overseas territories, Carthage was reduced to a regional territory, subservient to Rome. Nonetheless, Carthage paid off its heavy war indemnity and rebuilt its economy, which worried Cato the Elder, who considered the city to be a major threat.

Varro cites Mago several times in his work.

For there are two kinds of pasturing: one in the fields, which includes cattle-raising, and the other around the farmstead, which includes chickens, pigeons, bees and the like, which usually feed in the steading; the Carthaginian Mago, Cassius Dionysius, and others have left in their books remarks on them, but scattered and unsystematic. These Seius seem to have read; as a result he gets more revenue from such pasturing out of one villa than others receive from a whole farm. (*Varro.Rust.*3.2.13)

Carthage reinvested in farming after the Second Punic War and reemerged as an economic powerhouse that reactivated distrust and calls for its demise by Cato the Elder.

[Cato] also composed a book on farming, in which he actually gave recipes for making cakes and preserving fruit, so ambitious he was to be superior and peculiar in everything. The dinners, too, which he gave in the country, were quite plentiful. He always asked in congenial country neighbors, and made merry with them, and not only did those of his own age find in him an agreeable and much desired companion, but also the young. For he was a man of large experience, who had read and heard much that was well worth repeating. He held the table to be the very best promoter of friendship, and at his own, the conversation turned much to the praise of honorable and worthy citizens, greatly to the neglect of those who were worthless and base. About such Cato suffered no table-talk, either by way of praise or blame.

The last of his public services is supposed to have been the destruction of Carthage. It was Scipio the Younger who actually brought the task to completion, but it was largely in consequence of the advice and counsel of Cato that the Romans undertook the war. It was on this wise Cato was sent on an embassy to the Carthaginians and Masinissa the Numidian, who were at war with one another, to inquire into the grounds of their quarrel. Masinissa had been a friend of the Roman people from the first, and the Carthaginians had entered into treaty relations with Rome after the defeat which the elder Scipio had given them. The treaty deprived them of their empire, and imposed a grievous money tribute upon them. Cato, however, found the city by no means in a poor and lowly state, as the Romans supposed, but rather teeming with vigorous fighting men, overflowing with enormous wealth, filled with arms of every sort and with military supplies, and not a little puffed up by all this. He therefore thought it no time for the Romans to be ordering and arranging the affairs of Masinissa and the Numidians, but that unless they should repress a city which had always been their malignant foe, now that its power was so incredibly grown, they would be involved again in dangers as great as before. Accordingly, he returned with speed to Rome, and advised the Senate that the former calamitous defeats of the Carthaginians had diminished not so much their power as their foolhardiness, and were likely to render them in the end not weaker, but more expert in war; their present contest with Numidia was but a prelude to a contest with Rome, while peace and treaty were mere names wherewith to cover their postponement of war till a fit occasion offered. (*Plut.Vit.Cat.Mai.*25–26)

He [Cato] subsequently used dramatics to convince fellow senators of the dangers of a resurgent Carthage.

Burning with a mortal hatred to Carthage, anxious, too, for the safety of his posterity, and exclaiming at every sitting of the Senate that Carthage must be destroyed, Cato one day brought with him into the Senate House a ripe fig, the produce of that country. Exhibiting it to the assembled senators, "I ask you," said he, "when, do you suppose, this fruit was plucked from the tree?" All being of opinion that it had been but lately gathered,—"Know then," was his reply, "that this fig was plucked at Carthage but the day before yesterday—so near is the enemy to our walls." It was immediately after this occurrence that the Third Punic War commenced, in which Carthage was destroyed, though Cato had breathed his last, the year after this event. In this trait which are we the most to admire? Was it ingenuity and foresight on his part, or was it an accident that was thus aptly turned to advantage? Which, too, is the most surprising, the extraordinary quickness of the passage which must have been made, or the bold daring of the man? The thing, however, that is the most astonishing of all—indeed, I can conceive nothing more truly marvelous—is the fact that a city thus mighty, the rival of Rome for the sovereignty of the world during a period of one hundred and twenty years, owed its fall at last to an illustration drawn from a single fig!

Thus, did this fig effect that which neither Trebia nor Thrasimenus, not Cannæ itself, graced with the entombment of the Roman renown, not the Punic camp entrenched within three miles of the city, not even the disgrace of seeing Hannibal riding up to the Colline Gate, could suggest the means of accomplishing. It was left for a fig, in the hand of Cato, to show how near was Carthage to the gates of Rome! (*Plin. HN*.15.20)

Cato's deep hatred of Carthage prompted him to conclude each speech in the Senate by urging the removal of Rome's only rival. However, he did not live long enough to see its destruction.

And in one thing he was even more savage, namely, in adding to his vote on any question whatsoever these words: "In my opinion, Carthage must be destroyed." Publius Scipio Nasica, on the contrary, when called upon for his vote, always ended his speech with this declaration: "In my opinion, Carthage must be spared." He saw, probably, that the Roman people, in its wantonness, was already guilty of many excesses, in the pride of its prosperity, spurned the control of the Senate, and forcibly dragged the whole state with it, withersoever its mad desires inclined it. He wished, therefore, that the fear of Carthage should abide, to curb the boldness of the multitude like a bridle, believing her not strong enough to conquer Rome, nor yet weak enough to be despised. But this was precisely what Cato dreaded, when the Roman people was inebriated and staggering with its power, to have a city which had always been great, and was now but sobered and chastened by its calamities, forever threatening them. Such external threats to their sovereignty ought to be done away with altogether, he thought, that they might be free to devise a cure for their domestic fallings. In this way Cato is said to have brought to pass the third and last war against Carthage. But it had no sooner begun that he died. (*Plut. Vit. Cat.Mai*.27.1–4)

Rome subsequently proceeded to remove its archrival.

The Senate, which had been previously eager and prepared for war, having gained the accession of a city so strong and so conveniently placed, now disclosed its purpose. Assembling in the Capitol (where they were accustomed to deliberate on the subject of war), the senators voted to declare war against Carthage. (*App.Pun.*15.75)

The Carthaginians learned of the declaration of war and employed a desperate maneuver they thought might save their city.

[They] sent three hundred children of their noblest families as hostages, and would obey their orders in other respects, if the freedom and autonomy of Carthage should be preserved and that they should retain their lands in Africa. (*App.Pun.*16.77)

Despite this, Carthage was disarmed and complied with all of the demands of the Senate. Eventually, Carthage became fed up with the Romans because of the following speech of the consul Lucius Marcius Censorinus to the Carthaginian envoys in 149 BCE.

Your ready obedience up to this point, Carthaginians, in the matter of the hostages and arms, is worthy of all praise. In cases of necessity we must not multiply words. Bear bravely the remanding commands of the Senate. Yield Carthage to us and betake yourselves where you like within your own territory at a distance of at least fifteen kilometers from the sea, for we are resolved to raze your city to the ground. (*App.Pun.*17.81)

Carthage had no choice other than to prepare for war, as abandoning their city and way of life was tantamount to death.

The same day the Carthaginian Senate declared war and proclaimed freedom to the slaves. They also chose generals and selected Hasdrubal for the outside work, whom they had condemned to death, and who had already collected 30,000 men. They dispatched a messenger to him begging that, in the extreme peril of his country, he would not remember, or lay up against them, the wrong they had done him under the pressure of necessity from fear of the Romans.

Within the walls they chose for general another Hasdrubal, the son of a daughter of Masinissa. They also sent to the consuls asking a truce of thirty days in order to send an embassy to Rome. When this was refused a second time, a wonderful change and determination came over them, to endure everything rather than abandon their city.

Quickly all minds were filled with courage from this transformation. All the sacred places, the temples, and every other unoccupied space were turned into workshops, where men and women worked together day and night without pause, taking their food by turns on a fixed schedule. Each day they made 100 shields, 300 swords, 1,000 missiles for catapults, 500 darts and javelins, and as many catapults as they could. For strings to bend them the women cut off their hair for want of other fibers. (*App.Pun.*19.93)

After two years of fighting, the Romans still had not defeated the Carthaginians. They turned to Scipio Aemilianus. He blocked the city's harbor and breached the city walls.

Scipio's men cleared the city house by house. Many civilians were burned to death; others were crushed to death by the Roman cavalry. Fire raged for six days and nights. The last stand took place at the Temple of Eshmoun, where Hasdrubal's wife sacrificed herself and her children. Scipio ordered the city to be destroyed and burned. There is no mention of a curse. In fact, Scipio wept because he knew that Rome would one day face a similar fate.

Scipio, beholding this city, which had flourished 700 years from its foundation and had ruled over so many lands, islands, and seas, rich with arms and fleets, elephants and money, equal to the mightiest monarchies but far surpassing them in bravery and high spirit (since without ships or arms, and in the face of famine, it had sustained continuous war for three years), now come to its end in total destruction—Scipio, beholding this spectacle, is said to have shed tears and publicly lamented the fortune of the enemy.

After meditating by himself a long time and reflecting on the rise and fall of cities, nations, and empires, as well as of individuals, upon the fate of Troy that once proud city, upon that of the Assyrians, the Medes, and the Persians, greatest of all, and later the splendid Macedonian Empire, either voluntarily or otherwise the words of the poet escaped his lips:

"The day shall come in which our sacred Troy and Priam, and the people over whom spear-bearing Priam rules, shall perish all."

Being asked by Polybius in familiar conversation (for Polybius had been his tutor) what he meant by using these words, he said that he did not hesitate frankly to name his own country, for whose fate he feared when he considered the mutability of human affairs. And Polybius wrote this down just as he heard it.

Carthage being destroyed, Scipio gave the soldiers a certain number of days for plunder, reserving the gold, silver, and temple gifts. He also gave prizes to all who had distinguished themselves for bravery, except those who had violated the shrine of Apollo. Probably the Carthaginian god that is called Apollo was Rešef. He sent a swift ship, embellished with spoils, to Rome to announce the victory. He also sent word to Sicily that whatever temple gifts they could identify as taken from them by the Carthaginians in former wars they might come and take away. Thus, he endeared himself to the people as one who united clemency with power. He sold the rest of the spoils, and, in sacrificial cincture, burned the arms, engines, and useless ships as an offering to Mars and Minerva, according to the Roman custom.

When the people of Rome saw the ship and heard of the victory early in the evening, they poured into the streets and spent the whole night congratulating and embracing each other like people just now delivered from some great fear, just now confirmed in their worldwide supremacy, just now assured of the permanence of their own city, and winners of such a victory as never before. Many brilliant deeds of their own, many more of their ancestors, in Macedonia and Spain and lately against Antiochus the Great, and in Italy itself, had they celebrated; but no other war had so terrified them at their own gates as the Punic wars, which ever brought peril to them by reason of the perseverance, skill, and courage, as well as the bad faith, of those enemies. They recalled what they had suffered from the Carthaginians in Sicily and Spain, and in Italy itself for sixteen years, during which Hannibal destroyed 400 towns and killed 300,000 of their men in battles alone, more than once marching up to the city and putting it in extreme peril.

Pondering on these things, they were so excited over this victory that they could hardly believe it, and they asked each other over and over again whether it was really true that Carthage was destroyed. And so, they gabbled the whole night, telling how the arms of the Carthaginians were got away from them and how, contrary to expectation, they supplied themselves with others; how they lost their ships and built a great fleet out of old material; how the mouth of their harbor was closed, yet they managed to open another in a few days. They talked about the height of the walls, and the size of the stones, and the fires that so often destroyed the engines. They pictured to each other the whole war, as though it were just taking place under their own eyes, suiting the action to the word; and they seemed to see Scipio on the ladders, on shipboard, at the gates, in the battles, and darting hither and thither. In this way the people of Rome passed the night. (*App.Pun.27*.132–134)

Further Reading

Gainsford, Peter, "Salting the Earth," *Modern Myths about the Ancient World. Kiwi Hellenist.* December 12, 2016. http://kiwihellenist.blogspot.com/2016/12/salting-earth.html

Gevirtz, Stanley, "Jericho and Schechem: A Religio-Literary Aspect of City Destruction," *Vetus Testamentum*, Vol. 13, Fasc. 1 (1963), pp. 52–62.

Ridley, R. T., "To Be Taken with a Pinch of Salt: The Destruction of Carthage," *Classical Philology*, Vol. 81 (1986), pp. 140–146.

Stevens, S. T., "A Legend of the Destruction of Carthage," *Classical Philology*, Vol. 83 (1988), pp. 39–41.

Visonà, P., "Passing the Salt: On the Destruction of Carthage Again," *Classical Philology*, Vol. 83 (1988), pp. 41–42.

Warmington, B. H., "The Destruction of Carthage: A Retractatio," *Classical Philology*, Vol. 83 (1988), pp. 308–310.

2

Cato the Elder Hated Greek and Punic Culture

What People Think Happened

Cato the Elder has come to represent the embodiment of xenophobia and national politics in Roman history. His contentious relationship with the Scipio family highlights this image, to the point where people now assume he was vicious and bigoted and associate him with every kind of prejudice. In general, people typically assume that he despised non-Romans and therefore hated Romans who loved Greek culture (philhellenes) and Greek culture itself. He was misogynistic, abusive to slaves, and not above ruining someone else's political career or even extinguishing whole cultures. This image has survived over centuries. A popular piece of evidence toward supporting this idea was his practice of ending every speech in the Senate with "Carthage must be destroyed," a wish that came true after his death in 149 BCE (*Plut. Vit. Cat.Mai.*27).

Marcus Porcius Cato, also known as Cato the Elder, was born in 234 BCE. He "was well informed in political affairs" (*Nep. Cat.*2). He criticized the Scipio family relentlessly because they were philhellenes, hating them so much that he "even instigated some to begin prosecutions as for instance Petillius against Scipio." He also cooperated with the accusers of Scipio's brother Lucius (*Plut. Vit. Cat.Mai.*15.2). Cato's attacks caused Scipio Africanus, the hero of the Second Punic War, to step down to become a private citizen after his consulship ended (*Nep. Cat.*3).

People also believe Cato supported laws against adornments worn by elite females. He said, "If we had, each one of us, made it a rule to uphold the rights and authority of the husbands we should not now have this trouble with the whole body of our women" (*Livy.Ab.Urbe.Cond.*34.1.2).

Cato was stingy and mistreated his elderly slaves. Plutarch describes Cato's cruelty to elderly slaves and old animals "as the mark of a very mean nature" (*Plut.Vit.Cat.Mai.*5). Livy said, "Cato is a powerful speaker and sometimes almost menacing" (*Livy.Ab.Urbe.Cond.*34.5).

Worse yet in Cato's eyes, according to popular opinion, was Roman involvement in the East. Cato insulted King Eumenes II of Armenia by saying, "He is an excellent man, and a friend of Rome, but the animal known as king is by nature carnivorous" (*Plut.Vit.Cat.Mai.*8.8).

After his term as censor, Cato continued as the persistent opponent of Carthage and was unnerved by what he saw there. Plutarch reports: "In addition to this, it is said that Cato contrived to drop a Libyan fig in the Senate, as he shook out the folds of his toga, and then, as the senators admired its size and beauty, said that the country where it grew was only three days' sail from Rome. And in one thing he said was even more savage, namely, in adding to his vote on any question whatsoever these words, 'In my opinion, Carthage must be destroyed'" (*Plut.Vit.Cat.Mai.*27).

Pliny the Elder went into even more detail when he recounted this incident: Cato one day brought with him into the Senate House a ripe fig, the produce of that country. Exhibiting it to the assembled senators, "I ask you," said he, "when, do you suppose, this fruit was plucked from the tree?" All being of the opinion that it had been but lately gathered—"Know then," was his reply, "that this fig was plucked at Carthage but the day before yesterday—so near is the enemy to our walls." It was immediately after this occurrence that the Third Punic War commenced. Thus, "the rival of Rome for the sovereignty of the world during a period of one hundred and twenty years, owed its fall at last to an illustration drawn from a single fig!" (*Plin.HN.*15.20).

How the Story Became Popular

It was widely known that Cato the Elder believed Greek cultural influence would destroy Rome. People even knew that he especially loathed the Scipios for promoting philhellenism, and he hated Carthage as much as he despised the Greeks when he grumbled, "Carthage must be destroyed," after every speech.

Yet it was Plutarch who helped to spread a particularly negative image of Cato by describing him as: "Red-haired, snapper and biter, his eyes flashing defiance" (*Plut.Vit.Cat.Mai*.1.3). Pliny also contributed to this image when he quoted Cato's view of the Greeks: "They are a most iniquitous and intractable race." Furthermore, Pliny said, Cato warned that Greek literature would destroy Rome (*Plin.HN*.29.7). The popularity of this view of Greek culture helped spread Cato's acrimonious reputation. Elite Romans found Greeks treacherous: "[T]he words of the Greeks were born on their lips, but those of the Romans in their hearts" (*Plut.Vit.Cat. Mai*.12.5, *Cic.Tusc*.1.1.*Juv*.3). Moreover, Cato did not help himself when he was rude to Greeks by speaking Latin while in Athens (*Plut.Vit.Cat. Mai*.12.4).

Plutarch's unpleasant version of Cato had him declare that there was nothing admirable about Socrates, who, Cato said, enticed people to break laws. Furthermore, the famous Roman quipped, Socrates' sons were stupid (*Plut.Vit.Cat.Mai*.20.2).

Cato's reluctance to deal with Greeks also perpetuated the perception of his bigotry. For example, he taught his own son, refusing to allow a Greek to instruct him (*Plut.Vit.Cat.Mai*.20.3–4). Cato derided Greek doctors because he believed they swore to kill non-Greeks with their medicine (*Plut.Vit.Cat.Mai*.23, *Plin.HN*.29.7).

Naturally, Cato scorned philhellenes like Scipio Africanus and his family, lending the perception of viciousness to his character (*Plut.Vit. Flamm*.8.2). He accused Scipio of extravagance and of corrupting soldiers. Regardless, Scipio convinced officials he was innocent (*Plut.Vit.Cat. Mai*.3.5–8). Cato persisted, and Scipio eventually retired after being put on trial (*Livy.Ab.Urbe.Cond*.38.51–52). Cato was censured for mistreating Lucius, the brother of Scipio, out of spite (*Plut.Vit.Cat.Mai*.18.1, *Liv. Ab.Urbe.Cond*.38.54).

Cato's thoughts on Carthage also contributed to his cantankerous reputation. Often-repeated slogans, such as "Carthage must be destroyed" or "Furthermore, I consider Carthage must be destroyed," are variants of his desire to make it disappear. His nationalistic fear of a powerful, resurgent Carthage drove his vitriolic comments, which historians were only too eager to repeat. For instance, Cato stated, "I am declaring war on Carthage, for she has long been plotting mischief; and I shall not cease to fear her until I know that she has been utterly destroyed" (*Cic.Sen*.6.18).

Plutarch more strongly restated Cato's insistent desire: "[T]he last of his public services is supposed to have been the destruction of Carthage.

Cato showed figs to the Senate and uttered, 'It seems to me that Carthage should not exist anymore.'" Plutarch's dramatic wording was enhanced over time.

Diodorus Siculus also perpetuated Cato's reputation for an unreasonable desire for cultural extinction: "[W]henever he delivered his opinion in the Senate he always repeated that Carthage must be destroyed, even if the Senate was debating some other, unrelated matter; but Publius Nasica was ever of the opposite opinion, that Carthage should be preserved" (*Diod. Sic.*34/35.33G).

More crucially, Pliny the Elder's embellishment of the fig story provides the first link to the modern tradition. He placed the saying against a rhetorical backdrop:

> Burning with a mortal hatred to Carthage, anxious, too, for the safety of his posterity, and exclaiming at every sitting of the Senate that Carthage must be destroyed, Cato one day brought with him into the Senate House a ripe fig, the produce of that country. Exhibiting it to the assembled senators, "I ask you," said he, "when, do you suppose, this fruit was plucked from the tree?" All being of the opinion that it had been but lately gathered,—"Know then," was his reply, "that this fig was plucked at Carthage but the day before yesterday—so near is the enemy to our walls." It was immediately after this occurrence that the Third Punic War commenced, in which Carthage was destroyed. (*Plin.HN*.15.20)

Livy added, "Cato argued for, and Nasica against, war and the removal and sack of Carthage" (*Livy.Ab.Urbe.Cond.Per.*49.2).

Cicero imagined Cato's anxiety: "I am declaring war on Carthage, for she has long been plotting mischief; and I shall not cease to fear her until I know that she has been utterly destroyed" (*Cic.Sen.*6.18).

Velleius Paterculus declared, "Cato, the constant advocate of her destruction, died three years before the fall of Carthage" (*Vell.Pat.*1.13).

Cornelius Nepos tells the story: "But when he returned to Carthage, he realized that the state's condition was very different from what he had expected. For after such a long period of external war, a civil war flared up—Carthage would never face a more serious danger until it was destroyed" (*Nep.Hamil.*2.1).

Florus repeated Pliny almost verbatim: "Cato, with implacable hatred, kept declaring, even when he was consulted on other subjects, that Carthage must be destroyed" (*Flor.Epit.*1.31).

Appian indicated, "It is said that Cato, from time to time, continually expressed the opinion in the Senate that Carthage should not exist.

Scipio Nasica held the contrary view that 'Carthage should exist so that the Roman discipline, which was already relaxing, might be preserved through fear of her'" (*App.Pun.*14.69).

In the fourth century, Aurelius Victor reiterated the wish as "Carthage should be destroyed" (*Aur.Vict.Caes.*3.47.8).

Other ancient writers followed suit. Plutarch contributed indirectly regarding the myth of Carthage's destruction as his writings impacted historical writing in Europe from the sixteenth to the nineteenth centuries. These sources promoted the idea that Cato demanded the destruction of Carthage instead of just wishing it not to exist.

One form of the phrase appeared initially in the English-French translation of *Histoire Romaine depuis la foundation de Rome*, Amsterdam (1730, p. 126). It was translated into English by L. Echard as "Carthage must be destroyed," which is the commonly used quote in the English-speaking world to this day.

The Latin *ceterum censeo* ("I think, I am of the view") originated in the German-speaking world. The fixed phrase appears first in 1821 in Fiedler's *Geschichte des römischen Staates und Volkes* in the famous saying, "*Ceterum censeo, Carthaginem esse delendam*" (i.e., "Moreover, I think that Carthage must be destroyed"). Fiedler's quote resurfaces in 1853 in C. Peters's *Geschichte Roms* (Halle, 1853, p. 535): "The most enthusiastic of them was M. Porcius Cato, who for a time closed every speech in the Senate with the most famous words: 'By the way, I am of the opinion that Carthage must be destroyed.'"

The notion of Cato as hateful sourpuss has prevailed ever since. The modern phrasing is a rhetorical and dramatic description of the scenes in the Senate during the period preceding the Third Punic War.

PRIMARY DOCUMENTS

Plutarch's description of Cato the Elder declares:

As for his outward appearance, he had reddish hair, and keen green eyes, as the author of this well-known epigram naturally gives us to understand:

"Red-haired, snapper and biter, his grey eyes flashing defiance, Porcius, come to the shades, back will be thrust by their queen." (*Plut.Vit. Cat.Mai.*1.3)

Ginger-colored locks were looked upon with suspicion by some in the ancient world. For example, Martial has this to say about Zoilus, a social climber:

"With red hair, a black face, a cloven foot, and blear eyes, you show the world a prodigy, Zoilus, if you are an honest man."

Cato was not alone in his suspicion of Greeks. Juvenal's discomfort with foreigners is evident in Satire 3. Here he appears to categorize ancient Greeks according to common negative stereotypes, along with other non-Romans.

I cannot abide, Quirites [citizens of Rome], a Rome of Greeks; and yet what fraction of our dregs comes from Greece? The Syrian Orontes has long since poured into the Tiber, bringing with it its lingo and its manners, its flutes and its slanting harp-strings: bringing too, the timbrels of the breed, and the trulls [prostitutes] who are bidden ply their trade at the Circus. Out upon you, all ye that delight in foreign strumpets with painted headdresses! Your country clown, Quirinus, now trips to dinner in Greek-fangled slippers, and wears *niceterian* ornaments upon a *ceromatic* neck! One comes from lofty Sicyon, another from Amydon or Andros, others from Samos, Tralles or Alabanda; all making for the Esquiline, or for the hill that takes its name from osier-beds; all ready to worm their way into the houses of the great and become their masters. Quick of wit and of unbounded impudence, they are as ready of speech as Isaeus, and more torrential. Say, what do you think that fellow there to be? He has brought with him any character you please; grammarian, orator, geometrician; painter, trainer, or rope-dancer; augur, doctor or astrologer:

"All sciences a fasting monsieur knows,
And bid him go to Hell, to Hell he goes!"

In fine, the man who took to himself wings was not a Moor, nor a Sarmatian, nor a Thracian, but one born in the very heart of Athens!

Must I not make my escape from purple-clad gentry like these? Is a man to sign his name before me, and recline upon a couch above mine, who has been wafted to Rome by the wind which brings us our damsons and our figs? Is it to go so utterly for nothing that as a babe I drank in the air of the Aventine, and was nurtured on the Sabine berry?

What of this again, that these people are experts in flattery, and will commend the talk of an illiterate, or the beauty of a deformed, friend, and compare the scraggy neck of some weakling to the brawny throat of Hercules when holding up Antaeus from the earth; or go into ecstasies over a squeaky voice not more melodious than that of a cock when he pecks his spouse the hen? We, no doubt, can praise the same things that they do; but what they say is believed. Could any actor do better when he plays the part of Thais, or of a matron, or of the nude Doris? You would never think that it was an actor that was speaking, but a very woman, complete in all her parts. Yet, in their own country, neither Antiochus nor Stratocles, neither Demetrius nor the delicate Haemus, will be applauded: they are a nation of play-actors. If you smile, your Greek will split his sides with laughter; if he sees his friend drop a tear, he weeps, though without grieving; if you call for a bit of fire in winter-time, he puts on his cloak; if you say "I am hot," he breaks into a sweat. Thus, we are not upon a level, he and I; he has always the best of it, being ready at any moment, by night or by day, to take his expression from another man's face, to throw up his hands and applaud if his friend spit or hiccup nicely, or if his golden basin make a gurgle when turned upside down.

Besides all this, there is nothing sacred to his lusts: not the matron of the family, nor the maiden daughter, not the as yet un-bearded son-in-law to be, not even the as yet unpolluted son; if none of these be there, he will debauch the grandmother. These men want to discover the secrets of the family, and so make themselves feared. And now that I am speaking of the Greeks, pass on to the schools, and hear of a graver crime; the Stoic who informed against and slew his own young friend and disciple was born on that river bank where the Gorgon's winged steed fell to earth. No: there is no room for any Roman here, where some Protogenes, or Diphilus, or Hermarchus rules the roost—one who by a defect of his race never shares a friend, but keeps him all to himself. For when once he has dropped into a facile ear one particle of his own and his country's poison, I am thrust from the door, and all my long years of servitude go for nothing. Nowhere is it so easy as at Rome to throw an old client overboard. (*Juv.*3.58–125)

Cato hated Romans who were obsessed with Hellenic culture.

He also spent much time at Athens. And we are told that a certain speech of his is extant, which he addressed to the Athenian people in Greek, declaring that he admired the virtues of ancient Athenians, and was glad to behold a city so beautiful and grand as theirs. But this is not true. On the contrary, he dealt with Athenians through an interpreter. He could have spoken to them directly, but he always clung to his native ways, and mocked those who were lost in admiration for anything that was Greek. For instance, he poked fun at Postumius Albinus, who wrote a history in Greek, and asked the indulgence of his readers. Cato said they might have shown him indulgence had he undertaken his task in consequence of a compulsory vote of the Amphictyonic Assembly. Moreover, he says the

Athenians were astonished at the speed and pungency of his discourse. For what he himself set forth with brevity, the interpreter would repeat to them at great length and with many words: on the whole he thought the words of the Greeks were born on their lips, but those of the Romans in their hearts. (*Plut. Vit. Cat. Mai.*12.4–5)

Cato warned his son that Rome was in danger of being contaminated by Greek culture and the Philhellenes.

And seeking to prejudice his son against Greek culture, he indulges in an utterance all too rash for his years, declaring, in the tone of a prophet or a seer, that Rome would lose her empire when she had become infected with Greek letters. (*Plut. Vit. Cat. Mai.*23.2)

However, Plutarch remarks that the passage of time proved Cato the Elder to be wrong.

But time had certainly shown the emptiness of this ill-boding speech of his, for while the city was at the zenith of empire, she made every form of Greek learning and culture her own. (*Plut. Vit. Cat. Mai.*23.3)

Cicero criticizes Greeks because they prefer leisure affairs instead of military service.

What shall I say of our military affairs in which our ancestors have been most eminent in valor, and still more so in discipline? As to those things which are attained not by study, but nature, neither Greece, nor any nation, is comparable to us; for what people has displayed such gravity, such steadiness, such greatness of soul, probity, faith—such distinguished virtue of every kind, as to be equal to our ancestors. (*Cic. Tusc.*1.1)

Cato's remarks on Greek philosophers and Socrates (whom he believed undermined the ancient ways) suggest he is xenophobic.

This he did, not as some think, out of personal hostility to Carneades, but because he was totally averse to philosophy, and made mock of all Greek culture and training, out of patriotic zeal. He says, for instance, that Socrates was a mighty prattler, who attempted, as best he could, to be his country's tyrant, by abolishing its customs, and by enticing his fellow citizens into opinions contrary to the laws. (*Plut. Vit. Cat. Mai.*23.1)

Cato considered Greek doctors to be homicidal maniacs.

It was not only Greek philosophers that he hated, but he was also suspicious of Greeks who practiced medicine at Rome. He had heard, it would seem, of Hippocrates' reply when the Great King of Persia consulted him, with the promise of a fee of many talents, namely that he would never put his skill at the service of the Barbarians who were enemies of Greece. He said that all Greek physicians had taken a similar oath, and urged his son to beware of them all. (*Plut.Vit.Cat.Mai.*23.3–4)

Plutarch criticizes Cato for his cheapness, cruelty to animals, and abuse of slaves.

He tells us that he never wore clothing worth more than a hundred drachmas; that he drank, even when he was praetor of consul, the same wine as his slaves; that as for fish and meats, he would buy thirty asses' worth for his dinner from the public stalls, and even this for the city's sake, he might not live on bread alone, but strengthen his body for military service; that he once fell heir to an embroidered Babylonian robe, but sold it at once; that not a single one of his cottages had plastered walls; that he never paid more than fifteen hundred drachmas for a slave, since he did not want them to be delicately beautiful, but sturdy workers, as grooms and herdsmen, and these he thought it his duty to sell when they got oldish, instead of feeding them when they were useless; and that in general, he thought nothing cheap that one could do without, but that what one did not need, even if it cost but a penny, was dear; also that he bought lands where crops were raised and cattle herded, not those where lawns were sprinkled and paths swept.

These things were ascribed by some to the man's parsimony; but others condoned them in the belief that he lived in this contracted way only to correct and moderate the extravagances of others. However, for my part, I regard the treatment of his slaves like beasts of burden, using them to the uttermost, and then, when they were old, driving them off and selling them, as the mark of a very mean nature, which recognizes no tie between man and man but that of necessity. And yet we know that kindness has a wider scope than justice. Law and justice we naturally apply to men alone; but when it comes to beneficence and charity, these often flow in streams from the gentle heart, like water from a copious spring, even down to dumb beasts. A kindly man will take good care of his horses even when they are worn out with age, and of his dogs, too, not only in their puppyhood, but when their old age needs nursing. (*Plut.Vit.Cat.Mai.*4–5.1–2)

Cato also mistrusted women. He considered them inferior to men and might be considered a misogynist. He warned men about the dangers of women.

Again, he said the Romans were like sheep; for as these are not to be persuaded one by one, but all in a body blindly follow their leaders, "so, ye" he said, "though as individuals ye would not deign to the counsels of certain men, when ye are got together ye suffer to be led by them." Discoursing on the power of women, he said, "All other men rule their wives; we rule other men, and our wives rule us." This, however, is a translation from the sayings of Themistocles. He, finding himself much under his son's orders through the lad's mother, said: "Wife, the Athenians rule the Hellenes, I rule the Athenians, thou rulest me, and thy son thee. Therefore let him make sparing use of that authority which makes him, child though he is, the most powerful of the Hellenes." (*Plut.Vit.Cat.Mai.*8.2)

Likewise, Livy reveals that Cato blamed women and their love of luxury and excess for the decline of Rome.

You have often heard my complaints about the excessive spending of the women, and of the men, magistrates as well as private citizens, about the sorry state of our commonwealth because of two opposing vices, avarice and extravagance—plagues which have been the destruction of all great empires. As the fortune of our commonwealth grows better and happier day by day, and as our empire increases—and already we have crossed into Greece and Asia (regions full of all kinds of sensual allurements) and are even laying hands on the treasures of kings—I am the more alarmed lest these things should capture us instead of our capturing them; those statues brought from Syracuse, believe me, were hostile standards brought against this city. And now I hear far too many people praising the ornaments of Corinth and Athens, and jeering at the terracotta antefixes of the Roman gods. For my part, I prefer to have those gods propitious to us—as I trust they will be propitious, if we allow them to remain in their own abodes. (*Livy.Ab.Urbe.Cond.*34.4)

Cato was the archenemy of Scipio the Great.

The two men of his time who were most notable and had the greatest influence in the city, Scipio Africanus and Marcus Cato, were at variance with one another. Of these, Titus appointed Scipio to be dean of the Senate, believing him to be its best and foremost man; but with Cato he came into hostile relations, owing to the following unfortunate circumstances. Titus had a brother, Lucius, who was unlike him in all other ways, and especially in his shameful addiction to pleasure and his utter contempt of decency. (*Plut.Vit.Flamm.*18.2)

Cato denounced Scipio Africanus for his wasteful ways and perversion of young men.

He did not hesitate to oppose the great Scipio, a youthful rival of Fabius, and thought to be envious of him. When he was sent out with Scipio as quaestor for the war in Africa, he saw that the man indulged in wanton extravagance, and lavished money without stint on his soldiery. He therefore made bold to tell him that the matter of expense was not the greatest evil to be complained of, but the fact that he was corrupting the native simplicity of his soldiers, who resorted to wanton pleasures when their pay exceeded their actual needs. Scipio replied that he had no use for a parsimonious quaestor when the winds were bearing him under full sail to the war; he owed the city an account of his achievements, not of its moneys. Cato therefore left Sicily and joined Fabius in denouncing before the Senate Scipio's waste of enormous moneys, and his boys' addiction to palestras and theaters, as though he were not commander of an army, but master of a festival. (*Plut.Vit.Cat.Mai.*3.5–7)

Plutarch contributed indirectly to Cato's reputation as destroyer of Carthage.

In addition to this, it is said that Cato contrived to drop a Libyan fig in the Senate, as he shook out the folds of his toga, and then, as the senators admired its size and beauty, said that the country where it grew was only three days' sail from Rome. And in one thing he said was even more savage, namely, in adding to his vote on any question whatsoever these words: "In my opinion, Carthage should not exist." (*Plut.Vit.Cat.Mai.*27.1)

Pliny the Elder dramatized the event by placing it in a rhetorical setting.

Burning with a mortal hatred to Carthage, anxious, too, for the safety of his posterity, and exclaiming at every sitting of the Senate that Carthage must be destroyed, Cato one day brought with him into the Senate House a ripe fig, the produce of that country. Exhibiting it to the assembled senators, "I ask you," said he, "when, do you suppose, this fruit was plucked from the tree?" All being of the opinion that it had been but lately gathered,—"Know then," was his reply, "that this fig was plucked at Carthage but the day before yesterday—so near is the enemy to our walls." It was immediately after this occurrence that the Third Punic War commenced, in which Carthage was destroyed, though Cato had breathed his last, the year after this event. In this trait are we the most to admire? Was it ingenuity and foresight on his part, or was it an accident that was thus aptly turned to advantage? Which too, is the most surprising, the extraordinary quickness of the passage which must have been made, or the bold daring of the man? The thing, however, that is the most astonishing of all—indeed, I can conceive nothing more truly marvelous—is the fact that a city thus mighty, the rival of Rome for the sovereignty of the world during a period of one hundred and twenty years, owed its fall at last to an illustration drawn from a single fig! (*Plin.HN.*15.20)

Cicero channels his inner Cato's deepest fears.

But perhaps it seems to you that I who engaged in various kinds of warfare as private, captain, general and commander-in-chief, am unemployed now that I do not go to war. And yet I direct the Senate as to what wars should be waged and how: at the present time, far in advance of hostilities, I am declaring war on Carthage, for she has long been plotting mischief; and I shall not cease to fear her until I know that she has been utterly destroyed. And I pray the immortal gods to reserve for you, Scipio, the glory of completing the work which your grandfather left unfinished! (*Cic.Sen.*1.18)

What Really Happened

"Carthage must be destroyed" is a modern creation. Cato the Elder and the Scipios were symbols of the clash of culture that resulted from the Roman expansion in the East. Cato represents the simple Roman farmer-soldier-politician who contrasted with philhellenes like the Scipios. The narrative that Cato demanded Carthage to be destroyed while Scipio Nasica requested it to be saved is an embellished historical event, embodying a larger cultural rivalry.

Rome's conquests in Greece and the Hellenistic kingdoms resulted in the importation of art, luxury items, and Greek intellectuals and slaves to the city, but it also bred the fear of losing Roman culture. "Conquered Greece took captive her savage conqueror and brought her arts into rustic Latium" (*Hor.Epist.*1.156–157). Many elites adopted Greek culture while others struggled with the resulting changes and backlash. Romans criticized Greeks as lazy, weak cowards who cared more for leisurely activities than deeds that served the State. Polybius complained: "our men of action in Greece are relieved from the ambitions of a military or political career and have therefore ample means for inquiry and study" (*Polyb*.3.59.4).

Cato is the perfect example of this cultural tension because he lived through Rome's transition from city-state to empire. He was actually a much more complex personality than history sometimes reflects. For example, Plutarch personifies him as the epitome of a Roman. Cato practiced self-restraint and expected the same of others. He lived this way "to correct and moderate the extravagances of others" (*Plut.Vit.Cat.Mai.*5.1). Furthermore, Cato was a skilled orator and provided legal services gratis. His enemies hated him because he rose daily and devoted himself to public service.

Roman officials handled administrative duties in the provinces. Cato was the ideal magistrate in Sardinia. His predecessors "oppressed the province with the cost of their large retinues of servants and friends, and of their lavish and elaborate banquets" (*Plut.Vit.Cat.Mai.*6.2).

Because of his austerity, though, Cato had no shortage of enemies. His most famous rivalry involved Scipio Africanus. Their disagreement began during preparations for the African campaign in Sicily. Cato opposed Scipio's indulgence, which he thought corrupted young soldiers, so he convinced tribunes to recall Scipio. Cato used the negative stereotype of the luxury-loving Greek as a pejorative description of Scipio the Great in order to discredit him (*Plut.Vit.Cat.Mai.*3.5–8). Nevertheless, Africanus convinced the tribunes to allow him to proceed to his war in Africa.

Later Scipio Africanus, in response, tried to end Cato's command in Spain. Nonetheless, the Senate refused. Scipio's actions hurt his reputation, while Cato celebrated a triumph (*Plut.Vit.Cat.Mai.*11). Eventually Scipio Africanus was accused of accepting bribes (*Livy.Ab.Urbe.Cond.*38.51). "He [Scipio] saw before him envious attacks and contests with the tribunes and so after a somewhat lengthy adjournment had been agreed upon, he retired to Liternum" (*Livy.Ab.Urbe.Cond.*38.52). "With the death of Africanus, the courage of his enemies rose. The foremost of these was M. Porcius Cato, who even during Scipio's lifetime was constantly belittling his greatness" (*Livy.Ab.Urbe.Cond.*38.54).

Cato ousted Lucius, the brother of Scipio, from the equestrian order. For this he was heavily criticized because "he was thought to have done this as an insult to the memory of Scipio Africanus. But he was most obnoxious to the majority of his enemies because he lopped off extravagance in living" (*Plut.Vit.Cat.Mai.*18.1).

Cato and Cicero considered Roman culture to be superior. "I have often argued, the Latin language, so far from having a poor vocabulary, as is commonly supposed is actually richer than the Greek" (*Cic.Tusc.1.3, Cic.Fin.*1.1, 1.3, 10). "On the whole he [Cato] thought the words of the Greeks were born on their lips, but those of the Romans in their hearts" (*Plut.Vit.Cat.Mai.*12.5).

Cato's speech at Athens was meant to demonstrate the superiority of Latin and thus the Romans. It is not anti-Hellene. The Greek audience needed a translator. Cato's use of Latin signified the superiority of Latin's simplicity versus the wordiness of Greek (*Plut.Vit.Cat.Mai.*12.4–5).

Cato lampooned Greeks in part because they mocked Romans. He warned his son Marcus that "they are in the common habit, too, of calling us barbarians, and stigmatize us beyond all other nations, by giving us the abominable appellation of *Opici*" ("bumpkin" or "hick") (*Plin.HN.*29.7). Cato also decried the depravity when good looking slaves from Greece were more valuable than a traditional Roman farm.

Yet Cato actually had an ambivalent attitude regarding Hellenic culture. On the one hand, he admired Greek education and literature. At the same time, however, he considered Greeks a danger to Roman customs and values, which Romans considered superior to those of the people whom they conquered, as the examples above reflect.

Cato's admiration can be seen when Plutarch and Gellius mention Greek influence, at times verbatim, in Cato's writings (*Plut.Vit.Cat.Mai.* 2.4, *Gell.NA.*13.18.1–3). Cato's oratory also benefitted from Thucydides and Demosthenes (*Plut.Vit.Cat.Mai.*2.4). Cato's poetic history, *Origines*, was the first written in Latin. Previous to this, most Latin literature originated as translations from the Greek by authors such as Livius Andronicus, Naevius, Plautus, and Ennius, whom Cato brought to Italy.

Cato's rhetorical skills demonstrate his ambiguity regarding foreign policy. On the one hand he convinced the Senate not to attack Rhodes for not fighting against King Perseus of Macedon (*Cato.Orig.Frag.*5.3). On the other hand, he played a significant role in the demise of the city of Carthage.

Cato's ambivalent attitude is also evident regarding philosophy. He met Nearchus the philosopher, after which he "was eager to know of his doctrines" (*Plut.Vit.Cat.Mai.*2.3). Yet he believed philosophy could be subversive and destabilizing because it stressed argument versus substance. He feared that young men "should come to love a reputation based on mere words more than one achieved by martial deeds" (*Plut.Vit.Cat.Mai.* 22.4). He had philosophers expelled from Rome in order that "youth of

Rome give ear to their laws and magistrates, as heretofore" (*Plut.Vit.Cat. Mai*.22.4).

Some of Cato's supposed anti-Greek prejudice was misunderstood. For example, Cato stigmatized Greek doctors as homicidal in order to stress the superiority of Roman medicine. His most famous remarks may have actually just referred to the first Greek doctor to practice medicine in Rome. He was nicknamed *Carnifax* (executioner) (*Plin.HN*.29.6).

Cato objected to his son learning from his educated Greek slave because he was a slave (*Plut.Vit.Cat.Mai*.20.3–5), not because he was Greek.

Cato was a reactionary to Carthage. He fought in the Second Punic War and feared what he encountered in the city after returning from a diplomatic mission. In the Senate he expressed concern about a resurgent Carthage, but his alleged quote was dramatized and used in an oratory setting in order to emphasize his feud with the Scipios.

Plutarch's biography of Cato emphasizes the dilemma that took place in Rome regarding conquest and social changes in Rome. The struggle between traditional Roman ways and the adoption of Greek culture was personified in Cato the Elder and the Scipios.

PRIMARY DOCUMENTS

Cato the Elder came from a long line of common military soldiers. The family's original name was Priscus but was changed to Cato because of Cato's great wisdom and public service. He was an old-fashioned Roman patriot, a war hero and a new man, that is, the first man in his family to be a member of the Senate.

The family of Marcus Cato, it is said, was of Tusculan origin, though he lived, previous to his career as soldier and statesmen, on an inherited estate in the country of the Sabines. His ancestors commonly passed for men of no vote whatever, but Cato himself extols his father, Marcus, as a brave man and good soldier. He also says that his grandfather, Cato, often won prizes for soldierly valor, and received from the state treasury, because of his bravery, the prize of five horses which had been killed under him in battle. The Romans used to call men who had no family distinction, but were coming into public notice through their own achievements, "new men," and such they called Cato. But he himself used to say as far as office and distinction went, he was new, but having regard to ancestral deeds of valor, he was oldest of the old. His third name was not Cato at first, but Priscus.

Afterwards he got the surname of Cato for his great abilities. The Romans call a man who is wise and prudent, *catus*. (*Plut.Vit.Cat.Mai*.1.1–2)

Cato lived the Roman ideal of the citizen/soldier farmer. He was frugal, worked with his hands and was a brave soldier. He was also honest and did legal work for free. He lived as modestly as Roman heroes of the past, such as Manius Curius Dentatus, a frugal and incorruptible war hero of the Roman Republic.

His bodily habit, since he was addicted from the very first to labor with his own hands, a temperate mode of life, and military duties, was very serviceable, and disposed alike to vigor and health. His discourse—a second body, as it were, and for the use of a man who would live neither obscurely nor idly, an instrument with which to perform not only necessary, but also high and noble services—this he developed and perfected in the villages and towns about Rome, where he served as an advocate for all who needed him, and got the reputation of being, first a zealous pleader, and a capable orator. Thenceforth the weight and dignity of his character revealed themselves more and more to those who had dealings with him; they saw that he was bound to be a man of great affairs, and have a leading place in the state. For he not only gave his services in legal contests without a fee of any sort, as it would seem, but did not appear to cherish the repute won in such contests as his chief ambition. Nay, he was far more desirous of high repute in battles and campaigns against the enemy, and while he was yet a mere stripling, had his breast covered with honorable wounds. He says himself that he made his first campaign when he was seventeen years old, at the time when Hannibal was consuming Italy with the flames of his successes.

In battle, he showed himself effective of hand, sure and steadfast of foot, and of a fierce countenance. With threatening speech and harsh cries, he would advance upon the foe, for he rightly thought, and tried to show others, that often times such action terrifies the enemy more than the sword. On the march, he carried his own armor on foot, while a single attendant followed in charge of his camp utensils. With this man, it is said, he was never wroth, and never scolded him when he served up a meal, nay, he actually took hold himself and assisted in most such preparations, provided he was free from his military duties. Water was all he drank on his campaigns, except once in a while, in a raging thirst, he would call for vinegar, or when his strength was failing, would add a little wine.

Near his fields was the cottage which had once belonged to Manius Curius, a hero of three triumphs. To this he would often go, and the sight of the small farm and the mean dwelling led him to think of their former owner, who, though he had become the greatest of the Romans, had subdued the most warlike nations, and driven Pyrrhus out of Italy, nevertheless till this little patch of ground with his own hands and occupied this cottage, after three triumphs. Here it was that the ambassadors of the Samnites once found him seated at his hearth cooking turnips, and offered him as much gold; but he dismissed them, saying that a man whom such a meal satisfied had no need of gold, and for his part the thought that a more honorable thing than the possession of gold was the conquest of its possessors. Cato would go away with his mind full of these things, and on viewing again his own house and lands and servants and mode of life, would increase the labors of his hands and lop off his extravagancies. (*Plut. Vit.Cat.Mai.*1.3–2)

Cicero condemns Romans who see Greek literature as superior.

My dear Brutus,—The following essay, I am well aware, attempting as it does to present in a Latin dress subjects that philosophers of consummate ability and profound learning have already handled in Greek, is sure to encounter criticism from different quarters. Certain persons, and those not without some pretension to letters, disapprove of the study of philosophy altogether. Others do not so greatly object to it provided it be followed in dilettante fashion; but they do not think it ought to engage so large amount of one's interest and attention. A third class, learned in Greek literature and contemptuous of Latin, will say that they prefer to spend their time in reading Greek. Lastly, I suspect there will be some who will wish to divert me to other fields of authorship, asserting that this kind of composition, though a graceful recreation, is beneath the dignity of my character and position. To all of these objections I suppose I ought to make some brief reply. (*Cic.Fin.*1.1)

Cicero follows up with the following comments.

A more difficult task therefore is to deal with the objection of those who profess a contempt for Latin writings as such. What astonishes me first of all about them is this—why should they dislike their native language for serious and important subjects, when they are quite willing to read Latin plays translated word for word from the Greek? Who has such a hatred, one might almost say for the very name of Roman, as to despise and reject the *Media* of Ennius, or the *Antiope* of Pacuvius, and give as his reason that though he enjoys the corresponding plays of Euripides, he cannot endure books written in Latin? What, he cries, am I to read *The Young Comrades* of Caecilius, or Terence's *Maid of Andros*, when I might be reading the same two comedies of Menander? With this sort of person I disagree so strongly, that admitting the *Electra* of Sophocles to be a masterpiece, I think Atilius's poor translation of it worth my while to read. "An iron writer," Licinius called him; still, in my opinion, a writer all the same, and therefore deserving to be read. For to be entirely unversed in your own poets argues either the extreme of mental inactivity or else a refinement of taste carried to the point of caprice. To my mind no one can be styled a well-read man who does not know our native literature. If we read

Would that in forest glades

[J]ust as readily as the same passage in the Greek, shall we object to having Plato's discourses on morality and happiness set before the reader in Latin? And supposing that for our part we do not fill the office of a mere translator, but, while preserving the doctrines of our chosen authorities, add thereto our own criticism and our own arrangement: what ground have these objectors for ranking the writings of Greece above compositions that are at once brilliant in style and not mere translations from the Greek originals? Perhaps they will rejoin that the subject has already been dealt with the Greeks already. But then what reason have they for reading the multitude of Greek authors either that one has to read? Take Stoicism: what aspect of it has Chrysippus left untouched? Yet we read Diogenes, Antipater, Mnesarchus, Panaetius, and many others, not least our friend Posidonius. Again, Theophrastus handles topics previously treated by Aristotle, yet he gives us no small pleasure all the same. Nor do the Epicureans cease from writing as the spirit moves them on the same questions on which Epicurus and the ancient wrote. If Greek writers find Greek readers when presenting the same subject in a different setting, why should not Romans be read by Romans? (*Cic.Fin.*1.2)

Elite conservatives were indignant to Romans who preferred luxury instead of Roman simplicity. For example, Plutarch mentions that "He [Cato] poked fun at Postumius Albinus, who wrote a history in Greek, and asked the indulgence of his readers" (Plut.Vit.Cat.Mai.12.5).
   Likewise, Polybius mentions:

[Postumius] was a member of one of the first families, but naturally wordy, loquacious and vainglorious to excess. From childhood he had set his heart on acquiring Greek culture and the Greek tongue, and in both he was too much of an adept, so much that it was partly his fault that admiration for Greece became offensive in the eyes of the older and more distinguished Romans. He even went so far as to attempt to write in Greek a poem and a serious history, in the preface he begs his readers to excuse him, if, as a Roman, he has not a complete mastery of the Greek language and their method of treating the subject. Marcus Porcius Cato answered him, as I think, very properly on the subject. For he said he wondered what reason he had for making this apology. (*Polyb.*39.1.2–5)

Polybius, was a Greek noble taken hostage by the Romans in 167 BCE. He was also a client of the Scipios. He was blatantly partial to the Scipio family, as well as highly critical of their enemies. In the following excerpt, he criticizes Postumius for bad Greek and humiliating himself. "But to undertake of his own accord and under no compulsion to write a history, and then to get to be pardoned for his barbarisms, was obviously ludicrous" (Polyb.*39.1.7).*

"This man [Postumius] in the rest of his behavior likewise had adopted the worst vices of the Greeks. For he was both fond of pleasure and averse to toil" (Polyb.*39.1.10).*

Cato stigmatized the inferior Greeks because they called Romans Opici *or* Osci, *hick. "They are in the common habit of calling us barbarians and stigmatize us beyond all other nations by giving us the abominable appellation of* Opici*"* (Plin.HN.*29.6).*

Similarly, Cicero believed Romans to be superior. "We were very little, if at all, inferior to the Greeks" (Cic.Tusc.*1.2–3).*

Cato's speech stresses the superiority of Latin and thus the Romans. It is not anti-Hellene. The crowd needed a translator to understand its conquerors.

He [Cato] also spent much time at Athens. And we are told that a certain speech of his is extant, which he addressed to the Athenian people in Greek, declaring that he admired the virtues of the ancient Athenians, and was glad to behold a city so beautiful and grand as theirs. But this is not true. On the contrary, he dealt with Athenians through an interpreter. He could have spoken to them directly, but he always clung to his native ways, and mocked at those who were lost in admiration of anything that was Greek. (*Plut.Vit.Cat.Mai.*12.4)

Cicero also boasted of the preeminence of the Latin language. "I have often argued, the Latin language, so far from having a poor vocabulary, as is commonly supposed, is actually richer than the Greek" (Cic.Fin.*1.3.10*).

Cato was opposed to his son learning from a slave, not a Greek. Cato educated his own son instead of letting a slave teach him.

He had an accomplished slave, Chilo by name, who was a school-teacher, and taught many boys. Still, Cato thought it not right, as he tells us himself, that his son should be scolded by a slave, or have his ears tweaked when he was slow to learn, still less that he should be indebted to his slave for such a priceless thing as education. (*Plut.Vit.Cat.Mai.*20.3–5)

Cato was not completely averse to philosophy. Plutarch says he was a close friend of the philosopher Nearchus in his youth.

When Fabius Maximus took the city of Tarentum, it chanced that Cato, who was then a mere stripling, served under him, and being lodged with a certain Nearchus, of the sect of the Pythagoreans, he was eager to know his doctrines. When he heard this man holding forth as follows, in language which Plato also uses, condemning pleasure as "the greatest incentive to evil," and the body as "the chief detriment to the soul, from which she can release and purify herself only by such reasonings as most do wean and divorce her from bodily sensations," he fell still more in love with simplicity and restraint. (*Plut.Vit.Cat.Mai.*2.3)

Cato lashed out at philosophy's emphasis on argument as opposed to substance. Cato demanded their expulsion so that "these men may return to their schools and lecture to the sons of Greece, while the youth of Rome give ear to their laws and magistrates as heretofore" (Plut.Vit.Cat.Mai.*22.5*).

Cato mocks Greek medicine and stresses the superiority of Roman medicine by contrasting his home remedies.

It was not only Greek philosophers whom he hated, but he was also suspicious of Greeks who practiced medicine at Rome. He had heard, it would seem, of Hippocrates' reply when the Great King of Persia consulted him, with the promise of a fee of many talents, namely that he would never put his skill at the service of the Barbarians who were enemies of Greece. He said all Greek physicians had taken a similar oath and urged his son to beware of them all. He himself, he said, had written a book of recipes which he followed in the treatment and regimen of any who were sick in his family. He never required his patients to fast, but fed them on greens, on bits of duck, pigeon or hare. Such a diet, he said, was light and good for sick people, except that it often causes dreams. By following such treatment and regimen he said he had good health himself and kept his family in good health. (*Plut.Vit.Cat.Mai.*23.3–4)

Cato's remarks may refer to the first Greek doctor in Rome. He was nicknamed murderer.

That from his practice he received the name of "Vulnerarius" (wound-curer), that on his arrival he was greatly welcomed at first, but that soon afterwards, from the cruelty displayed by him in cutting and searing his patients, he acquired the new name of *Carnifex* (the executioner) and brought his art and physicians in general into considerable disrepute. (*Plin.HN.*29.6)

*Cato approved of Greek education and rhetoric. He was fluent in Greek despite Plutarch's claim that he [Cato] "did not learn Greek till late in life, and was quite well on in years when he took to reading Greek books" (*Plut.Vit.Cat. Mai.*2.3–4). Plutarch adds:*

Then he profited from oratory somewhat from Thucydides, but most from Demosthenes. However, his writings are moderately embellished with Greek sentiments and stories, and many literal translations from the Greek have found a place among his maxims and proverbs. (*Plut.Vit.Cat. Mai.*2.4)

Gellius reports that Cato was also familiar with Greek sayings.

There is a speech by Marcus Cato Censorius, on the Improper Election of Aediles. In that oration is this passage: "Nowadays they say that the standing-grain, still in the blade, is a good harvest. Do not count too much upon it. I have heard that many things may come *inter os atque offam*, or 'between the mouth and the morsel,' but there certainly is a long distance between a morsel and the blade." Erucius Clarus, who was prefect of the city and twice consul, a man deeply interested in the customs and literature of early days, wrote to Sulpicius Apollinaris, the most learned man within my memory, begging and entreating that he would write him the meaning of those words. Then in my presence, for at that time I was a young man in Rome and was in attendance upon him for the purposes of instruction, Apollinaris replied to Clarus very briefly, as was natural when writing to a man of learning, that "between mouth and morsel" was an old proverb, meaning the same as the poetic Greek adage: "Twixt cup and lip there's many a slip." (*Gell.NA*.13G)

Further Reading

Adcock, F. E., "Delenda Est Carthago," *The Cambridge Historical Journal*, Vol. 8, No. 3 (1946), pp. 117–128. https://www.jstor.org/stable/3020657?seq=1#page_scan_tab_contents

Gruen, Erich S., "Cato and Hellenism," *Culture and National Identity in Republican Rome*. Cornell University Press, Ithaca, NY, 1992.

Little, Charles E., "The Authenticity and Form of Cato's Saying 'Carthago Delenda Est,'" *The Classical Journal*, Vol. 29, No. 6 (March 1934), pp. 429–435.

O'Gorman, Ellen, "Cato the Elder and the Destruction of Carthage," *Helios*, Vol. 31 (2004), pp. 96–123.

Ruebel, James S., "Cato and Scipio Africanus," *The Classical World*, Vol. 71, No. 3 (November 1977), pp. 161–173. https://www.jstor.org

Thürlemann, Silvia, "Ceterum censeo Carthaginem esse delendam," *Gymnasium*, Vol. 81 (1974), pp. 79–95.

Van de Casteele, Bruno, "Furthermore, I Am of the Opinion That Carthage Should Be Destroyed," *Skeptoid Blog*. May 10, 2015. https://skeptoid.com/blog/2015/05/10/furthermore-i-am-of-the-opinion-that-carthage-should-be-destroyed/

Vogel-Weidemann, Ursula, "Carthago Delenda Est: Aita and Prophasis," *Acta Classica*, Vol. 32 (1989), pp. 79–95.

3

Caesar's Last Words Were "Et Tu, Brute"

What People Think Happened

Julius Caesar, a brilliant but arrogant and ambitious general, lived and died by the sword. Because Caesar's aspirations extended to the desire to become king, a group of wealthy men assassinated him. In his last moments, as he turned to face his attacker, Caesar reputedly uttered, "*Et tu, Brute*" ("You too, Brutus") and then died at the hands of his young protégé, Brutus. Today the phrase "*et tu, Brute*" means the ultimate betrayal by a close friend.

Julius Caesar succeeded both in politics and in battle. His final rival having been routed at Pharsalus in 49 BCE, he became the undisputed master of Rome.

As Suetonius reports, "having ended the civil wars, he celebrated five triumphs, four in a single month" (*Suet.Caes.*37.1). However, not all were happy, "for it commemorated no victory over foreign commanders or barbarian kings, but the utter annihilation of the sons, and the family of the mightiest of Romans" (*Plut.Vit.Caes.*56.8).

Over time Caesar consolidated power and behaved as a royal despot. He was appointed dictator for life in February of 44 BCE, which endowed him with incredible executive, military, and judicial authority. Many senators even feared he would do away with the Republic, as his actions often suggested that he disregarded the Senate. First, he abused his power and filled vacancies in the Senate and magistracies with his supporters. The

Senate and his cronies awarded him unprecedented honors and titles. For example, he accepted an uninterrupted consulship, Imperator as a forename, the title of Father of His Country, a golden throne, and coins with his face on them. These actions strained his relationship with the upper class.

His utterances also revealed arrogance and disdain for the Senate. At one triumph he bragged about the swiftness of his conquests with the three words: "*Veni, vidi, vici*" ("I came, I saw, I conquered") (*Suet.Jul.* 37.2). Titus Ampius records "the State was nothing, a mere name without body or form" (*Suet.Jul.* 77.1).

Furthermore, Caesar demanded an increasing number of privileges and acted with utter contempt toward the Senate. For example, once after receiving several honors from the senators, he remained sitting (rather than standing in their presence) in the Temple of Venus Genetrix (*Dio. Cass.*44.8.1–2, *Suet.Caes.*78, *Plut.Vit.Caes.*60.4).

Another mark of his hubris was the fact that Caesar dressed like a king but, even though greeted as such, responded, "I am Caesar and no king." Mark Antony even tried to place the crown on his head. Popular belief held that only a king could conquer the Parthians. Because Caesar was planning to conduct a military campaign to Parthia on March 18, 44 BCE, his enemies feared that victory would render him invincible.

Several senators resented him and feared his popularity and power would lead to the return of a monarchy. They convinced Brutus, Caesar's protégé, to join them as "the noblest Roman of them all." Brutus killed Caesar because he imagined he would free Rome, just as his ancestor had freed Rome from tyrannical kings in 509 BCE.

As the story goes, Caesar arrived late at the Senate because of Calpurnia's worries and warnings on the Ides of March. Decimus convinced Caesar that the Senate would be disappointed. One conspirator distracted Caesar by presenting him with a petition, and then Casca attacked, joined quickly by the others. Caesar tried to fight, but when he saw his closest friend Brutus, whom he loved like a son, he felt betrayed and uttered, "*Et tu, Brute*." These famous final words have echoed in the annals of history.

How the Story Became Popular

William Shakespeare is the major source for many misperceptions regarding the assassination of Julius Caesar on the Ides of March, 44 BCE. Written in 1599, *The Tragedy of Julius Caesar*, about a tyrant whose friend betrays and then assassinates him, is one of Shakespeare's most popular works.

Shakespeare's *Julius Caesar* draws mainly from Plutarch's *The Lives of Noble Greeks and Romans*. Plutarch of Chaeronea, who was born before 50 and died after 120 CE, was a philosopher and biographer who wrote rhetorical works, treatises, dialogues, antiquarian works, and *Parallel Lives*. Without a doubt, his *Lives* is his finest work. In it he exemplified the individual virtues or vices of the careers of the great men in history, including information on family, education, beginning of public life, pinnacle, reversals of fortune, and final years. Plutarch's work was popular and considered a classic by the fourth century. He was a favorite of Byzantine scholars, who preserved much of his work. As a result, Plutarch heavily influenced Renaissance figures such as Jaques Amyot, a French scholar and translator, along with Sir Thomas North, an English judge and translator. In 1579, North published an English translation of Jacques Amyot's *Vies des hommes illustres*. Shakespeare closely followed the wording of North's translation from the *Lives* of Caesar, Brutus, and Mark Antony to write the play. North's translation also furnished material for *Antony and Cleopatra*, *Coriolanus*, and *Timon of Athens*. In *Julius Caesar*, Shakespeare used some of North's wording, with minor changes.

Another influence on Shakespeare was the poet Lucan's *Pharsalia*, which presented Caesar as a man deserving to die for destroying the Republic. Lucan's epic is a grim account of the civil war between Caesar and Pompey that led to destruction, the loss of freedom, and the end of the Republic. Shakespeare's conspirators are heroes in this play.

Julius Caesar has produced well-known quotes such as, "Friends, Romans, countrymen lend me your ears," "It was Greek to me," and "Beware the Ides of March." The idea that the Ides was a perilous time of the month originates from *Julius Caesar*. The soothsayer's warning to Julius Caesar to "Beware the Ides of March" implies that the fifteenth of that month was something perilous that should be avoided.

In *The Tragedy of Julius Caesar*, Shakespeare gives Caesar the line, "You too, Brutus" in Latin. Used in Act Three, Scene 1, lines 75–78, these words form part of the macaronic (mixing the vernacular with Latin) phrase, "*Et tu, Brute? Then fall, Caesar.*" Shakespeare's play is the source of the modern misperception that the phrase was Caesar's last words.

Shakespeare was not the first to use the very well-known phrase, however. Richard Edes is probably the original source for *Et tu, Brute?* Edes was an English churchman and one of the translators of King James's Bible. He wrote a now-lost Latin tragedy called *Caesar Interfectus*, performed by students at Christ Church in 1582. The popular phrase also appears in *The True Tragedie of Richard Duke of Yorke and the Death of*

Good King Henrie the Sixth, with the Whole Contention betweene the two Houses Lancaster and Yorke (1595), which is the earliest printed version of *Henry VI. Part 3*.

Samuel Nicholson used the phrase verbatim in "Acolastus, His Afterwitte," a poem dated to 1600. Additionally, a similar line occurs in the anonymous play, *The Tragedy of Caesar's Revenge*, which was performed in the 1590s.

Shakespeare's ancient source was Suetonius, who states that Brutus rushed at Caesar and that unnamed sources allege that his response was, "You too, my child?" Dio's account includes anonymous individuals asserting that "when he (Brutus) struck him a powerful blow, he said: 'Thou, too, my son?'"

An adaptation from a commonly used Greek phrase, the quote is used by Tacitus, Suetonius, and Dio in writings regarding the future emperor Galba, who was somewhat of a child prodigy.

Galba was wealthy and from an ancient, noble patrician family. However, he was not well connected. His grandfather had been a protégé of Empress Livia. Galba was so talented as a young man that many predicted he would one day sit on the imperial throne.

"I must not pass over a prognostication of Tiberius respecting Servius Galba, then consul. Having sent for him and sounded him on various topics, he at last addressed him in Greek to this effect. 'You too, Galba, will some day have a taste of empire'" (*Tac.Ann.*6.20.2).

Galba's good fortune was known to Suetonius, who said, "It is well known that when he was still a boy and called to pay his respects to Augustus with others of his age, the emperor pinched his cheek and said in Greek, 'Thou too child, wilt have a nibble of this power of mine'" (*Suet. Galb.*4.1). Dio Cassius's form of the phrase is, "You too will one day taste command" (*Dio.Cass.*57.19.4).

So well-known was the prophecy that Josephus mentioned it: "Accordingly, when he once saw Galba coming in to him, he said to his most intimate friends that there came in a man that would one day have the dignity of the Roman Empire" (*Jos.AJ.*18.6.9).

When Tiberius said, "*et tu, Galba*'will one day taste command," he was not praising Galba. Tiberius was not happy being the emperor. Tiberius claimed that "a wretched and burdensome slavery was being forced upon him, he accepted the empire, but in such fashion as to suggest the hope that he would one day lay it down" (*Suet.Tib.*24.2). He also compared ruling Rome to "holding a wolf by the ears" (*Suet.Tib.*25.1).

In Charles François Lhomond's *De viris illustribus Urbis Romae a Romulo ad Augustum*, published in 1779, Caesar's last words appear as: "*Tu quoque, mi fili.*" Lhomond's work was a standard text and was influential in promoting the myth.

Modern artists have used the phrase as it is found in Shakespeare. The band Red Hot Chili Peppers recorded "Even You, Brutus?" The phrase is inscribed in the arms of Taylor Swift's throne in her "Look What You Made Me Do" video.

"Et tu, Brute?" persists as an urban myth and is widely quoted to mean the ultimate betrayal of a close friend. Nonetheless, no evidence exists that Caesar ever said those words.

PRIMARY DOCUMENTS

William Shakespeare has had a massive influence on the modern perception of ancient Rome, but especially on Julius Caesar. Most of what people think they know about Caesar comes from Shakespeare's Julius Caesar. *For example, his play is the major source of the myth that Caesar's last words were "Et tu, Brute?" Shakespeare was, in turn, heavily influenced by Lucan's* Pharsalia, *which documents the civil war between Pompey and Caesar, which Caesar eventually won in 46 BCE and afterward ended the Republic. In Thomas May's 1631 translation of Lucan, Julius Caesar is an evil, impatient despot whose sole ambition is to rule the world.*

Caesar now mad for war loves not to finde,
But make his way by blood, nor is his minde
Ioy'd that in Italy hee sees no foes,
No Countreys guarded from him, meets no blowes:
But counts his journey lost; desires to breake,
Not open gates, and loves his march to make
By fire and sword, not sufferance; thinkes it shame
To tread permitted paths and beare the name Of Citizen. (*Luc. Civil Wars*. 2)

Lucan thus presents Caesar as a ruthless, power-hungry tyrant whose assassination was completely deserved. The conspirators are selfless individuals trying to save the Republic from Caesar's tyranny.

Thomas North's 1579 translation of Amyot's Vies des hommes illustres *was a major influence on Shakespeare. The book was widely read. There is no doubt that Shakespeare used North's translation of Plutarch's* Parallel Lives of Julius Caesar and Marcus Brutus *for Julius Caesar, Coriolanus, and* Antony and Cleopatra. *In* Antony and Cleopatra, *entire speeches are borrowed from North's work. In the following example, Shakespeare did not copy North verbatim, but keeps the gist of the narrative. Like Plutarch, Shakespeare emphasized how the exploits of individuals impacted history.*

There Brutus, being afraid to be besieged, sent back again the noblemen that came thither with him, thinking it no reason that they, which were no partakers of the murder, should be partakers of the danger. (*Plutarch* 126)

Cassius: And leave us Publius; lest that the people,
Rushing on us, should do your age some mischief.
Brutus: Do so; and let no man abide this deed
But we the doers.
(*JC*.III.i89–92)

In this scene Brutus is planning his suicide.

Brutus as he sat bowed towards Clitus, one of his men and told him somewhat in his ear; the other answered him not, but fell a-weeping. Thereupon he proved Dardanus, and said somewhat also to him. At length he came to Volumnius himself, and, speaking to him in Greek, prayed him . . . that he would help him to put his hand to his sword, to thrust it in him to kill him. (*Plutarch* 170)

Brutus: Sit thee down, Clitus; slaying is the word,
It is a deed in fashion. Hark Thee, Clitus.
Clitus: What, I, my lord? No, not for all the world.
Brutus: Peace then, no words.
Clitus: I'll rather kill myself.
Whispering
Brutus: Hark thee, Dardanius [*sic*]
Dardanius: Shall I do such a deed? (V.v.4–8)

Here Plutarch's narration formed the basis of Caesar's speech to Calpurnia, who is upset because of omens.

And when some of his friends did consul him to have a guard for the safety of his person, and some of them did offer themselves to serve him, he would never consent to it, but said, it was better to die once than be afraid of death. (*Plutarch* 78)

Caesar: Cowards die many times before their deaths
The valiant never taste of death but once,
Of all the wonders that I have yet heard,
It seems to me most strange that men should fear;
Seeing that death, a necessary end,
Will come when it will come. (*JC*.II.ii.32–37)

Shakespeare uses Plutarch's words literally in Act V, while Brutus's troops plan for the impending skirmish.

The greatest and chiefest things among men are most uncertain, and that, if the battle fall out otherwise today than we wish or look for, we shall hardly meet again, what are thou then determined to do. (*Plutarch* 154)

Cassius: Now, most noble Brutus,
The gods to-day stand friendly, that we may,
Lovers in peace, lead our days to age!
But since the affairs of men rest still incertain
Let's reason with the worst that may befall.
If we do lose this battle, then is this
The very last time we shall speak together:
What are you then determined to do? (*JC*.V.i.93–100)

Shakespeare's line sounds eerily familiar to North's translation.

He should wear his diadem in all other places by sea and land. (*Plutarch* 90)
   Casca: And he shall wear his crown both by sea and land. (*JC*.I.iii.87)

Likewise, the scene where Antony reveals Caesar's last wishes for the citizens of Rome is lifted directly from Plutarch.

He bequeathed unto every citizen of Rome seventy-five drachmas a man and that he left his gardens and arbours unto the people, which he had this side of the river of Tiber. (*Plutarch* 128)

Antony: To every Roman citizen he gives,
To every several man, seventy-five drachmas. (*JC*.III.ii.139, 140)

Moreover, he hath left you all his walks,
His private arbours and new-planted orchards,
On this side Tiber; he hath left them to you. (*JC*.III.ii 245–247)

In Act II, Scene 2, Caesar expressed reservation about going to the Senate, because "Thrice hath Calpurnia in her sleep cried out, 'Help, ho! They murder Caesar!'" A servant made a sacrifice. Since the animal was missing its heart, it was a bad omen. At Calpurnia's urging, Caesar said, "I will stay home." Decius convinced Caesar that Calpurnia's dream was misinterpreted. He also told him, "[T]he Senate have concluded to give this day a crown to mighty Caesar. If you send them word you will not come, their minds may change."

In Act III, Scene 1, Caesar went to the Senate. The conspirators, Casca, Brutus, Cassius, Decius, Cinna, and Metellus Cimber followed him. Caesar said, "[T]he Ides of March are come," to the soothsayer, indicating that his prediction had not come true. The soothsayer replied, "[A]ye, Caesar, but not gone." Artemidorus desperately tried to reach him to read his letter, which contains the names of all the conspirators.

Artemidorus:	O Caesar, read mine first; for mine's a suit.
	That touches Caesar nearer: read it Great Caesar.
Caesar:	What touches us ourself shall be last served.
Artemidorus:	Delay not Caesar; read it instantly.
Caesar:	Is the fellow mad?
Publius:	Sirrah, give place.
Cassius:	What, urge you your petitions in the street?
	Come to the Capitol.

At Cassius's urging, Caesar proceeded to the Capitol.

One of the plotters approached Caesar under the false pretense of requesting that Caesar read his petition. Then, the collaborators gathered around Caesar and drew their weapons. Brutus delivered the final blow.

Caesar: Et tu, Brute?! Then fall, Caesar!

However, the phrase "Et tu, Brute?" had been previously used in Richard Eedes' lost Latin play, Caesar Interfectus, *from 1582.*

The saying is also found in Shakespeare's history play The True Tragedy of Richard Duke of York 1595, *which is the earliest printed version of* Henry VI, Part 3. *Here Clarence criticizes Edward for favoring his wife's family over him.*

Clarence:
Clarence, Clarence for Lancaster.
Edward:
Et tu, Brute, wilt though stab Caesar too?
A parley sir, to George of Clarence.
[Sound a parley, and Richard and Clarence whisper together, and then Clarence takes his red rose out of his hat, and throws it at Warwick]
Warwick:
Come Clarence come, if thou wilt Warwick call.
Clarence:
Father of Warwick, know you what this means?
I throw mine infamy at thee.

Here is the version from Henry VI, Part 3. King Edward said, "Et tu, Brute? Wilt thou stab Caesar too? A parley, sirrah, to George of Clarence" (Henry VI Part 3, Act. V. Scene 1.81–82).

In addition, the quote appears in Samuel Nicholson's poem Acolastus, His After-witte, *written in 1600. Nicholson's work, a pastoral satire consisting of 250 stanzas, is a dialogue between Acolastus and Eubulus, an older shepherd, on the dishonesty of female affection. Acolastus was a young shepherd who was rejected by a young woman because he was poor. Acolastus spoke of the dangers of love, women, and money. The poem is best known for the author's borrowings from Shakespeare, including the saying, "Et tu, Brute?"*

Et tu, Brute,
Wilt thou stab Caesar too?
Thou err my friend
And wilt not see me wrong'd
I pray thee leave me without adoo
For with my life my sorrowes are prolong'd
I know thou pleasurst not in my distresse,
Then rob me not of death's true happinesse.

Similarly, its use in the Tragedy of Caesar's Revenge *indicates that the phrase was commonly used during the Elizabethan period.*

Cæsar. "What Brutus Too? Nay, nay, then let me die,
Nothing wounds deeper than ingratitude."
Brutus. "Aye, bloody Caesar, Caesar, Brutus, too,

Doth give thee this, and this, to quiet Rome's wrongs." (*Caesar's Revenge*, Act 3, Scene 6, Lines 1726–1730)

Shakespeare used North's translation of Plutarch's Lives of Noble Grecians and Romans *for most of his Roman plays. However, Suetonius wrote the only historical source that reports that "some have written that when Marcus Brutus rushed at him, he said in Greek, 'You too, my son?'" (Suet.Caes.82.1–3).*

Similarly, Dio Cassius, writing in the third century mentions, "to Brutus, when he struck him a powerful blow, he said, 'Thou too, my son?'" (Dio.Cass. 44.19.5).

Julius Caesar's last words are generally interpreted as a statement of shock at Brutus for the ultimate betrayal. However, the saying, "You too, my son" was derived from ancient Greek literature. The original saying was, "You too, my son, will have a taste of power." It was a Roman proverb and denoted a curse or a warning. Caesar spoke these words to Brutus as a threat. He meant to tell Brutus, "Your turn will come."

In the following passage, Tacitus credited the proverb to Tiberius and evoked a similar understanding of the phrase as a dire warning. Galba had a meteoric rise to might but did not "taste power" for long.

About the same time, Gaius Caesar [Caligula], who had accompanied his grandfather on the departure to Capreae, received in marriage Claudia, the daughter of Marcus Silanus. His monstrous character was masked by a hypocritical modesty: not a word escaped him at the sentencing of his mother or the destruction of his brethren; whatever the mood assumed for the day by Tiberius, the attitude of his grandson was the same, and his words not greatly different. Hence, a little later, the epigram of the orator Passenius—that the world never knew a better slave, nor a worse master.

I cannot omit the prophecy of Tiberius with regard to Servius Galba, the consul. He sent for him, sounded him in conversations on a variety of subjects, and finally addressed him in a Greek sentence, the purport of which was, "Thou, too, Galba, shalt one day have thy taste of empire": a hint of belated and short-lived power, based on knowledge of the Chaldean art, the acquirement of which he owed to the leisure of Rhodes and the instructions of Thrasyllus.

His tutor's capacity he had tested as follows:

For all consultations on such business he used the highest part of his villa and the confidential services of one freedman. Along the pathless and broken heights (for the house overlooks a cliff) this illiterate and robust guide led the way in front of the astrologer whose art Tiberius sought to investigate, and on his return, had any suspicion arisen of incompetence or fraud, hurled him into the sea below, lest he should turn betrayer of the secret. Thrasyllus, then, introduced by the same rocky path, after he had impressed his questioner by adroit revelations of his empire to be and of the course of the future, was asked if he had ascertained his own horoscope—what was the character of that year—what the complexion of the day. A diagram which he drew up of the positions and distances of the stars at first gave him pause; then he showed signs of fear: the more careful his scrutiny, the greater his trepidation between surprise and alarm; and at last he exclaimed that a doubtful, almost a crisis was hard upon him. He was promptly embraced by Tiberius, who, congratulating him on the fact that he had divined, and was about to escape, his perils, accepted as oracular truth the predictions he had made, and retained him among his closest friends. (*Tac.Ann.*6.20–21)

Suetonius attributed the quote to Augustus in his Life of Galba. *Galba was emperor of Rome from 68–69 CE. Galba was born into a wealthy family and later gained the imperial throne with the help of the praetorian guard.*

It would be a long story to give in detail his illustrious ancestors and the honorary inscriptions of the entire race, but I shall give a brief account of his immediate family. It is uncertain why the first of the Sulpicii who bore the surname Galba assumed the name, and whence it was derived. Some think that it was because after having a long time unsuccessfully besieged a town in Spain, he at last set fire to it by torches smeared with *galbeum*, that is to say of remedies wrapped in wool; still others, because he was a very fat man, such as the Gauls term *galba*, or because he was, on the contrary, as slender as the insects called *galbae*, which breed in oak trees.

The family acquired distinction from Servius Galba, who became consul and was decidedly the most eloquent speaker of his time. This man, they say, was the cause of the war with Viriathus, because while governing Spain as proprietor, he treacherously massacred thirty thousand of the Lusitanians. His grandson had been one of Caesar's lieutenants in Gaul, but angered because his commander caused his defeat for the consulship, he joined the conspiracy with Brutus and Cassius, and was consequently condemned to death by the Pedian law. From him were descended the grandfather and father of the emperor Galba. The former, who was more eminent for learning than for his rank—for he did not advance beyond the grade of praetor—published a voluminous and painstaking history. The father attained the consulship, although he was short of stature and even hunchbacked, besides being only an indifferent speaker, [but] was an industrious pleader at the bar. He married Mummica Achaica, the granddaughter of Catulus, and great-granddaughter of Lucius Mummius who destroyed Corinth; and later Livia Ocellina, a very rich and beautiful woman, who however is thought to have sought marriage with him because of his high rank, and the more eagerly when, in response to her frequent advances, he took off his robe in private and showed her his deformity, so as not to seem to deceive her by concealing it. By Achaica he had sons Gaius and Servius. Gaius, who was the elder, left Rome after squandering the greater part of his estate, and committed suicide because Tiberius would not allow him to take part in the allotments of the provinces in his year.

The emperor Servius Galba was born in the consulship of Marcus Valerius Messala and Gnaeus Lentulus, on the ninth day before the Kalends of January, in a country house situated on a hill near Tarracina, on the left as you go towards Fundi. Adopted by his stepmother Livia, he took her name and the surname Ocella, and also changed his forename; for he used Lucius instead of Servius, from that time until he became emperor. It is well known that when he was still a boy and called to pay his respects to Augustus with others of his age, the emperor pinched his cheek and said in Greek: "Thou too, child, wilt have a nibble of this power of mine." Tiberius too, when he heard that Galba was destined to be emperor, but in his old age, said: "Well, let him live then, since that does not concern me." Again, when Galba's grandfather was busy with a sacrifice for a stroke of lightning, and an eagle snatched the intestines from his hand and carried them to an oak full of acorns, the prediction was made that the highest dignity would come to the family, but late; whereupon he said with a laugh: "Very likely, when a mule has a foal." Afterwards when Galba was beginning his revolt, nothing gave him so much encouragement as the foaling of a mule, and while the rest were horrified and looked on it as an unfavorable omen, he alone regarded it as most propitious, remembering the sacrifice and his grandfather's saying. (*Suet. Galb.* 3–4)

Tiberius was unhappy to be emperor and predicted a similar fate for Galba.

Tiberius became cruel and bitter over time. He charged many with *maiestas* [treason] for improper acts or speech against Augustus, Livia or himself.

And towards those who were suspected of plotting against him he was inexorable.

Tiberius was stern in his chastisement of persons accused of any offence. He used to remark: "Nobody willingly submits to being ruled, but a man is driven to it against his will; for not only do subjects delight in refusing obedience, but they also enjoy plotting against their rulers." And he would accept accusers indiscriminately, whether it was a slave denouncing his master or a son his father.

Indeed, by indicating to certain persons his desire for the death of certain others, he brought about the destruction of the latter at the hands of the former, and his part in these deaths was no secret.

Not only were slaves tortured to make them testify against their own masters, but freemen and citizens as well. Those who had accused or testified against persons, divided by lot the property of the convicted and received in addition both offices and honors. In the case of many, he took care to ascertain the day and hour of their birth, and on the basis of their character and fortune as thus disclosed would put them to death; for if he discovered any unusual ability or promise of power in anyone, he was sure to slay him. In fact, so thoroughly did he investigate and understand the destiny in store for every one of the more prominent men, that on meeting Galba (the later emperor), when the latter had a wife betrothed to him, he remarked: "You shall one day taste of the sovereignty." He spared him, as I conjecture, because this was settled as his fate, but as he explained it to himself, because Galba would reign only in old age and long after his death. (*Dio. Cass.*57.19.1–2)

What Really Happened

Julius Caesar was assassinated on March 15, 44 BCE, by jealous conspirators. He was persuaded to attend a senatorial session despite warnings to stay away as well as the concerns of his wife. Although he was stabbed twenty-three times, Brutus did not inflict the final and fatal blow. That he said, "Et tu, Brute?" is pure fiction. In fact, most scholars report that Caesar did not say anything. Shakespeare used the phrase in order to dramatize what really happened. Moreover, the phrase might be considered as a warning, meaning, "you will get yours, too."

The Ides of March is synonymous with bad luck, thanks to Shakespeare's soothsayer's plea that Caesar "Beware the Ides of March." There is actually nothing sinister about the date. Ides was simply another way of saying the fifteenth of any month. In fact, Caesar had been warned about a thirty-day period from February 15 to March 15. He was supposed to go to a senatorial session on the Ides of March, but Suetonius reported that "the soothsayer Spurinna warned him to beware of danger, which would come not later than the Ides of March" (*Suet.Caes*.81.2). Shakespeare used this Roman tradition in order to create an alarming situation.

The plotters were "envious of his fortune and power, now grown to enormous proportions" (*App.B.Civ*.2.111). They decided to act before Caesar's Parthian campaign to thwart his ambitions, because "that if he should conquer these nations also he would indeed be indisputably king" (*App.B.Civ*.2.111).

Despite Caesar's kindness, the conspirators "never abandoned their hope of doing him harm," and "some of them had hopes of becoming leaders themselves in his place if he were put out of the way" (*Nic.Dam*.19). The senators felt insulted because they had given Caesar honors. "But he did not rise when they approached nor while they remained there, and this, too, afforded his slanderers a pretext for accusing him of wishing to be greeted as a king" (*App.B.Civ*.2.107).

However, the plotters were not idealists who desired to save the Republic. Rather, they met in secret and discussed various ways of killing Caesar, such as attacking him as he walked along the "Via Sacra" at the gladiatorial shows. Most exhorted that he be killed during the session of the Senate because Caesar would be alone. Since many plotters were senators, this plan was implemented (*Nic.Dam*.23).

The more than sixty collaborators included former enemies of Caesar such as Brutus, whom Shakespeare has made out to be the ultimate traitor. In Dante's *Inferno* 34.61–7, Judas is described as the ultimate traitor along with Brutus and Cassius.

However, the real villain was Decimus Brutus, "one of his dearest friends" (*App.B.Civ*.2.111), who "was so trusted by Caesar that he was entered in his will as his second heir" (*Plut.Vit.Caes*.64.1, *Suet.Caes*.83.2). The "day before the meeting Caesar went to dine with Lepidus, his master of the horse, taking Decimus Brutus Albinus with him to drink wine after dinner" (*App.B.Civ*.2.115). It was Decimus, whom Shakespeare mistakenly called Decius in *Julius Caesar*, who escorted Caesar to his meeting that fateful day. He also detained Mark Antony and "purposely engaged him in a lengthy conversation" (*Plut.Vit.Caes*.66.4). Suetonius revealed that the morning of the plot, Caesar was "urged by Decimus Brutus not to disappoint the full meeting which had for some time been waiting for him" (*Suet.Caes*.81.4).

Many factors could have prevented Caesar's murder. That Ides night, his wife Calpurnia had a nightmare. Worse yet, "when he offered sacrifice there were many unfavorable signs" (*App.B.Civ.*2.115). Naturally, Caesar's friends and family tried to stop him from going to the senatorial meeting that day. Furthermore, Caesar was handed a tablet informing him of the plot, but he had no time to read it. He entered the Senate after disregarding additional bad omens.

While Antony was engaged by the conspirators, Tullius presented Caesar with a petition to recall his exiled brother. He grabbed Caesar's toga, to which Caesar angrily replied, "Why, this is violence!" Casca was the first to stab him. Caesar fought back, but soon the other conspirators were stabbing him. It was a sloppy and chaotic affair. "Cassius Longinus was eager to give another stroke, but he missed and struck Marcus Brutus on the hand. Minucius, too, made a lunge at Caesar but he struck Rubrius on the thigh. It looked as if they were fighting over Caesar" (*Nic.Dam.*24). Caesar tried fighting but tripped and fell before the statue of Pompey, still holding the unread letter warning him of the plot. "They continued their attack after he had fallen until he received twenty-three wounds. Several of them while thrusting with their swords wounded each other" (*App.B.Civ.*2.117).

Roman authors claim that Caesar did not speak. Nicolaus of Damascus reported that "he fell, under many wounds, before the statue of Pompey" (*Nic.Dam.*24). Similarly, Appian described Caesar's last actions as "he at last despaired, and veiling himself with his robe, composed himself for death and fell at the foot of Pompey's statue" (*App.B.Civ.*2.117). Suetonius said he did not say anything, but reported that some heard him say *kai su teknon*? ("You too, my child?" or, "You too, my son?") (*Suet.Caes.*82.2). Plutarch wrote that Caesar did not utter a word but that "[w]hen he saw Brutus had drawn his dagger, he pulled his toga down over his head and sank" (*Plut.Vit.Caes.*66.12). Likewise, Dio reported, "Caesar was unable to say or do anything but veiling his face" (*Dio.Cass.*44.19.4–5).

Like Shakespeare, Suetonius probably added the phrase for dramatic effect. He used "Et tu, Bruté?" to mean, "Have you joined my enemies too? Woe is me," as in Shakespeare. In Suetonius, though, the phrase is a threat. When Caesar uttered his last words, he was foretelling Brutus's eventual death. The quotation was used similarly to predict Galba's eventual death after becoming emperor.

Shakespeare was writing for a Renaissance audience, who would have been familiar with Latin, so he added the line in order to spice up the play. He also staged the murder in the Senate instead of in the Theater of Pompey for dramatic effect. *The Tragedy of Julius Caesar* may reflect concerns about the uncertainties of royal succession and the possibility of civil war.

PRIMARY DOCUMENTS

Although the phrase Ides of March is best known from Julius Caesar, it also occurs in John Capgrave's Life of St. Gilbert, circa 1451. Here there is nothing scary about the fifteenth. This reference serves to mark the date of the saint's death.

The Ides of March is associated with doom and gloom because Shakespeare used a scary soothsayer, warning Caesar to "Beware the Ides of March." In reality, the Ides was neither positive nor negative but was simply a means of marking the middle of the month. Suetonius reports that a soothsayer cautioned Caesar that harm would come to him no later than March 15.

Now Caesar's approaching murder was foretold to him by unmistakable signs. A few months before, when the settlers assigned to the colony at Capua by the Julian Law were demolishing some tombs of great antiquity, to build country houses, and plied their work with the greater vigor because as they rummaged about they found a quantity of vases of ancient workmanship, there was discovered a tomb, which was said to be that of Capys, the founder of Capua, a bronze tablet, inscribed with Greek words and characters to this purport: "Whenever the bones of Capys shall be moved, it will come to pass that a son of Ilium shall be slain at the hands of his kindred, and presently avenged at heavy cost to Italy." And let no one think this tale is a myth or a lie, for it is vouched for by Cornelius Balbus, an intimate friend of Caesar. Shortly before his death, as he was told, the herds of horses which he had dedicated to the river Rubicon when he crossed it, and had let loose without a keeper, stubbornly refused to graze and wept copiously.

Again, when he was offering sacrifice, the soothsayer Spurinna warned him to beware of the danger, which would come no later than the Ides of March; and on the day before the Ides of that month a little bird called the king bird flew into the Hall of Pompey with a sprig of laurel, pursued by others of various kinds from the grove hard by, which tore it to pieces in the hall. In fact the very night before his murder he dreamt that he was flying about the clouds, and now that he was clasping the hand of Jupiter; and his wife Calpurnia thought that the pediment of their house fell, and that her husband was stabbed in her arms; and on a sudden the door of the room flew open of its own accord. (*Suet.Caes.*81.1–3)

At first Caesar was going to stay home but then foolishly ignored the soothsayer's dire predictions.

Both for these reasons and because of poor health he hesitated for a long time whether to stay at home and put off what he had planned to do in the Senate; but at last urged by Decimus Brutus not to disappoint the full meeting which had for some time been waiting for him, he went forth almost at the end of the fifth hour; and when a note revealing the plot was handed him by someone on the way, he put it with others which he held in his left hand, intending to read them presently. Then, after several victims had been slain, and he could not get favorable omens, he entered the House in defiance of portents, laughing at Spurinna and calling him a false prophet, because the Ides of March were come without bringing him harm; though Spurinna replied that they had of a truth come, but they had not gone. (*Suet.Caes.*81.4)

Julius Caesar was not a man who rested on his laurels. He was in competition with himself and wanted to outdo his previous successes. Subsequently, the assassins had to act, as Caesar was soon to leave on another military expedition.

Caesar's many successes, however, did not divert his natural spirit of enterprise and ambition to the enjoyment of what he had laboriously achieved, but served as fuel and incentive for future achievements, and begat in him plans for greater deeds and a passion for fresh glory, as though he had used up what he already had. What he felt was therefore nothing else than emulation of himself, as if he had been another man, and a sort of rivalry between what he had done and what he proposed to do. For he planned and prepared to make an expedition against the Parthians. And after subduing these and marching around the Euxine by way of Hyrcania, the Caspian Sea, and the Caucasus, to invade Scythia, and after overrunning the countries bordering on Germany and Germany itself, to come back by way of Gaul to Italy, and so to complete this circuit of his empire, which would then be bounded by all sides of the ocean. During this expedition, moreover, he intended to dig through the Isthmus of Corinth, and had already put Anienus in charge of this work; he intended also to divert the Tiber just below the city into a deep channel, give it a bend towards Circeium, and make it empty into the sea at Terracina, thus contriving for merchant men a safe as well as an easy passage to Rome; and besides this, to convert marshes about Pomentinum and Setia into a plain which many thousands of men would cultivate; and further, to build moles which should barricade the sea where it was nearest to Rome, to clear away the hidden dangers on the shore at Ostia, and then construct harbors and roadsteads sufficient for the great fleets that would visit them. And all these things were in preparation. (*Plut.Vit.Caes.*58.4–10)

However, the conspirators were not idealists. Moreover, Caesar threatened the power of the elite, who had previously dominated Roman politics.

At first a few men started the conspiracy, but afterwards many took part, more than are remembered to have taken part in any earlier plot against a commander. They say that there were more than eighty who had a share in it. Among those who had the most influence were: Decimus Brutus, a particular friend of Caesar; Gaius Cassius; and Marcus Brutus, second to none in the estimations of the Romans at that time. All these were formerly members of the opposite faction, and they had tried to further Pompeius's interests, but when he was defeated, they came under Caesar's jurisdiction and lived quietly for the time being; but they never abandoned their hope of doing him harm. He on his part was naturally without grudge against the beaten party, because of a certain leniency of disposition, but they, using to their own advantage his lack of suspicion, by seductive words and the pretense of deeds treated him in such a way as to more readily escape detection in their plot. There were various reasons which affected each and all of them and impelled them to lay their hands on the man. Some of them had hopes of becoming leaders themselves in his place if he were put out of the way; others were angered over what had happened to them in the war, embittered over the loss of their relatives, property or offices of State. They concealed the fact that they were angry, and made the pretense of something more seemingly, saying they were displeased at the rule of a single man and that they were striving for a republican form of government. Different people had different reasons, all brought together by whatever pretext they happened upon.

At first the ringleaders conspired; then many more joined, some of their own accord because of personal grievances, some because they had been associated with the others and wished to show plainly the good faith of their long-standing friendship, and accordingly became their associates. There were some who were neither of these types, but who had agreed because of the worth of the others, and who resented the power of one man after the long-standing republican constitution. They were very glad not to start the affair themselves, but were willing to join such company when someone else had initiated proceedings, not even hesitating to pay the penalty if need be. The reputation which had long been attached to the Brutus family was very influential in causing the uprising, for Brutus' ancestors had overthrown the kings who ruled from the time of Romulus, and they had first established republican government in Rome. Moreover, men who had been friends of Caesar were no longer similarly well disposed toward him when they saw people who were previously his enemies saved and given honors equal to their own. In fact, even these others were not particularly well disposed toward him, for their ancient grudges took precedence over gratitude and made them forgetful of their good fortune in being saved, while, when they remembered the good things they had lost in being defeated, they were provoked. Many also hated him because they had been saved by him, although he had been irreproachable in his behavior toward them in every respect; but nevertheless, the very thought of receiving as a favor the benefits which as victors they would readily have enjoyed, annoyed them very much.

There was another class of men, namely those who had served with him, whether as officers or privates, and who did not get a share of glory. They asserted that prisoners of war were enrolled among the veteran forces and that they received identical pay. Accordingly, his friends were incensed at being rated equal to those whom they themselves had taken prisoners, and indeed they were even outranked by some of them. To many, also, the fact that they had benefitted at his hands, both by gifts of property and by appointment to offices, was a special source of grievance, since he alone was able to bestow such benefits, and everyone else was ignored as of no importance. When he became exalted through many notable victories (which was fair enough) and began to think himself superhuman the common people worshipped him, but he began to be obnoxious to the optimates and to those who were trying to obtain a share in the government. And so, every kind of man combined against him: great and small, friend and foe, military and political, every one of whom put forward his own particular pretext for the matter in hand, and as a result of his own complaints each lent a ready ear to the accusations of the others. They all confirmed each other in their little conspiracy and they furnished as surety to one another the grievances which they held severally in private against him. Hence, though the number of conspirators became so great, no one dared to give information of the fact. Some say, however, that a little before his death, Caesar received a note in which warning of the plot was given, and that he was murdered with it in his hands before he had a chance to read it, and that it was found among other notes after his death. (*Nic.Dam.*19)

More than sixty people joined the conspiracy against him, led by Gaius Cassius and Marcus and Decimus Brutus. (*Suet.Caes.*80.4)

Shakespeare credits Brutus as the ultimate betrayer. The real traitor was "Decimus Brutus, surnamed Albinus," who "was so trusted by Caesar that he was entered in his will as his second heir but was partner in the conspiracy of the other Brutus and Cassius" (Plut.Vit.Caes.*64.1*).

Decimus Junius Brutus Albinus was a distant relative of Julius Caesar and was like a son to Caesar. He was also one of Caesar's soldiers and served during the Gallic Wars.

Caesar, having delayed two days in that place, because he had anticipated that, in the natural course of events, such would be the conduct of Vercingetorix, leaves the army under pretense of raising recruits and cavalry: he places Brutus, a young man, in command of these forces; he gives him instructions that the cavalry should range as extensively as possible in all directions; that he would exert himself not to be absent from the camp longer than three days. Having arranged these matters, he marches to Vienna by as long journeys as he can, when his own soldiers did not expect him. Finding there a fresh body of cavalry, which he had sent on to that place several days before, marching incessantly night and day, he advanced rapidly through the territory of the Aedui into that of the Lingones, in which two legions were wintering, that, if any plan affecting his own safety should have been organized by the Aedui, he might defeat it by the rapidity of his movements. When he arrived there, he sends information to the rest of the legions, and gathers all his army into one place before intelligence of his arrival could be announced to the Arverni. Vercingetorix, on hearing this circumstance, leads back his army into the country of the Bituriges; and after marching from it to Gergovia, a town of the Boii, whom Caesar had settled there after defeating them in the Helvetian War, and had rendered tributary to the Aedui, he determined to attack it. (*Caes.B.Gall.*7.9)

Dante considered Cassius and Brutus as the equal of Judas Iscariot.

"That soul up there which has the greatest pain,"
The Master said, "is Judas Iscariot;
With head inside, he plies his legs without.

Of the two others, who head downward are,
The one who hangs from the black jowl is Brutus;
See how he writhes himself and speaks no word.

And the other, who so stalwart seems, is Cassius.
But night is reascending, and 'tis time
That we depart, for we have seen the whole." (Dante's *Inferno* 34.61–7)

Caesar almost stayed home the Ides of March but was "urged by Decimus Brutus not to disappoint the full meeting which had for some time been waiting for him" (Suet.Caes.*81.4*).

Caesar's end came quickly. He was stabbed to death in the Theater of Pompey. Nicolaus of Damascus wrote the earliest account and describes the chaotic commotion.

First Servilius Casca stabbed him on the left shoulder a little above the collarbone, at which he had aimed but missed through nervousness. Caesar sprang up to defend himself against him and Casca called to his brother, speaking in Greek in his excitement. The latter obeyed him and drove his sword into Caesar's side. A moment before, Cassius struck him obliquely across the face. Decimus Brutus struck him through the thigh. Cassius Longinus was eager to give another stroke, but he missed and struck Marcus Brutus on the hand. Minucius, too, made a lunge at Caesar but he struck Rubrius on the thigh. It looked as if they were fighting over Caesar. He fell under many wounds, before the statue of Pompey, and there was not one of them but struck him as he lay lifeless, to show that each of them had a share in the deed, until he had received thirty-five wounds, and breathed his last. (*Nic.Dam*.24)

Suetonius states that Caesar probably said nothing.

Cimber caught his toga by both shoulders; then as Caesar cried, "Why, this is violence!" one of the Cascas stabbed him from one side just below the throat. Caesar caught Casca's arm and ran it through with his stylus, but as he tried to leap to his feet, he was stopped by another wound. When he saw that he was beset on every side by drawn daggers, he muffled his head in his robe, and at the same time drew down its lap to his feet with his left hand, in order to fall more decently, with the lower part of his body also covered. And in this wise he was stabbed with three and twenty wounds, uttering not a word, but merely a groan at the first stroke, though some have written that when Marcus Brutus rushed at him, he said in Greek, "You too, my child?" (*Suet.Caes*.82.1–2)

Plutarch on Caesar's last moments:

Hemmed in on all sides, whichever way he turned confronting blows of weapons aimed at his face and eyes, driven hither and thither like a wild beast, was entangled in the hands of all; for all had to take part in the sacrifice and taste of the slaughter. Therefore, Brutus also gave him one blow in the groin. And it is said by some writers that although Caesar defended himself against the rest and darted this way and that and cried aloud, when he saw that Brutus had drawn his dagger, he pulled his toga over his head and sank. (*Plut. Vit. Caes.*66.10–12)

Appian reveals that Caesar put up a fight but does not mention that he spoke.

Then first Casca, who was standing over Caesar's head, drove his dagger at his throat, but swerved and wounded him in the breast. Caesar snatched his toga from Cimber, seized Casca's hand, sprang from his chair, turned around, and hurled Casca with great violence. While he was in this position another one stabbed him with a dagger in the side, which was stretched tense by his strained position. Cassius wounded him in the face, Brutus smote him in the thigh, and Bucolianus in the back. With rage and outcries Caesar turned now upon one and another like a wild animal, but after receiving the wound from Brutus he at last despaired and, veiling himself with his robe, composed himself for death and fell at the foot of Pompey's statue. They continued their attack after he had fallen until he received twenty-three wounds. Several of them while thrusting with their swords wounded each other. (*App. B. Civ.*2.117)

Dio Cassius's narrative is similar and makes no reference to any utterance by Caesar.

There upon they attacked him from many sides at once and wounded him to death, so that by reason of their numbers Caesar was unable to say or do anything, but veiling his face, was slain with many wounds. This is the truest account, though some have added that to Brutus, when he struck him a powerful blow, he said, "Thou, too, my son?" (*Dio. Cass.*44.19.4–5)

Further Reading

Edwards, P., "6 Myths about the Ides of March, and Killing Caesar," *Vox.* March 15, 2017. https://www.vox.com/2015/3/15/8214921/ides-of-march-caesar-assassination

Gainsford, P., "Caesar's Birth and Death," *Modern Myths about the Ancient World. Kiwi Hellenist.* September 29, 2017. http://kiwihellenist.blogspot.com/2017/09

Gershenson, D. E., "*Kai su teknon*: Caesar's Last Words," *Shakespeare Quarterly*, Vol. 43, No. 2, (1 July 1992), pp. 218–219. https://doi.org/10.2307/2870883

Woodman, A. J., "Tiberius and the Taste of Power: The Year 33 in Tacitus," *Classical Quarterly*, Vol. 59 (2006), pp. 175–189.

Ziogas, I., "Famous Last Words: Caesar's Prophecy on the Ides of March," *Antichthon*, Vol. 50 (2016), pp. 134–153.

4

Livia Murdered Augustus's Heirs to Make Tiberius Emperor

What People Think Happened

Livia Drusilla is routinely believed to be the epitome of a devious, scheming, evil stepmother. Moreover, she is seen as a selfish, cruel bully. She avoided the funeral of her grandson, persecuted his wife, and was responsible for the banishment of her stepdaughter Julia. She also was viewed as a cold-blooded killer.

Tacitus is the major contributing source for the view of Livia as the conniving, wicked stepmother. More than any other work, the *Annals* of Tacitus greatly impacted the modern perception of the imperial men as well as that of Empress Livia Drusilla. He claimed to write "without either bitterness or partiality" (*Tac.Ann.*1.1.2), but his work is a hostile commentary on the Julio-Claudian Dynasty. Tacitus was a member of the senatorial class who lost power and influence after the establishment of the imperial system, which Augustus created.

Tacitus was very hostile toward ambitious, imperial women and spoke negatively about the empress throughout his writings. He accomplished this primarily by applying the stereotype of the evil stepmother to Livia (*Tac.Ann.*1.33).

The wicked, cunning stepmother was a particularly despised character in Roman literature and law since the earliest times. Typically, she was depicted as a mean, murderous individual. In *Pseudolus* by Plautus, a request for money is compared to petitioning to a stepmother. The Latin word for stepmother, *noverca*, is related to the Latin word *nouus*, new, and suggests "novel" or "strange." It also stresses the intrusive manner in which stepmothers insert themselves into the family. They are depicted as trying to rob a rightful heir of his inheritance in favor of their own children. From the earliest periods, stepmothers were seen as nonmaternal. The ancient Romans were particularly preoccupied with the stepmother who deprives a rightful heir of his inheritance in favor of her own children. Roman literature is full of instances when evil women requested the elimination of stepchildren as a condition of marriage. Sallust reveals that Aurelia Orestilla would marry Catiline only if he agreed to have his son killed. "He was smitten with a passion for Aurelia Orestilla, in whom no good man, at any time of her life, commended anything but her beauty, it is confidently believed that because she hesitated to marry him, from the dread of having a grown-up stepson, he cleared the house for their nuptials by putting his son to death" (*Sall.Cat.*15.2). By the Augustan Age, the stepmother's reputation as a scheming murderer was firmly established. In the first ten chapters of his *Annals,* Tacitus skillfully exploited "stepmother" stereotypes, with Livia perfidiously doing away with competitors for the imperial throne and exploiting her senile husband.

The adoption of Gaius and Lucius by Augustus in 17 BCE presented Livia with the first obstacle to her quest for power. Tacitus left no doubt that Livia had a hand in their deaths. Lucius and Gaius "were prematurely cut off by destiny, or by their stepmother Livia's treachery" (*Tac.Ann.*1.3). Their deaths left only her son Tiberius and the grandson Postumus as possible heirs. Postumus had been banished to an island for no cause, thanks to Livia who, according to Tacitus, "had the aged Augustus firmly under her control" (*Tac.Ann.*1.3). He also claimed that Livia was involved in Germanicus's poisoning through her friend Plancina (*Tac.Ann.*3.17).

According to Tacitus, Augustus wished to reconcile with his grandson, Postumus. However, Augustus died before he could restore Postumus as his heir. Tacitus reported that when the emperor got sick, people suspected Livia of dirty deeds (*Tac.Ann.*1.5). Postumus was soon removed from the picture. "Tiberius and Livia, the one from fear, the other from a stepmother's enmity, hurried on the destruction of a youth whom they suspected and hated" (*Tac.Ann.*1.6.2). Readers familiar with the anti-stepmother imagery would recognize how Tiberius profited from the deaths of Augustus and his grandson.

Tacitus also condemned Livia for not attending the funeral of her popular grandson Germanicus. "Tiberius and Augusta kept away from the public [either] because they felt it inferior to their majesty if they lamented openly, or because hypocrisy would be discerned if everyone's eyes focused on their countenances" (*Tac.Ann.*3.3).

Tacitus added that Livia persecuted Agrippina: "Then, there were feminine jealousies, Livia feeling a stepmother's bitterness towards Agrippina" (*Tac.Ann.*1.33).

Tacitus did not create the stereotype of the wicked, murdering stepmother. However, he exploited this term shamelessly. His constant references to stepmother and stepmotherly behavior would have been understood as code words for Livia's plotting to steal Augustus's throne from his rightful heirs.

How the Story Became Popular

Dio Cassius and Suetonius are two sources who have shaped and influenced the misperception of Livia. Both were elite males who supported the Republic and wrote anti-imperial literature.

Dio Cassius's *Roman History* discusses the Roman empire from the Trojan War to the reign of Severus Alexander (222–235 CE). He cited Tacitus, Suetonius, and others. Politically involved women figure prominently in his moralizing. Suetonius claimed familiarity with numerous sources but failed to name a source in reference to Livia. Lacking critical judgment, like Tacitus, he made use of "some say" or "it is believed" in order to create a damaging image of Livia.

Tacitus's take on Livia was purely gossip/innuendo. His hostility toward Livia had a great impact on Dio Cassius, who blamed her for several imperial heirs' suspicious deaths. He reported on her responsibility in the suspicious death of Marcellus but added that many people died of disease that year. He agreed with Tacitus and suspected that Livia was connected with the deaths of Lucius and Gaius because their deaths occurred when Tiberius returned to Rome from Rhodes, where Augustus had exiled him (*Dio.Cass.*53.33.4, *Tac.Ann.*1.3).

Augustus died in 14 CE at Nola. Dio claimed that Livia murdered him with poisoned figs. He also claimed that Livia delayed announcing his death because Tiberius was not in Rome (*Dio.Cass.*56.31.1). She did it because "he [Augustus] had secretly sailed over to the island to see Agrippa and seemed about to become completely reconciled with him" (*Dio.Cass.*56.30).

Dio blamed Tiberius for Postumus's death but said that "still others [said] that Livia instead of Tiberius had ordered his death" (*Dio.Cass.*57.3.6).

Unlike Tacitus, Dio did not blame Livia for the death of her grandson Germanicus. However, he reported that "at the death of Germanicus, Tiberius and Livia were thoroughly pleased, but everybody else was deeply grieved" (*Dio.Cass.*57.18.6). Tacitus did, however, claim that Livia and Tiberius prevented the inconsolable Antonia from going to her son's funeral in order to make it appear as if they were too distraught to attend (*Tac.Ann.*3.3).

Suetonius published imperial biographies and had much to say about Livia in reference to her relationships with her husband Augustus, son Tiberius, grandson Claudius, and great-grandson Gaius (Caligula). Regarding the death of Germanicus, he agreed with Dio Cassius that the body showed signs of poison. Suetonius was ambiguous as to who killed Postumus. "There is uncertainty about those instructions, as to whether the dying Augustus left them to eliminate a pretext for insurrection after him; or if Livia dictated [them] in Augustus's name, and whether Tiberius was aware or ignorant thereof" (*Suet.Tib.*22).

Suetonius said that at every mention of him (Postumus) and the Julias [daughter and granddaughter of Augustus], Augustus "would sigh deeply and cry out: 'would that I had ne'er wedded and would that I had died without offspring,' and he never alluded to them except as his three boils and his three ulcers" (*Suet.Aug.*65.4). Dio agreed that Augustus was unfortunate in marriage, that is, he was unhappy with Livia (*Dio.Cass.Frag.*56.108–109). Suetonius accused Livia of supplying Augustus with maidens from all quarters for him to "deflower" (*Suet.Aug.*71.1).

He reported that Livia tried to exercise influence in matters of state and tried to control Tiberius and be his equal or even superior. Suetonius concluded that Tiberius avoided his overbearing mother because she wanted to be coruler. "Vexed at his mother Livia, alleging that she claimed an equal share in the rule, he shunned frequent meetings with her and long and confidential conversations, to avoid the appearance of being guided by her advice; though in point of fact he was wont every now and then to need and to follow it. He was greatly offended, too, by a Decree of the Senate, which provided that 'son of Livia' as well as 'son of Augustus' should be written in his honorary inscriptions" (*Suet.Tib.*50.2).

Dio Cassius concurred with Suetonius: "For in the time of Augustus she had possessed the greatest influence and she always declared that it was she who made Tiberius emperor; consequently, she was not satisfied to rule on equal terms with him but wished to take precedence over him. As a result, various extraordinary measures were proposed, many persons expressing the opinion that she should be called the Mother of her Country, and many that she should be called Parent. Still others proposed that Tiberius should be named after her" (*Dio.Cass.*12.3–5).

Livia and Tiberius argued about a new citizen whom she wanted to be registered as a potential juror. Tiberius agreed to do so on the condition that the entry be marked as "forced upon the emperor by his mother" (*Suet. Tib.*51.1).

Livia's negative reputation continued into the Christian period. Sextus Aurelius Victor was born in Africa and was the imperial governor of Pannonia in 361 and urban prefect of Rome in 389. His highly abbreviated *Book about the Caesars* begins with the lives of Roman emperors from the time of Julius Caesar the dictator to Constantine. According to Victor, Augustus was unlucky in marriage.

These rumors about Livia became very influential in the modern era. Robert Graves wrote *I, Claudius* in the 1930s. He relied on the salacious tales from Tacitus, Dio, and Suetonius. Graves's Livia is a monster who killed Marcellus, Agrippa, Gaius, Lucius, and her son Drusus, as well as her first husband and anyone else who got in her way.

Augustus is portrayed as a kind but blundering individual who is completely under the control of his wife. She convinced him to exile his daughter Julia and grandson Postumus. Livia is particularly evil and framed her grandson for raping her granddaughter, Livilla. Postumus escaped by impersonating a slave but was eventually executed by Tiberius.

BBC/PBS Masterpiece Theater's 1976 presentation of *I, Claudius*, based primarily on the works of Tacitus and Suetonius, is one of the most popular portrayals of Livia, where she was even more evil than in the book. Livia was a great schemer who would do anything to get her way. She killed nearly everyone in the imperial family in her quest to see that the Roman Republic would never rise from the ashes. Livia believed that one-man rule was the only way to prevent the return of the disastrous century of civil wars that Augustus finally ended. Sian Phillips's portrayal of Livia as the quintessential villain has had a massive impact on the modern perception of Livia. In the series, Livia was very funny and quite likeable despite her murderous ways. Consequently today, when people think of Livia, Sian Philips comes to mind. This association has perpetuated the misconception of Livia as a power-hungry, ruthless killer.

PRIMARY DOCUMENTS

Romans viewed stepmothers as vicious, selfish, and cruel monsters. Nothing stops her from killing her stepchild out of jealousy.

But all credibility, and it is with credibility that the great majority of arguments are concerned, turns on questions such as the following: whether it is credible that a father has been killed by his son, or that a father has committed incest with his daughter, or to take questions of an opposite character, whether it is credible that a stepmother has poisoned her stepchild, or that a man of luxurious life has committed adultery; or again whether a crime has been openly committed, or false evidence given for a small bribe, since each of these crimes is the result of a special cast as a rule, though not always; if it were always so, there would be no room for doubt, and no argument. (*Quint.Inst.*5.10.19)

Despite the fact that many Roman children had stepmothers, popular belief perpetuated the negative, murderous stereotype.

Modern authors, however, more especially the declaimers, are bolder, indeed they show the utmost animation in giving rein to their imagination; witness the following passages from Seneca's treatment of the controversial theme in which a father, guided by one of his sons, finds another son in the act of adultery with his stepmother and kills both culprits. (*Quint.Inst.*9.3.42)

Public opinion viewed the noverca *as an outsider who committed the vilest crimes. Moreover, by her nature she is the worst of all women.*

Nature herself will have proved not a mother, but a stepmother to what we deem her greatest gift to man, the gift that distinguishes her from other living things, if she devised the power of speech to be the accomplice of crime, the foe to innocence, and the enemy of truth. For it had been better for men to be born dumb and devoid of reason than to turn to the gifts of providence to their moral destruction. (*Quin.Inst.*12.1.2–3)

Livia has gone down in history as an evil stepmother thanks to Tacitus, who presents a stepmother in her worst behavior form: the deprivation of an heir from his inheritance. Augustus met Livia when she had already had a son and was pregnant with another child by her former husband Tiberius Claudius Nero. Augustus had to ask the pontiffs for permission to marry Livia. Mothers should be loving and supportive of the family. Tacitus did not approve, and describes how Augustus kidnapped Livia from her husband. In the following passages, Tacitus uses double entendre. The term gravis *can mean important or significant but cursed or dreadful as well. Tacitus uses* gravis *to emphasize Livia's overbearing personality. The verb* abducere *suggests rape. Tacitus distances himself and blames Augustus for forcefully removing Livia from her former husband.*

His domestic adventures were not spared; the abduction of Nero's wife, and the farcical questions to the pontiffs, whether with a child conceived but not yet born, she could legally wed; the debaucheries of Vedius Pollio; and lastly, Livia, as a mother, a curse to the realm; as a stepmother, a curse to the house of the Caesars. (*Tac.Ann.*1.10)

In this passage from Livia's obituary, Tacitus stresses the scandalous start of the marriage but avoids mention of the long marriage of Livia and Augustus. His wording suggests the forceful removal of Livia based on Augustus's lust for her. Augustus's desire for Livia brings up the brutal rapists from Roman history, such as Sextus Tarquin. It also conjures up images of tyranny and kingship. Augustus is depicted as a man who takes whatever he wants. It is the opposite of what life was like during the Republic, according to Tacitus.

In the consulate of Rubellius and Fufius, both surnamed Geminus, Julia Augusta departed this life in extreme old age; by membership of the Claudian family and by adoption into the Livian and Julian houses, associated with the proudest nobility of Rome. Her first marriage and only children went to Tiberius Nero, who, exiled in the Perusian War, returned to the capital on the conclusion of peace between Sextus Pompeius and the Triumvirate. In the sequel, Augustus, smitten by her beauty, took her away from her husband. Her regrets are doubtful, and his haste was such that, without even allowing an interval for her confinement, he introduced her to his hearth while pregnant. (*Tac.Ann.*5.1)

Suetonius also used the verb abducare. *Suetonius stresses Augustus's domination over his wife.*

Shortly after he [Augustus] married Scribonia, who had been wedded before to two ex-consuls, and was a mother by one of them, "he divorced her also, 'unable to put up with her shrewish position,' as he himself writes, and at once took Livia Drusilla from her husband Tiberius Nero, although she was with child at the time; and he loved and esteemed her to the end without rival." (*Suet.Aug.*62.2)

In the next passage from the Life of Tiberius, *Suetonius indicates that Livia was not taken from her husband. Here his purpose is to portray Livia as the overbearing stepmother who dominates her passive husband, Augustus. Moreover, he depicts Livia as a domineering wife vis-a-vis her wimpy ex-husband.*

He (Tiberius Claudius Nero) returned to Rome, on the conclusion of a general peace, and gave up to Augustus at his request, his wife Livia Drusilla, who was pregnant at the time and had already borne him a son. Not long afterwards, he died, survived by his sons, Tiberius Nero and Drusus Nero. (*Suet. Tib.*4)

Mark Antony may have started the rumor that Augustus carried off the wife of an ex-consul from her husband's dining room in his presence and removed her to the bedroom. Livia returned with disheveled hair and glowing ears. Suetonius depicts Caligula as a depraved tyrant in a similarly disparaging account. Like Tacitus, Suetonius was not a fan of the imperial system. He describes how Caligula picked his second wife, Livia Orestilla, while she was still engaged to another man. Caligula claimed he was following in the tradition of Rome's founder as well as that of his great-grandfather.

It is not easy to decide whether he acted more basely in contracting his marriages, in annulling them, or as a husband. At the marriage of Livia Orestilla to Gaius Piso, he attended the ceremony himself, gave orders that the bride be taken to his own house, and within a few days divorced her; two years later he banished her, because of a suspicion that in the meantime she had gone back to her former husband. Others write that being invited to the wedding banquet, he sent word to Piso, who reclined opposite to him: "Don't take liberties with my wife," and at once carried her off with him from the table, the next day issuing a proclamation that he had got himself a wife in the manner of Romulus and Augustus. (*Suet. Calig.*25)

In the next quote Livia is introduced to readers for the first time. Livia was not a stepmother in the usual sense but rather in that Lucius and Gaius were adopted by Augustus as his heirs. Tacitus exploits a loaded term that equated stepmothers with poisoners and murderers of their stepchildren. He leaves no doubt in the mind of the reader that Livia had a hand in the deaths of Augustus's grandsons.

Meanwhile, to consolidate his power, Augustus raised Claudius Marcellus, his sister's son and a mere stripling, to the pontificate and curule aedileship: Marcus Agrippa, no aristocrat, but a good soldier and his partner in victory, he honored with two consecutive consulates, and a little later, on the death of Marcellus, selected him as his son-in-law. Each of his step-children, Tiberius Nero and Claudius Drusus, was given the title of Imperator, though his family proper was still intact: for he had admitted Agrippa's children, Gaius and Lucius, to the Caesarian hearth, and even during their minority had shown, under a veil of reluctance, a consuming desire to see them consuls designate with the titles Princes of the Youth. When Agrippa gave up the ghost, untimely fate, or the treachery of their stepmother Livia, cut off both Lucius and Caius Caesar, Lucius on his road to the Spanish armies, Caius—wounded and sick—on his return from Armenia. Drusus had long been dead, and of the stepsons Nero [Tiberius] survived alone. On him all centered. Adopted as son, as colleague in the empire, as consort of the tribunician power, he was paraded through all the armies, not as before by the secret diplomacy of his mother, but openly at her injunction. (*Tac.Ann.*1.3)

Tacitus blames Livia for the banishment of Postumus, the brother of Lucius and Gaius. Livia manipulated the elderly, senile Augustus into exiling his last surviving male relative to an isolated island. Romans would have been familiar with the evils of the wicked stepmother.

A stepmother's hate is presented as responsible for the death of Postumus who was with difficulty killed by a centurion, Sallustius Crispus, a knight who was the grandson of the sister of the famous Roman historian Sallust. Suetonius insinuates that Sallustius Crispus was somehow privy to the demise of Agrippa Postumus.

The opening crime of the new principate was the murder of Agrippa Postumus; who, though off his guard and without his weapons, was dispatched by a resolute centurion. In the Senate Tiberius made no reference to the subject: his pretense was an order from his father, instructing the tribune in charge to lose no time in making away with his prisoner, once he himself should have looked his last on the world. It was beyond question that by his frequent and bitter strictures on the youth's character Augustus had procured the senatorial decree for his exile: on the other hand, at no time did he harden his heart to the killing of a relative, and it remained incredible that he should have sacrificed the life of a grandchild in order to diminish the anxieties of a stepson. More probably, Tiberius and Livia, actuated in the one case by fear, and in the other by step-motherly dislike, hurriedly procured the murder of a youth whom they suspected and detested. To the centurion who brought the usual military report, the emperor rejoined that he had given no instructions and the deed would have to be accounted for in the Senate. The remark came to the ears of Sallustius Crispus, a partner in the imperial secrets—it was he who had forwarded the note to the tribune—he feared the charge might be fastened on himself, with the risks equally great whether he spoke the truth or lied. He therefore advised Livia not to publish the mysteries of the palace, the counsels of her friends, the services of the soldiery; and also to watch that Tiberius did not weaken the powers of the throne by referring everything and all things to the senate—"It was a condition of sovereignty that the account balanced only if rendered to a single auditor." (*Tac.Ann.*1.6)

Here Tacitus uses the term in the same context as above. The next case really stretches the point, as Livia was not Agrippina's stepmother. Livia was the stepmother of Agrippina's mother, Julia the Elder. Here the term conjures up images of the stereotypical, hateful and jealous stepmother.

Meantime Germanicus, while, as I have related, he was collecting the taxes of Gaul, received news of the death of Augustus. He was married to the granddaughter of Augustus, Agrippina, by whom he had several children, and he himself was the son of Drusus, brother of Tiberius, and the grandson of Augusta, he was troubled by the secret hatred of his uncle and grandmother, the motives for which were the more venomous because unjust. For the memory of Drusus was held in honor by the Roman people, and they believed that had he obtained the empire, he would have restored freedom. Hence, they regarded Germanicus with favor for the same hope. He was indeed a young man of unaspiring temper, and of wonderful kindliness, contrasting with the proud and mysterious reserve that marked the conversation and features of Tiberius. Then, there were feminine jealousies, Livia feeling a stepmother's bitterness toward Agrippina, herself too being rather excitable, only her purity and love of her husband gave her a right direction to her otherwise imperious disposition. (*Tac.Ann.*1.33)

Dio Cassius associates Livia with the stepmotherly image of the removal of the rightful heir and theft of legal legacy.

The reason why he sent Germanicus and not Agrippa [Postumus] to take the field was that the latter possessed an illiberal nature, and he spent most of his time fishing, by virtue of which he used to call himself Neptune.

He [Postumus] used to give way to violent anger, and spoke ill of Livia as a stepmother, while he often reproached Augustus himself for not giving him the inheritance his father had left him. When he could not be made to moderate his conduct, he was banished and his property was given to the military treasury; he himself was put ashore on Planasia, the island near Corsica. (*Dio.Cass.*55.32.1–2)

Dio Cassius hints that Livia is responsible for several deaths in the imperial family, starting with Marcellus, who was the popular nephew of Augustus.

Livia, now, was accused of having caused the death of Marcellus, because he had been preferred before her sons; but the justice of this suspicion became a matter of controversy by reason of the character both of that year and the year following, which proved so unhealthful that great numbers perished during them. And, just as it usually happens that some sign occurs before such events, so on this occasion a wolf was caught in the city, fire and storm damaged many buildings, and the Tiber, rising, carried away the wooden bridge and made the city navigable for boats during three days. (*Dio.Cass.*53.33.4)

Similar to Tacitus, Dio Cassius sees Livia as responsible for the deaths of Lucius and Gaius.

So, Gaius resigned at once all the duties of his office and took a trading vessel to Lycia, where at Limrya, he passed away. But even before Gaius' death the spark of life in Lucius had been quenched at Massilia. He, too, was being trained to rule by being dispatched on missions to many places, it was his custom to personally read the letters of Gaius to the senate, whenever he was present. His death was due to a sudden illness. In connection with both deaths, therefore, suspicion attached to Livia and particularly because it was just at this time that Tiberius returned to Rome from Rhodes. (*Dio.Cass.*55.10A9–10)

Tacitus agrees but does not give details. Instead, he implies that Livia was involved in the demise of Augustus and his grandson, along with Maximus.

While these topics and the like were under discussion, this malady of Augustus began to take a graver turn; and some suspected foul play on the part of his wife. For a rumor had gone the round that, a few months earlier, the emperor, confiding in a chosen few, and attended only by Fabius

Maximus, had sailed for Planasia on a visit to Agrippa. "There tears and signs of affection on both sides had been plentiful enough to raise a hope that the youth might yet be restored to the house of his grandfather. Maximus disclosed the incident to his wife Marcia; Marcia, to Livia. It had come to the Caesar's knowledge, and after the death of Maximus, which followed shortly, possibly by his own hand, Marcia had been heard at the funeral, sobbing and reproaching herself as the cause of her husband's destruction." Whatever the truth of the affair, Tiberius had hardly set foot in Illyricum, when he was recalled by an urgent letter from his mother; and it is not certainly known whether on reaching the town of Nola, he found Augustus still breathing or lifeless. For house and street were jealously guarded by Livia's ring of pickets, while sanguine notices were issued at intervals, until the measures dictated by the crisis had been taken: then one report announced simultaneously that Augustus had passed away and that Nero [Tiberius] was master of the empire. (*Tac.Ann.*1.5)

Dio Cassius does not directly accuse Tiberius or Livia as responsible for the death of Germanicus. However, both are evil because they took pleasure in others' suffering. Germanicus is presented as the ideal ruler who died too young.

At the death of Germanicus Tiberius and Livia were thoroughly pleased, but everybody else was deeply grieved. He was a man of the most striking physical beauty and likewise of the noblest spirit, and was conspicuous alike for his culture and for his strength. Though the bravest of men against the foe, he showed himself most gentle with his countrymen; and though as a Caesar he had the greatest power, he kept his ambitions on the same plane as weaker men. He never conducted himself oppressively toward his subjects or with jealousy toward Drusus or in any reprehensible way toward Tiberius. In a word, he was one of the few men of all time who have neither sinned against the fortune allotted them nor been destroyed by it. Although on several occasions he might have obtained imperial power, with the free consent not only of the soldiers but of the people and Senate as well, he refused to do so. His death occurred at Antioch as the result of a plot formed by Piso and Plancina. For bones of men that had been buried in the house where he dwelt and sheets of lead containing curses together with his name were found while he was yet alive; and that poison was the means of his carrying off was revealed by the condition of his body, which was brought into the Forum and exhibited to all who were present. Piso later returned to Rome and was brought before the Senate on the charge of murder by Tiberius himself, who thus endeavored to clear himself of the suspicion of having destroyed Germanicus; but Piso secured a postponement of the trial and committed suicide. (*Dio.Cass.*57.18.6)

What Really Happened

Livia's reputation as a murdering, evil stepmother has been greatly exaggerated. The claims are based more on innuendo than hard evidence. Livia was unlikely to have been near any of her alleged victims. Marcellus probably died from malaria. The other deaths were accidental. Livia was an easy target because she lived in a society that frowned upon too public a role for women. Livia was upheld as a paragon of virtue throughout her life. She was married to Augustus for more than fifty years, despite the fact that they never had any children together. Livia was adored by her husband and served as his closest advisor. Livia was also a quiet mover and shaker behind the scenes. She was very wealthy and was famous for her altruism and patronage to friends and clients. Livia had considerable influence after the death of her husband in 14 CE and was awarded many honors. She continued to be a force to be reckoned with until her death at the age of eighty-six in 29 CE.

Ancient and modern authors alike have accused Livia of murder, of cruelty to her stepchildren as well as of being power hungry. Despite a lack of evidence, she has been convicted by public opinion of killing Marcellus, Gaius, Lucius, Germanicus, Postumus, and Augustus.

Marcellus died as the result of an epidemic that spread throughout Rome. After he became ill, he was treated by Augustus's private physician, to no avail (*Dio.Cass.*53.30.1–4). Dio Cassius accused Livia of killing him but offered no evidence. He seems indecisive in that he admitted that during the pandemic "so many perished" (*Dio.Cass.*53.33.4).

Velleius Paterculus (*Vell.Pat.*2.93), Suetonius (*Suet.Aug.*63), and Tacitus (*Tac.Ann.*1.3.1) do not mention Livia in connection with Marcellus's demise.

False rumors by Tacitus and Dio suggest Livia had a hand in the demise of Lucius and Gaius. Suetonius does not attribute their deaths to Livia (*Suet.Aug.*65). Neither heir was murdered. Lucius died suddenly at Massilia, while his brother Gaius succumbed from a wound.

Augustus bequeathed the use of his name, his property, and bloodline to Postumus but did not make him heir to the throne. Postumus was actually banished to the island of Planasia because of his bad behavior (*Vell.Pat.*2.112.7). Tacitus reported that "a rumor had gone the round, that a few months earlier, the emperor, confiding in a chosen few, and attended only by Fabius Maximus, had sailed for Planasia, on a visit to Agrippa" (*Tac.Ann.*1.5). It is highly unlikely he was well enough to make such a voyage.

Livia did not poison her husband. The first source of this rumor stems from the fact she had her own garden of medicinal plants and mixed her own remedies. Livia developed an autumn-ripening fig called the *Liviana*, which probably added fuel to the fire. Augustus died peacefully.

According to Suetonius: "Then he sent them all off and while he was asking some newcomers from the city about the daughter of Drusus, who was ill, he suddenly passed away, uttering these last words: 'Live mindful of our wedlock, Livia, and farewell,' thus blessed with an easy death and such a one he had always longed for" (*Suet.Aug.*99.1).

Livia is also falsely accused of the downfall of Agrippina, the widow of Germanicus. Livia raised her children after Agrippina was sent into exile. Sejanus is to blame for her banishment and eventual demise, all of which occurred after the death of Livia in 29 CE.

Livia's friction with Tiberius is greatly exaggerated. She successfully mediated between her son and Quintus Haterius, who no doubt approached Livia because of her reputation for assisting people. She had good relations with Tiberius until 22 CE. Tiberius frowned upon her public appearances but may have done so because of concern about her health (Livia was very ill that year).

In contrast to all the nasty rumors and gossip, many Roman authors present Livia as a faithful wife, who is poised and dignified. She wore little jewelry and dressed modestly in garments that covered her completely. She also made her husband's clothes (*Suet.Aug.*2.73). She was extolled by Velleius Paterculus as the most noble because of her family, beauty, and modesty (*Vell.Pat.*2.75). In the anonymous *Consolation to Livia*, she was cast as the devoted mother devastated by the loss of her son Drusus. She also was especially praised for having led a chaste life (*pudicitia*). Dio Cassius reported: "Once when some had asked her how and by what course she had obtained such a commanding influence over Augustus, she answered that it was by being scrupulously chaste herself, doing gladly whatever pleased him, not meddling with any of his affairs, and in particular, by pretending neither to hear nor to notice the favorites of his passion. Such was the character of Livia" (*Dio.Cass.*58.2.3–6). Dio also said: "For is there anything better than a wife who is chaste, domestic, a good house-keeper, a rearer of children; one to gladden you in health, to tend you in sickness, to be your partner in good fortune, to console you in misfortune, to restrain the mad passion of youth and to temper the unseasonable harshness of old age?" (*Dio.Cass.*56.3.1–3).

Livia literally did not meddle in Augustus's numerous affairs. Augustus was a notorious womanizer. Nonetheless, Suetonius claimed that "he (Augustus) loved and esteemed her to the end without a rival" (*Suet.Aug.*62.1–2).

Livia was not only the epitome of the Roman *matrona* but also an advisor and confidant to her husband in state decisions as well as personal ones. Both Seneca and Dio Cassius reported that Livia effectively counseled her husband to pardon Cinna. Augustus discovered that Cornelius Cinna was plotting against him, and Livia recommended clemency instead of punishment. The result was that Cinna became a loyal retainer. She also used her influence to get her husband to grant the island of Samos independence.

Augustus passed laws that provided opportunities for Livia (and his sister Octavia). The laws gave her authority over property and wealth and freedom from any form of male guardianship. Livia had considerable power and influence that enabled her to promote many of her clients, such as Severus Sulpicius Galba and the Plautii, into politics. Wealthy women such as Urgulania sought her influence. Urgulania's son was made consul in 2 BCE because of Livia's influence. She successfully intervened on behalf of Plancina, the wife of Piso, the man who had been posthumously condemned for the death of Germanicus. After Livia's death, Plancina committed suicide. Livia's overseas clients included Salome, the sister of Herod the Great.

Livia was very generous to her extended family and opened her home to them and visitors from abroad, such as Julia and her sons Lucius and Gaius, to name a few. Julia Drusilla and Julia Livilla stayed with Livia while their mother, Agrippina the Elder, was exiled. The grandfather of the future emperor Otho, Marcus Salvius Otho, was raised in Livia's home.

Livia remained influential after the death of Augustus. She inherited one-third of his estate as well as the title of Augusta. She was also a priestess in the cult of Augustus. The Senate wished to grant her the title *Mater Patriae* (Mother of the Fatherland), but Tiberius refused. Notably, he also refused similar honors for himself.

Livia's friction with Tiberius is greatly exaggerated. Tiberius gave his mother a reserved seat with the Vestal Virgins (*Tac.Ann.*4.16). Livia was seriously ill in 22 CE, and Tacitus reported that her son rushed back to Rome to be at her side. Livia fell ill again in 29 CE but did not recover. She was eighty-six years old. Tiberius refused to execute her will and also canceled the honors granted to her by the Senate. Her great-grandson

Gaius (Caligula) delivered her eulogy. He executed her will when he became emperor. Livia finally was deified by her grandson Claudius.

PRIMARY DOCUMENTS

The first excerpt is from Velleius Paterculus. Written to commemorate the aedileship of Marcus Vinicius in 30 CE, it consists of two volumes, the first of which outlines the history of Rome from the fall of Troy to the end of the Punic Wars in 146 BCE. Volume 2 begins at 133 BCE and ends at the death of Livia in the year 29 CE. Velleius extols the virtue, selflessness, and modesty of Livia, who, prior to her marriage, was the wife of an enemy of Augustus.

Who can adequately express his astonishment at the changes of fortune, and the mysterious vicissitudes in human affairs? Who can refrain from hoping for a lot different from that which he now has, or from dreading the one that is the opposite of what he expects? Take, for example, Livia. She, the daughter of the brave and noble Drusus Claudianus, most eminent of Roman women in birth, in sincerity and in beauty, she, whom we later saw as the wife of Augustus, and as his priestess and daughter after his deification, was then a fugitive before the arms and forces of the very Caesar who would soon be her husband, carrying in her bosom her infant of two years, the present emperor Tiberius Caesar, destined to be the defender of the Roman Empire and the son of this same Caesar. Pursuing by-paths that she might avoid the swords of the soldiers and accompanied by but one attendant, so as more readily to escape detection in her flight, she finally reached the sea, and with her husband Nero made her escape by ship to Sicily. (*Vell.Pat.*2.75.2)

Velleius does not connect anyone with the death of Marcellus.

Some three years before the plot of Egnatius was exposed, about the time of the conspiracy of Murena and Caepio, fifty years from the present date, Marcus Marcellus died, the son of Octavia, sister of Augustus, after giving a magnificent spectacle to commemorate his aedileship and while still a youth. (*Vell.Pat.*2.93)

Tacitus's image of Livia as a scheming and ruthless stepmother is at odds with her positive portrait in Velleius's work. Paterculus praises Livia as "a woman pre-eminent among women, and who in all things resembled the gods more than mankind, whose power no one felt except for the alleviation of trouble or the promotion of rank" (Vell.Pat.2.130.5).

Seneca extols Livia for her love of family as well as how she dealt with loss. He wrote this letter to Marcia, who like Livia, was coping with the death of her son Drusus, who died in an accident in Germany. Octavia, similar to his friend, was unable to move on with her life.

I am aware that all who wish to give anyone advice begin with precepts, and end with examples: but it is sometimes useful to alter this fashion, for we must deal differently with different people. Some are guided by reason, others must be confronted with authority and the names of celebrated persons, whose brilliancy dazzles their mind and destroys their power of free judgment. I will place before your eyes two of the greatest examples belonging to your sex and your century: one, that of a woman who allowed herself to be entirely carried away by grief; the other, one who, though afflicted by a like misfortune, and an even greater loss, yet did not allow her sorrows to reign over her for a very long time, but quickly restored her mind to its accustomed frame. Octavia and Livia, the former Augustus's sister, the latter his wife, both lost their sons when they were young men, and when they were certain of succeeding to the throne. Octavia lost Marcellus, whom both his father-in-law and his uncle had begun to depend upon, and to place upon his shoulders the weight of the empire—a young man of keen intelligence and firm character, frugal and moderate in his desires to an extent which deserved especial admiration in one so young and so wealthy, strong to endure labor, averse to indulgence, and able to bear whatever burden his uncle might choose to lay, or I may say to pile upon his shoulders. Augustus had well-chosen him as a foundation, for he would not have given way under any weight, however excessive. His mother never ceased to weep and sob during her whole life, never endured to listen to wholesome advice, never even allowed her thoughts to be diverted from her sorrow. She remained during her whole life just as she was during the funeral, with all the strength of her mind intently fixed upon one subject. I do not say that she lacked the courage to shake off her grief, but she refused to be comforted, thought that it would be a second bereavement to lose her tears, and would not have any portrait of her darling son, nor allow any allusion to be made to him. She hated all mothers, and raged against Livia with especial fury, because it seemed as though the brilliant prospect once in store for her own child was now transferred to Livia's son. Passing all her days in darkened rooms and alone, not conversing even with her brother, she refused to accept the poems which were composed in memory of Marcellus, and all the other honors paid him by literature, and closed her ears against all consolation. She lived buried and hidden from view, neglecting her accustomed duties, and actually angry with the excessive splendor of her brother's prosperity, in which she shared. Though surrounded by her children and grandchildren, she would not lay aside her mourning garb, though by retaining it she seemed to put a slight upon all her relations, in thinking herself bereaved in spite of their being alive. (*Sen.Helv.*4.2)

Seneca begs Marcia to follow Livia's example and to bury her grief with her son. Marcia would be neglecting her duties as a mother if she cannot emerge from her loss.

Livia lost her son Drusus, who would have been a great emperor, and was already a great general: he had marched far into Germany, and had planted the Roman standards in places where the very existence of the Romans was hardly known. He died on the march, his very foes treating him with respect, observing a reciprocal truce, and not having the heart to wish for what would do them most service. In addition to his dying thus in his country's service, great sorrow for him was expressed by the citizens, the provinces, and the whole of Italy, through which his corpse was attended by the people of the free towns and colonies, who poured out to perform the last sad offices to him, till it reached Rome in a procession which resembled a triumph. His mother was not permitted to receive his last kiss and gather the last fond words from his dying lips: she followed the relics of her Drusus on their long journey, though every one of the funeral pyres with which all Italy was glowing seemed to renew her grief, as though she had lost him so many times. When, however, she at last laid him in the tomb, she left her sorrow there with him, and grieved no more than was becoming to a Caesar or due to a son. She did not cease to make frequent mention of the name of her Drusus, to set up his portrait in all places, both public and private, and to speak of him and listen while others spoke of him with the greatest pleasure: she lived with his memory; which none can embrace and consort with who has made it painful to himself. Choose, therefore, which of these two examples you think the more commendable: if you prefer to follow the former, you will remove yourself from the number of the living; you will shun the sight both of other people's children and of your own, and even of him whose loss you deplore; you will be looked upon by mothers as an omen of evil; you will refuse to take part in honorable, permissible pleasures, thinking them unbecoming for one so afflicted; you will be loath to linger above ground, and will be especially angry with your age, because it will not straightway bring your life abruptly to an end. I here put the best construction on what is really most contemptible and foreign to your character. I mean that you will show yourself unwilling to live, and unable to die. If, on the other hand, showing a milder and better regulated spirit, you try to follow the example of the latter most exalted lady, you will not be in misery, nor will you wear your life out with suffering. Plague on it! what madness this is, to punish oneself because one is unfortunate, and not to lessen, but to increase one's ills! You ought to display, in this matter also, that decent behavior and modesty which has characterized all your life: for there is such a thing as self-restraint in grief also. You will show more respect for the youth himself, who well deserves that it should make you glad to speak and think of him, if you make him able to meet his mother with a cheerful countenance, even as he was wont to do when alive. (*Sen.Helv.*4.3)

After the death of Drusus, Livia turned to philosophy to help her recover from grief. This enabled her to fulfill her duties as a mother.

I will not invite you to practice the sterner kind of maxims, nor bid you bear the lot of humanity with more than human philosophy; neither will I attempt to dry a mother's eyes on the very day of her son's burial. I will appear with you before an arbitrator: the matter upon which we shall join issue is, whether grief ought to be deep or unceasing. I doubt not that you will prefer the example of Julia Augusta, who was your intimate friend: she invites you to follow her method: she, in her first paroxysm, when grief is especially keen and hard to bear, betook herself for consolation to Areus, her husband's teacher in philosophy, and declared that this did her much good; more good than the thought of the Roman people, whom she was unwilling to sadden by her mourning; more than Augustus, who, staggering under the loss of one of his two chief supporters, ought not to be yet more bowed down by the sorrow of his relatives; more even than her son Tiberius, whose affection during that untimely burial of one for whom whole nations wept made her feel that she had only lost one member of her family. This was, I imagine, his introduction to and grounding in philosophy of a woman peculiarly tenacious of her own opinion:—"Even to the present day, Julia, as far as I can tell—and I was your husband's constant companion, and knew not only what all men were allowed to know, but all the most secret thoughts of your hearts—you have been careful that no one should find anything to blame in your conduct; not only in matters of importance, but even in trifles you have taken pains to do nothing which you could wish common fame, that most frank judge of the acts of princes, to overlook. Nothing, I think, is more admirable than that those who are in high places should pardon many shortcomings in others, and have to ask it for none of their own. So also, in this matter of mourning you ought to act up to your maxim of doing nothing which you could wish undone, or done otherwise." (*Sen.Helv.*4.4)

Suetonius's account of the death of Augustus contrasts with the accusations of Tacitus and Dio Cassius.

On the last day of his life he asked every now and then whether there was a disturbance without on his account; then calling for a mirror, he had his hair combed and his falling jaws set straight. After that, calling in his friends and asking whether it seemed to them that he had played the comedy of life fitly, he added the tag:

"Since, well I've played my part, all clap your hands.
And from the stage dismiss me with applause."

Then he sent them all off, and while he was asking some newcomers from the city about the daughter of Drusus, who was ill, he suddenly passed away as he was kissing Livia, uttering these last words: "Live mindful of our wedlock, Livia, and farewell." Thus, blessed with an easy death and such a one as he had always longed for. For almost always on hearing that anyone had died swiftly and painlessly, he prayed that he and his might have a like euthanasia, for that was the term he was wont to use. (*Suet.Aug.*99.1–2)

Suetonius ends by emphasizing that "he [Augustus] loved her and esteemed her to the end without a rival" (Suet.Aug.62.1–2).
  Augustus valued his wife's advice. Dio Cassius presents their discussion on the practicalities of clemency, which Livia recommended. The result was that Cinna became a loyal supporter of Augustus.

"You are indeed right," answered Livia, "and I have some advice to give you—that is, if you are willing to receive it, and will not censure me because I, though a woman, dare suggest to you something which no one else, even of your most intimate friends, would venture to suggest—not because they are not aware of it, but because they are not bold enough to speak."

"Speak out," replied Augustus, "whatever it is." "I will tell you," said Livia, "without hesitation, because I have an equal share in your blessings and your ills, and as long as you are safe I also have my part in reigning, whereas if you come to any harm, (which Heaven forbid!) I shall perish with you." (*Dio.Cass.*55.16.1–2)

Augustus turned an enemy, Cinna, into a friend. Cinna also came out ahead, as he was pardoned of plotting and parricide.

Then, after an interval of silence, he would say to himself in a far louder, angrier tone than he had used to Cinna, "Why do you live, if it be to so many men's advantage that you should die? Is there no end to these executions? to this bloodshed? I am a figure set up for nobly born youths to sharpen their swords on. Is life worth having, if so many must perish to prevent my losing it?" At last his wife Livia interrupted him, saying: "Will you take a woman's advice? Do as the physicians do, who, when the usual remedies fail, try their opposites. Hitherto you have gained nothing by harsh measures: Salvidienus has been followed by Lepidus, Lepidus by Muraena, Muraena by Caepio, and Caepio by Egnatius, not to mention others of whom one feels ashamed of their having dared to attempt so great a deed. Now try what effect clemency will have: pardon Lucius Cinna. He has been detected, he cannot now do you any harm, and he can do your reputation much good." Delighted at finding someone to support his own view of the case, he thanked his wife, straightaway ordered his friends, whose counsel he had asked for, to be told that he did not require their advice, and summoned Cinna alone. After ordering a second seat to be placed for Cinna, he sent everyone else out of the room, and said:—"The first request which I have to make of you is, that you will not interrupt me while I am speaking to you: that you will not cry out in the middle of my address to you: you shall be allowed time to speak freely in answer to me. Cinna, when I found you in the enemy's camp, you who had not become but were actually born my enemy, I saved your life, and restored to you the whole of your father's estate. You are now so prosperous and so rich, that many of the victorious party envy you, the vanquished one: when you were a candidate for the priesthood I passed over many others whose parents had served with me in the wars, and gave it to you: and now, after I have deserved so well of you, you have made up your mind to kill me." When at this word the man exclaimed that he was far from being so insane, Augustus replied, "You do not keep your promise, Cinna; it was agreed upon between us that you should not interrupt me. I repeat, you are preparing to kill me." He then proceeded to tell him of the place, the names of his accomplices, the day, the way in which they had arranged to do the deed, and which of them was to give the fatal stab. When he saw Cinna's eyes fixed upon the ground, and that he was silent, no longer because of the agreement, but from consciousness of his guilt, he said, "What is your intention in doing this? Is it that you yourself may be emperor? The Roman people must indeed be in a bad way if nothing but my life prevents your ruling over them. You cannot even maintain the dignity of your own house: you have recently been defeated in a legal encounter by the superior influence of a freedman: and so, you can find no easier task than to call your friends to rally round you against Caesar. Come, now, if you think that I alone stand in the way of your ambition; will Paulus and Fabius Maximus, will the Cossi and the Servilii and all that band of nobles, whose names are no empty pretense, but whose ancestry really renders them illustrious—will they endure that you should rule over them?" Not to fill up the greater part of this book by repeating the whole of his speech—for he is known to have spoken for more than two hours, lengthening out this punishment, which was the only one which he intended to inflict—he said at last: "Cinna, I grant you your life for the second time: when I gave it you before you were an open enemy, you are now a secret plotter and parricide. From this day forth let us be friends: let us try which of us is the more sincere, I in giving you your life, or you in owing your life to me." After this he of his own accord bestowed the consulship upon him, complaining of his not venturing to offer himself as a candidate for that office, and found him ever afterwards his most grateful and loyal adherent. Cinna made the emperor his sole heir, and no one ever again formed any plot against him. (*Sen.Clem.*1.9)

Even Tacitus praises Livia as an accommodating wife.

In the sequel, Augustus, smitten by her beauty, took her from her husband. Her regrets are doubtful, and his haste was such that, without even allowing an interval for her confinement, he introduced her to his hearth while pregnant. After this, she had no issue; but the union of Agrippina and Germanicus created a blood connection between herself and Augustus, so that her great-grandchildren were shared with the prince. In domestic virtue, she was of the old school, though her affability went further than was approved by women of the elder world. An imperious mother, she was an accommodating wife, and an excellent match for the subtleties of her husband and the insincerities of her son. (*Tac.Ann.*5.1.1)

Livia was the ideal Roman wife who did not complain about the fact that:

[Augustus] was given to adultery not even his friends deny, although it is true that they excuse it as committed not from passion but from policy, the more readily to get track of his adversaries' designs through the women of their households. (*Suet.Aug.*69.1)

Livia was held in high regard for leading a chaste life. Dio Cassius reports that she saved some naked men that she chanced upon.

Among the many excellent utterances of hers that are reported are the following. Once, when some naked men met her and were to be put to death in consequence, she saved their lives by saying that to chaste women such men are no whit different from statues. (*Dio.Cass.*58.2.3)

Augustus valued his wife's advice. Dio Cassius presents their discussion on the practicalities of clemency, which Livia recommended. The result was that Cinna became a loyal supporter of Augustus.

"You are indeed right," answered Livia, "and I have some advice to give you – that is, if you are willing to receive it, and will not censure me because I, though a woman, dare suggest to you something which no one else, even of your most intimate friends, would venture to suggest—not because they are not aware of it, but because they are not bold enough to speak." "Speak out," replied Augustus, "whatever it is." "I will tell you," said Livia, "without hesitation, because I have an equal share in your blessings and your ills, and as long as you are safe I also have my part in reigning, whereas if you come to any harm, (which Heaven forbid!) I shall perish with you." (*Dio.Cass.*55.16.1–2)

Livia intervened in the rift between her son Tiberius and Haterius and is credited with saving the life of the latter. "Haterius appealed to Augustus, and was saved by the urgency of her prayers" (Tac.Ann.*1.13*).

Livia had a good relationship with her son for quite a while. Tiberius saw to it that "Augusta, whenever she entered the theater, was to take her place among the seats reserved for the Vestals" (Tac.Ann.*4.16.1*).

After the death of Augustus, the Senate wanted to grant honors to Livia, but Tiberius denied such distinction for his mother as well as himself.

For in the time of Augustus she had possessed the greatest influence and she always declared that it was she who had made Tiberius emperor; consequently, she was not satisfied to rule on equal terms with him, but wished to take precedence over him. As a result, various extraordinary measures were proposed, many persons expressing the opinion that she should be called Mother of her country, and many that she should be called Parent. Still others proposed that Tiberius should be named after her, so that, just as the Greeks were called by their father's name, he should be called by that of his mother. All this vexed him, and he would neither sanction the honors voted her, with a very few exceptions, nor otherwise allow her any extravagance of conduct. For instance, she had once dedicated in her house an image to Augustus, and in honor of the event wished to give a banquet to the Senate and the knights together with their wives, but he would not permit her to carry out any of this program until the Senate had so voted, and not even then to receive the men at dinner; instead, he entertained the men and she the women. Finally, he removed her entirely from public affairs but allowed her to direct matters at home; as she was troublesome even in that capacity, he proceeded to absent himself from the city and to avoid her in every way possible; indeed, it was chiefly on her account that he removed to Capreae. Such are the reports that have been handed down about Livia. (*Dio. Cass.* 57.12.3–6)

Further Reading

Barrett, Anthony A., *Livia: First Lady of Imperial Rome*. Yale University Press, New Haven and London, 2002.

Barrett, Anthony A., "Tacitus, Livia and the Evil Stepmother," *Rheinisches Museum für Philologie*, Neue Folge, 144. Bd., H. 2 (2001), pp. 171–175.

Gray-Fow, Michael, "The Wicked Stepmother in Roman Literature and History: An Evaluation," *Latomus*, Vol. 47, No. 4 (1988), pp. 741–757.

Hillard, Tom, "Livia Drusilla," *Groniek*, Vol. 198 (2013), pp. 5–22.

Mudd, Mary, *I. Livia, The Counterfeit Criminal*. Trafford Publishing, Victoria, BC, 2005.

Noy, David, "Wicked Stepmothers in Roman Society and Imagination," *Journal of Family History*, Vol. 16 (1991), pp. 345–361.

Watson, P. A., *Ancient Stepmothers: Myth, Misogyny and Reality* (Mnemosyne, Suppl. 143). E. J. Brill, Leiden, 1995.

5

Caligula Made His Horse, Incitatus, a Consul

What People Think Happened

Caligula, who ruled from 37–41 CE as Rome's most infamous emperor, is popularly thought of as a monster. His name is synonymous with madness, cruelty, tyranny, and incest. People often cite his most peculiar deed as that of appointing his horse to the Senate.

Born in 12 CE, Gaius Julius Caesar Augustus Germanicus (Caligula) was the son of Germanicus, a military hero, and Agrippina the Elder, granddaughter of Augustus. When he was a child, his mother dressed him up as a little soldier, and he became the mascot of the soldiers, who adored him and called him Caligula, or "little boots" (*Suet. Calig.* 9.1), a name he hated. Caligula became emperor after the death of his uncle, Tiberius, in 37 CE.

Caligula's behavior was extremely erratic. He also abused his power. Instead of ruling the empire, he indulged in his passions. For example, Caligula was very fond of chariot racing, a very popular Roman spectator sport. Four teams, the Reds, Blues, Whites, and Greens, competed for cash prizes. According to Suetonius: "He (Caligula) was so passionately devoted to the Green faction that he constantly dined and spent the night in their stable (club)" (*Suet. Calig.* 55.2). Caligula was said to be so wicked that he poisoned the horses and drivers of the other teams so that the Greens would win.

An example of his outlandishness was his obsession with his favorite horse, Incitatus, meaning "Swifty" or "Speedy." Suetonius reported that

Caligula "used to send his soldiers on the day before the games and order silence in the neighborhood to prevent the horse Incitatus from being disturbed" (*Suet. Calig.* 55.3). Caligula was so deranged and wasteful he bestowed sumptuous gifts on the horse. Incitatus had a marble stable complete with fancy furniture, very expensive purple blankets and his own personal slaves to wait on him (*Suet. Calig.* 55.3). Even more degenerate is the fact that Suetonius reported, "it is also said that he (Caligula) planned to make him consul, a promise he would have kept if he had lived longer" (*Suet. Calig.* 55.3, *Dio. Cass.* 59.14.7).

Dio Cassius also mentioned that Caligula appointed his horse to be a fellow-priest (*Dio. Cass.* 59.28.6). Caligula used to invite his horse to dinner, where Incitatus reportedly dined on golden barley. Caligula would toast to his health from golden goblets.

The bridge at Baiae is one of the most sensational tales. Caligula built a pontoon bridge across the Bay of Baiae that extended over three Roman miles "to the mole [breakwater] at Puteoli" (*Suet. Calig.* 19.1, *Dio. Cass.* 59.17.1). With Caligula's image as the epitome of excess and greed, it is also not surprising that he chose Baiae, the Sin City of the ancient Roman world. Like Caligula, it was synonymous with scandals and decadent behavior. Seneca said it "was a place to be avoided" and "a resort of vice" (*Sen. Lucil.* 51.1–3).

Caligula's wasteful procession lasted for two days. He used so many boats that none were left for grain transport. He rode Incitatus and wore the breastplate of Alexander the Great. Suetonius reported: "Gaius devised this kind of bridge in rivalry to Xerxes" (*Suet. Calig.* 19.3). Xerxes had a reputation for excess and tyranny. Similarly, Caligula, like Xerxes, Suetonius suggested, is the epitome of the extravagant, arrogant Eastern despot.

Dio Cassius added that Caligula had a great banquet but threw many of the guests, some of whom perished, overboard (*Dio. Cass.* 59.17.9–10). Josephus mentioned that Caligula built the bridge because "he was a god" (*Jos. AJ.* 19.1).

For Suetonius, Caligula was the paradigm of excess cruelty. He noted that Caligula kept wild animals as pets. Once, during a gladiatorial show, because the cost of cattle was too high, he fed criminals to his pets (*Suet. Calig.* 27.1).

Caligula is thus thought to be the epitome of insanity. One popular story says that he marched his legionnaires to the seashore to invade Britain but suddenly abandoned the mission. Instead of crossing the channel, he declared war on Neptune and ordered his soldiers to pick up seashells in their helmets. After they finished, he declared victory over Neptune, marching back home to Rome with the shells as spoils from the ocean (*Suet.Calig.*46, *Dio.Cass.* 59.25.1–3). Suetonius suggested that Caligula was so desperate for a military victory that he used imaginary Germans to march in his triumph (*Suet.Calig.*47.1).

Caligula behaved more depravedly as time went on, says popular thought. He had incestuous relationships with his three sisters, cross-dressed, and even claimed to be a god and demanded to be worshipped in a temple in Rome. People began to hate him. Caligula threatened to move his capital to Alexandria so he could be worshipped as a god. The Romans had had enough. He was stabbed to death by his own Praetorian guards on January 24, 41 CE.

How the Story Became Popular

The misperception that Caligula made his favorite horse a consul was created by Roman writers in order to discredit Caligula and to justify his assassination. Under Caligula, the Senate and upper classes had become irrelevant. The madman stereotype was used both to explain his cruelty and bizarre behavior and to show his incompetence.

Early works by historians such as Cluvius Rufus, who was involved in the assassination of Caligula (*Jos.AJ*.13), were unkind. Cluvius's *Historiae* perpetuated this negative view by its use in the works of Tacitus, Suetonius, and Josephus.

Even the limited information on Caligula that survives in Tacitus is negative. For example, he described Caligula as having had a "troubled brain" (*Tac.Ann.*13.3).

Philo of Alexandria also has contributed to the misperception of Caligula as mad. As were the histories before his work, Philo's portrayal of the emperor is completely negative. He reviled Caligula for his insanity (*Philo.Leg.*13.93–94). In 39/40 CE he went to Rome to speak with Caligula regarding conflict between Jews and Greeks in Alexandria. Caligula was very angry that Philo would not worship him as a god. "You are haters of God, inasmuch as you do not think I am a god, I who already am confessed to be a god by every other nation, but who is refused that appellation by you" (*Philo.Leg.*44.353). Another Jewish historian, Josephus, attributed Caligula's insanity to the desire to become a god (*Jos.AJ.* 19.13). Juvenal mentioned a love potion as a possibility (*Juv.*6.610–626).

The philosopher Seneca was nearly executed by the emperor. Fortunately for Seneca, Caligula rescinded the death sentence "because he believed the statement of one of his female associates, to the effect that

Seneca had a consumption in an advanced stage and would die before a great while" (*Dio. Cass.* 59.19.7–8). Seneca described Caligula's behavior as *dementia* (madness) but was more concerned about his tyranny.

It was Suetonius who established Caligula as the archetypical mad tyrant (*Suet. Calig.* 51.1). "He was neither sound of mind nor body" (*Suet. Calig.* 50.2). Suetonius shocked his readers with Caligula's many transgressions. He even denied Caligula's humanity when he referred to him as a "monster." Suetonius found this term useful to describe Caligula's extremely vile deeds. For example, when Caligula was struck ill in 37 CE, people vowed to give their lives if the emperor would recover. In response to this, Caligula made some fight as gladiators and hurled others off of embankments (*Suet. Calig.* 27.1–2, *Dio. Cass.* 59.8.3).

Suetonius presented the following actions as typical of Caligula's insanity: "he never rested more than three hours at night, and even for that length of time he did not sleep quietly, but was terrified by strange apparitions, once for example, dreaming that the spirit of the Ocean talked with him" (*Suet. Calig.* 50.3).

Another incident also supposedly proved he was mad and deranged: "Once he (Caligula) summoned three consulars to the palace at the close of the second watch, and when they arrived in great and deathly fear, he seated them on a stage and then, on a sudden, burst out with great din of flutes and clogs, dressed in a cloak and tunic reaching to his heels, and after dancing a number, went off again" (*Suet. Calig.* 54.2).

Suetonius revealed how disrespectful Caligula was to Livia Augusta when he accused his great-grandmother of low birth and called her "Ulysses in petticoats" (*Suet. Calig.* 23.2). Other statements asserted that Caligula was sadistic and enjoyed tormenting people. He once said to his wife, "Off comes this beautiful head whenever I give the word" (*Suet. Calig.* 33). Purportedly he enjoyed killing a person slowly and commanded the executioner to "[s]trike so he may feel that he is dying" (*Suet. Calig.* 30). He was self-centered as well. Once when the crowd cheered for a faction he opposed, he cried, "I wish the Roman people had but a single neck" (*Suet. Calig.* 30.2).

Suetonius's Caligula is truly a beast. Claims of incest with his sisters, and his bizarre cross dressing emphasized Caligula's mad follies (*Suet. Calig.* 24.1–3, 52, *Dio. Cass.* 59.11.1–4).

Caligula was so removed from reality that he completely denied his humanity and demanded to be worshipped as a god himself (*Suet. Calig.* 22).

Dio Cassius depicted Caligula as a crazy, outlandish despot. He attributed Caligula's madness to be the result of his character flaws (*Dio. Cass.*

59.4–5). For example, he described him thus: "So capricious was he; and no one could easily suit him" (*Dio.Cass.*59.23.4). According to him, Caligula invited his horse to dinner, fed him golden barley and promised to appoint him as consul. Caligula was delusional because "he pretended to be a god" (*Dio.Cass.*59.26.10).

Dio also expressed horror at the thought of the emperor donning women's clothing. "He also impersonated Hercules, Bacchus, Apollo, and all the other deities, not merely males but also females, often taking the role of Juno, Diana or Venus" (*Dio.Cass.*59.26.6). Caligula did this "to appear to be anything other than a human being or an emperor" (*Dio.Cass.*59.26).

Caligula was also portrayed as excessive regarding finances. The treasury was full when he became emperor. However, he squandered the money in less than a year (*Suet.Calig.*37.1–3, *Suet.Ner.*30.1, *Dio.Cass.* 59.2.5–6). Suetonius reported that in Caligula's reckless extravagance he would "drink pearls of great price dissolved in vinegar; and set before his guests, loaves and meat of gold, declaring that a man ought to be frugal or Caesar." In addition, "He built villas and country houses without regard to expense" (*Suet.Calig.*37.1–2).

Suetonius claimed that two men were involved in Caligula's assassination (*Suet.Calig.*58), while Dio Cassius said that most of the court was involved (*Dio.Cass.*59.29.1).

Eutropius mentioned that Caligula's incestuous relationship with his sisters produced a child (*Eutr.*7.12). In the fourth century, Sextus Aurelius Victor showed how the mad Caligula became ingrained in the Roman world (*Aur.Vict.Caes.*3). He agreed that Caligula's bizarre behavior was something to be avoided. Orosius revealed that Caligula "committed the crime of violating his own sisters" (*Oros.*7.5).

Villains never really die. Caligula's next appearance was in Robert Graves's *I, Claudius*, published in 1934. Graves adapted the writings of Suetonius and Dio Cassius and made Caligula even crazier. In this book, Caligula has absolutely no semblance of humanity and is completely insane. He killed his father and slept with and murdered his sister. Graves's Caligula went to war with Poseidon and ordered his soldiers to throw spears at the water. The book was later adapted to television in a BBC production. All this leaves the popular impression that Caligula was evil since his childhood. He was called a monster when caught in bed with his sister Drusilla. Caligula's popular reputation continued to decline throughout the twentieth century to such an extent that he was depicted as killing Christians in *The Robe* (1953) and committing bestiality in 1979's *Caligula*.

In short, he was portrayed as completely egomaniacal and deranged from day one of his rule. He wanted to be worshipped as a god, made his horse a consul, and was despicable to all. The negative image of Caligula, painted in works that are now lost, lived on in the writings of Tacitus, Suetonius, and Dio Cassius, who added gossip and exaggerated claims that further smeared Caligula's name. Modern books, television, and motion pictures have subsequently established Caligula as the archetype of the insane tyrant, a popular conception that continues even today.

PRIMARY DOCUMENTS

Caligula did not like competition and did away with whomever he considered to be his rival. Domitius Afer was a Roman orator accused of offending Caligula in the Senate. He played down his rhetorical skills and feigned being highly impressed with Caligula's speaking skills. The emperor was so thrilled that he rewarded Afer with a consulship in 39 CE.

Domitius Afer came near losing his life for an extraordinary reason, and was saved in a still more remarkable manner. Gaius hated him in any case, because in the reign of Tiberius he had accused a woman who was related to his mother Agrippina. Hence Agrippina, when she afterwards met Domitius and perceived that out of embarrassment he stood aside from her path, called to him and said: "Fear not, Domitius; it isn't you that I hold to blame, but Agamemnon." At the time in question, Afer had set up an image of the emperor and had written an inscription for it to the effect that Gaius in his twenty-seventh year was already consul for the second time. This vexed Gaius, who felt that the other was reproaching him for his youth and his illegal conduct. Hence for this action, for which Afer had looked to be honored, the emperor brought him at once before the Senate and read a long speech against him. For Gaius always claimed to surpass all the orators, and knowing that his adversary was an extremely gifted speaker, he strove on this occasion to excel him. And he certainly would have put Afer to death, if the latter had entered into the least competition with him. As it was, the man made no answer or defense, but pretended to be astonished and overcome by the ability of Gaius, and repeating the accusation point by point, praised it as if he were a mere listener and not on trial. When the opportunity was given to him to speak, he had recourse to entreaties and lamentations; and finally he threw himself to the ground and lying there prostrate played the suppliant to his accuser, pretending to fear him more as an orator than as Caesar. Gaius, accordingly, when he saw and heard all this, was melted, believing that he had really overwhelmed Domitius by the eloquence of his speech. For this reason, then, as well as for the sake of Callistus, the freedman, whom he was wont to honor and whose favor Domitius had courted, he gave up his resentment. And when Callistus later blamed him for having accused the man in the first place, he answered: "It would not have been right for me to keep such a speech to myself." Thus, Domitius was saved by being convicted of being no longer a skillful orator. On the other hand, Lucius Annaeus Seneca, who was superior in wisdom to all the Romans of his day and to many others as well, came near to being destroyed, though he had neither done anything wrong nor had the appearance of doing so, but merely because he pleaded a case well in the Senate while the emperor was present. (*Dio.Cass.*59.19)

Seneca the Younger found Caligula to be insane and cruel. Caligula was said to be jealous of Seneca's oratorical skills. The emperor ordered Seneca to commit suicide but Seneca was ill at the time. It comes as no surprise that Seneca has nothing good to say about the imperial monster.

Gaius Caesar, among the other vices with which he overflowed, was possessed by a strange, insolent passion for marking everyone with some note of ridicule, he himself being the most tempting subject for derision; so ugly was the paleness which proved him mad, so savage the glare of the eyes which lurked under his old woman's brow, so hideous his misshapen head, bald and dotted about with a few cherished hairs besides the neck set thick with bristles, his monstrous feet. It would be endless were I to mention all the insults which he heaped upon his parents and ancestors, and people of every class of life. I will mention those which brought him to ruin. An especial friend of his was Asiaticus Valerius, a proud-spirited man and one hardly likely to put up with another's insults quietly. At a drinking bout, that is, a public assembly, Gaius, at the top of his voice, reproached this man with the way his wife behaved in bed. Good gods! that a man should hear that the emperor knew this, and that he, the emperor, should describe his adultery and his disappointment to the lady's husband, I do not say to a man of consular rank and his own friend. Chaerea, on the other hand, the military tribune, had a voice not befitting his prowess, feeble in sound, and somewhat suspicious unless you knew his achievements. When he asked for the watchword Gaius at one time gave him "Venus," and at another "Priapus," and by various means reproached the man-at-arms with effeminate vice; while he himself was dressed in transparent clothes, wearing sandals and jewelry. Thus, he forced him to use his sword, that he might not have to ask for the watchword oftener; it was Chaerea who first of all the conspirators raised his hand, who cut through the middle of Caligula's neck with one blow. After that, many swords, belonging to men who had public or private injuries to avenge, were thrust into his body, but he first showed himself a man who seemed least like one. The same Gaius construed everything as an insult (since those who are most eager to offer affronts are least able to endure them). He was angry with Herennius Macer for having greeted him as Gaius—nor did the chief centurion of *triarii* [a Roman military unit] get off scot-free for having saluted him as Caligula; having been born in the camp and brought up as the child of the legions, he had been wont to be called by this name, nor was there any by which he was better known to the troops, but by this time he held "Caligula" to be a reproach and a dishonor. Let wounded spirits, then, console themselves with this reflection that, even though our easy temper may have neglected to revenge itself, nevertheless that there will be someone who will punish the impertinent, proud, and insulting man, for these are vices which he never confines to one victim or one single offensive act. Let us look at the examples of those men whose endurance we admire, as, for instance, that of Socrates, who took in good part the published and acted jibes of the comedians upon himself, and laughed no less than he did when he was drenched with dirty water by his wife Xanthippe. Antisthenes was reproached with his mother being a barbarian and a Thracian; he answered that the mother of the gods, too, came from Mount Ida. (*Sen.Dial.*2.18.1)

Philo said that an illness caused a sudden change.

But in the eighth month a severe disease attacked Gaius who had changed the manner of his living which was a little while before, while Tiberius was alive, very simple and on that account more wholesome than one of great sumptuousness and luxury; for he began to indulge in abundance of strong wine and eating of rich dishes, and in the abundant license of insatiable desires and great insolence, and in the unseasonable use of hot baths, and emetics, and then again in winebibbing and drunkenness, and returning gluttony, and in lust after boys and women, and in everything else which tends to destroy both soul and body, and all the bonds which unite and strengthen the two; for the rewards of temperance are health and strength, and the wages of intemperance are weakness and disease which bring a man near to death. (*Philo.Leg.*2.14)

Philo also condemned Caligula's abhorrent claim of divinity.

But the madness and frenzy to which he gave way were so preposterous, and so utterly insane, that he went even beyond the demigods, and mounted up to and invaded the veneration and worship paid to those who are looked upon as greater than they, as the supreme deities of the world, Mercury, and Apollo, and Mars. And first of all, he dressed himself up with the caduceus, and sandals, and mantle of Mercury, exhibiting a regularity in his disorder, a consistency in his confusion, and a ratiocination in his insanity. (*Philo.Leg.*13.93–94)

Caligula was a modest and good ruler for the first few years of his reign. However, Josephus said that Caligula's arrogance led him to believe that he was divine.

Now Caius managed public affairs with great magnanimity during the first and second year of his reign, and behaved himself with such moderation that he gained the good-will of the Romans, and of his other subjects. But, in process of time, he went beyond the bounds of human nature in his conceit of himself, and by the reason of the vastness of his dominions made himself a god. (*Jos.AJ.*18.245)

Josephus considered the emperor to be depraved and evil. He is also the first to mention Caligula's alleged incest.

He was, even before he came to be Emperor, ill natured; and one that had arrived at the utmost pitch of wickedness. A slave to his pleasures; and a lover of calumny. Greatly affected by every terrible accident; and on that account of a very murderous disposition, where he durst shew it. He enjoyed his exorbitant power to this only purpose, to injure those who least deserved it, with unreasonable insolence, and got his wealth by murder and injustice. He labored to appear above regarding either what was divine, or agreeable to the laws: but was a slave to the commendations of the populace. And whatsoever the laws determined to be shameful, and punished, that he esteemed more honorable than what was virtuous. He was unmindful of his friends, how intimate so ever; and though they were persons of the highest character. And if he was once angry at any of them, he would inflict punishment upon them, on the smallest occasions: and esteemed every man that endeavored to lead a virtuous life his enemy: and whatsoever he commanded he would not admit of any contradiction to his inclinations. Whence it was said he had criminal conversation with his own sister. (*Jos.AJ.*19.2.5)

Suetonius was the first writer who claimed that Caligula was insane, possibly from sickness or from poisoning.

He was sound neither of body nor mind. As a boy he was troubled with the falling sickness, and while in his youth he had some endurance, yet at times because of sudden faintness he was hardly able to walk, to stand up, to collect his thoughts, or to hold up his head. He himself realized his mental infirmity and thought at times of going into retirement and clearing his brain. It is thought that his wife Caesonia gave him a drug intended for a love potion, which however had the effect of driving him mad. (*Suet.Calig.*50.2–3)

Caligula is also impious for wishing to be worshiped as a god and replacing the heads of deities with his own.

But on being reminded that he had risen above the elevation of both princes and kings, he began from that time on to lay claim to divine majesty; after giving orders that such statues of the gods as were especially famous for their sanctity or their artistic merit, including that of Jupiter of Olympia should be brought from Greece in order to remove their heads and put his own in their place. (*Suet.Calig.*22.2)

In the eyes of his contemporaries, Caligula was obviously not normal, because he was a cross-dresser, among other things. Therefore, in the eyes of Suetonius, he was an incompetent ruler.

In his clothing, his shoes and the rest of his attire he did not follow the usage of his country and his fellow-citizens; not always even that of his sex; or in fact, that of an ordinary mortal. He often appeared in public in embroidered cloaks covered with precious stones, with a long-sleeved tunic and bracelets; sometimes in silk and in a woman's robe, now in slippers or buskins, again in boots, such as the emperor's body-guard wear, and at times in the low shoes which are used by females. But oftentimes he exhibited himself with a golden beard, holding in his hand a thunderbolt, a trident, or a caduceus, emblems of the gods, and even in the garb of Venus. (*Suet.Calig.*52.1)

Next Suetonius repeats Josephus's claim of incest.

He lived in habitual incest with all of his sisters, and at a large banquet he placed each of them in turn below him, while his wife reclined above. Of these he is believed to have violated Drusilla when he was still a minor, and even to have been caught lying with her by his grandmother Antonia, at whose house they were brought up in company. (*Suet.Calig.*24.1)

Suetonius showed how brutal and sadistic Caligula could be. His viciousness and cruelty knew no bounds.

He forced parents to attend the executions of their sons, sending a litter for one man who pleaded ill health, and inviting another to dinner immediately after witnessing the death, and trying to rouse him to gaiety and jesting by a great show of affability. He had the manager of his gladiatorial shows and beast-baitings beaten to death with chains in his presence for several successive days, and would not kill him until he was disgusted at the stench of his putrefied brain. He burnt a writer of Atellan [improvised affairs with crude jokes] farces alive in the middle of the arena of the amphitheater because of a humorous line of double meaning. When a Roman knight on being thrown to the wild beasts loudly protested his innocence, he took him out, cut off his tongue, and put him back again.

Having asked a man who had been recalled from an exile of long standing, how in the world he spent his time there, the man replied by way of flattery: "I constantly prayed the gods for what has come to pass, that Tiberius might die and you become emperor." Thereupon Caligula, thinking that his exiles were likely praying for his death, sent emissaries from island to island to butcher them all. Wishing to have one of the senators torn to pieces, he induced some of the members to assail him suddenly, on his entrance to the House, with the charge of being a public enemy, to stab him with their styles, and turn him over to the rest to be mangled; and his cruelty was not sated until he saw the man's limbs, members, and bowels dragged through the streets and heaped up before him. (*Suet.Calig.* 27.4–28)

Dio Cassius reported on Caligula's demands to be treated as a god. "For to most of the senators, even, he merely extended his hand or foot for homage" (Dio.Cass.59.27.1).

Romans hated Tiberius because of his gloomy disposition and treason trials. Nonetheless, Dio Cassius claimed: "Hence the deeds of Tiberius, though they were felt to have been very harsh, were nevertheless superior to those of Gaius [Caligula] as the deeds of Augustus to those of his successor" (Dio.Cass.59.5).

Caligula killed Tiberius's grandson Gemellus because he hated competition. "He caused the death of Tiberius [Gemellus], who had assumed the toga virilis, had been given the title of Princeps Iuventutis, *and finally had been adopted into his family" (Dio.Cass.59.8.1).*

His barbarity knew no limits. He murdered people for his own amusement. "It was not the large number who perished that was so serious, though that was serious enough, but his excessive delight in their death and his insatiable desire for the sight of blood" (Dio.Cass.59.10.2).

Like other incompetent emperors, Caligula was also financially irresponsible. Caligula's expedition to Gaul was just an excuse to squeeze more money out of the wealthy provinces in order to support his lavish, wasteful lifestyle.

Gaius had now spent practically all the money in Rome and the rest of Italy, gathered from every source from which he could in any way get it, and as no source of revenue in considerable amount or practical to collect could be found there, and his expenses were pressing him hard, he set out for Gaul, ostensibly because the hostile Germans were stirring up trouble, but in reality, with the purpose of exploiting both Gaul with abounding wealth and Spain also. However, he did not openly announce his expedition beforehand, but went first to one of the suburbs and then suddenly set out on the journey, taking with him many actors, many gladiators, horses, women, and all the other trappings of luxury. (*Dio.Cass.*59.21)

Subsequently Dio Cassius reported that he began "collecting money in most shameful and dreadful ways": "One might indeed, pass over in silence the wares and the taverns, the prostitutes and the courts, the artisans and the wage-earning slaves, and other such sources, from which he collected every conceivable tribute" (Dio.Cass.59.28.8).

Caligula indulged himself with delusions of military greatness. However, instead of conquering Britain:

He took his seat on a lofty platform and gave the soldiers the signal as if for battle, bidding the trumpeters urge them on; then of a sudden he ordered them to gather up the shells. Having secured these spoils (for he needed booty, of course, for his triumphal procession), he became greatly elated, as if he had enslaved the very ocean; and he gave his soldiers many presents. The shells he took back to Rome for the purpose of exhibiting the booty to the people there as well. (*Dio.Cass.*59.25, 2–3)

Suetonius depicted Caligula as cowardly and inept.

Finally, as if he intended to bring the war to an end, he drew up a line of battle on the shore of the ocean, arranging his ballistas and other artillery; and when no one knew or could imagine what he was going to do, he suddenly bade them to gather shells and fill their helmets and the folds of their gowns, calling them "spoils from the Ocean, due to the Capitol and Palatine." As a monument of his victory he erected a lofty tower, from which lights were to shine at night to guide the course of the ships, as from the Pharos. Then promising the soldiers a gratuity of a hundred denarii each, as if he had shown unprecedented liberality, he said, "Go your happy way; go your way rich." (*Suet.Calig.*46.1)

What Really Happened

Caligula did not make his horse a consul; it was a joke. Suetonius and Dio Cassius claim only that Caligula *planned* to make his horse a consul. In fact, Caligula made the comment only to humiliate the senators. Rather than being insane, Caligula was an autocratic ruler with a sarcastic sense of humor.

After his father died in 19 CE, Caligula's mother and brothers were exiled and eventually killed. He was summoned to Capri by Tiberius and eventually made co-heir with Gemellus. Though some accused Caligula of Tiberius's death in 37 CE, contemporary accounts clear him. With help from the Praetorian Prefect Macro, Caligula became emperor over Gemellus.

Caligula was the golden boy (*Suet.Calig.*13, *Philo.Leg.*2). He showed reverence and brought the ashes of his mother and brothers back to Rome. He gave amnesty to people who were condemned or banished under Tiberius (*Suet.Calig.*15.4), and, unlike Tiberius, he sponsored games. More importantly, he restored democratic elections (*Suet.Calig.*16.2). He ordered banished writings to be circulated, completed building projects, erected aqueducts, and abolished the sales tax.

Caligula's decisions were sane, well-reasoned, and designed for the benefit of the empire. As evidence, the provinces were peaceful, he appointed efficient commanders such as Galba to Upper Germany, and he also named Petronius governor of Syria in 39 CE.

Salacious tales, written by members of the upper classes, are unanimously hostile toward Caligula, given their stance toward authority. Elite Romans believed that the Senate should control Rome. They also thought that the emperor ruled only with their permission. Moreover, during the time that Tiberius ruled from Capri (26–37 CE), the Senate enjoyed great freedom, which they were loath to surrender. By the time of Caligula, the myth of the Republic was just a charade. In addition, Caligula enjoyed making sarcastic jokes and playing extravagant pranks. He also took great pleasure in humiliating and taunting members of the Senate. Once, at a banquet, one of the aristocrats asked Caligula why he was laughing so hard, to which he responded, "What do you suppose, except that at a single nod of mine both of you could have your throats cut on the spot?" (*Suet.Calig.*32.3). Caligula had a prisoner killed before them to make them feel really uncomfortable. The story about the horse stems from a sarcastic comment Caligula made to humiliate the Senate, namely, "[Y]ou are so useless that a horse could do your job." It was also the expression of an autocratic ruler who did whatever he wanted. Other stories involving the horse may stem from the fact it was the emperor's pampered pet. In any case, Suetonius and Dio Cassius never stated that the horse was actually appointed to any office.

Caligula also had a dark sense of humor. His interaction with Philo was not violent but, rather, mocking. Caligula was merely being rudely sarcastic when he called Jews "god-haters" (*Philo.Leg.*44.353). He also thought he was being funny when he asked the Jews why they did not eat pork. Caligula's final comments show how he thought it was humorous to make people feel uncomfortable: "[T]hese men do not appear to me to be wicked so much as unfortunate and foolish, in not believing that I have been endowed with the nature of a god" (*Philo.Leg.*45.367).

All evidence suggests that Caligula was not any more extravagant than any other emperor. Suetonius and Dio Cassius added details to give the appearance of Caligula's military incompetence. Although sources agree that Caligula built a pontoon bridge, he did it in imitation of Alexander the Great, whose breastplate he wore during the event.

On the other hand, acting more like his war-hero father than a madman, Caligula put down an uprising led by the governor of Upper Germany and strengthened the army. Caligula eliminated Macro and Gemellus, banished his sisters, and disposed of others who were involved in political plotting against him.

Caligula's troops mutinied, refusing to go to Britain because they considered it the edge of the world. Picking up shells was his way of teaching them a humiliating lesson. Another explanation for the narrative on the beach is that the Latin word for seashells (*musculi*) was soldiers' slang for engineering huts. Caligula grew up in a soldiers' camp and probably meant "pack up the huts," and not seashells. As a further vindication, Caligula's expedition paved the way for Claudius' eventual conquest of Britain (*Suet. Vesp.*4).

Caligula most likely did not commit incest. Philo and Seneca do not mention it at all. Josephus' overall view of Caligula was negative and greatly exaggerated, casting some questions on the historian's credibility. Furthermore, Caligula presented his sisters with high honors, which no doubt precipitated such a rumor. He was also devastated at the death of his sister Drusilla. Tales of the emperor sleeping with other men's wives and rating their performances are probably false; Suetonius reported that Caligula was faithful to his wife.

Caligula liked to dress up as various gods and goddesses. He ordered the construction of a temple in Rome for his own worship (*Suet. Calig.* 22.3). It is possible that he portrayed himself as king and god in order to legitimate his rule. All Roman emperors were worshipped as gods in the East. Excavations in Rome show that Caligula incorporated the ancient temple of Castor and Pollux within his temple.

Although Caligula began favorably with the Senate, the relationship eventually soured. In the end, a conspiracy between the Praetorian guard and members of the Senate succeeded in assassinating him.

Scholars have treated Caligula unfairly, to say the least. He was not insane; rather, he had a bad sense of humor. Most of the incidents used to present him as insane have been taken out of context to make him appear in the worst light possible, in order to justify his removal. He was autocratic but was probably no better or worse than many other emperors.

PRIMARY DOCUMENTS

Romans looked forward to Caligula's reign. After all, Caligula had the right pedigree. His father was the beloved Germanicus.

Germanicus, father of Gaius Caesar, son of Drusus and the younger Antonia, after being adopted by his paternal uncle Tiberius, held the quaestor-ship five years before the legal age and passed directly into the consulship. When the death of Augustus was announced, he was sent to the army in Germany, where it is hard to say whether his filial piety or his courage was more conspicuous; for although all the legions obstinately refused to accept Tiberius as emperor, and offered him the rule of state, he held them to their allegiance. And later he won a victory over the enemy and celebrated a triumph. Then chosen consul for a second time, before he entered on his term he was hurried off to restore order in the Orient, and after vanquishing the king of Armenia and reducing Cappadocia to the form of a province, died of a lingering illness at Antioch, in the thirty-fourth year of his age. There was some suspicion that he was poisoned; for besides the dark spots which appeared all over his body and the froth that flowed from his mouth, after he had been reduced to ashes his heart was found among his bones; and it is supposed to be a characteristic of that organ that when steeped in poison it cannot be destroyed by fire. (*Suet. Calig.* 1)

*Furthermore, Suetonius adds: "It is the general opinion that Germanicus possessed all the highest qualities of body and mind, to a degree never equaled by anyone; a handsome person, unequalled valor, surpassing ability in the oratory of Greece and Rome, unexampled kindliness, and a remarkable desire and capacity for winning men's regard and inspiring their affection" (*Suet. Calig.3*).*

The citizens of Rome were devasted when they first became aware that Germanicus was ill. Some believed Tiberius was responsible because he was secretly jealous of Germanicus.

At Rome when the community, in grief and consternation at the first report of his illness, was awaiting further news, and suddenly after nightfall a report at last spread abroad, on doubtful authority, that he had recovered, a general rush was made from every side to the Capitol with torches and victims, and the temple gates were all but torn off, that nothing might hinder them in their eagerness to pay their vows. Tiberius was roused from sleep by the cries of the rejoicing throng, who were all united in singing:—"Safe is Rome, safe too is our country, for Germanicus is safe."

But when it was at last made known that he was no more, the public grief could be checked neither by any consolation nor edict, and it continued even during the festal days of the month of December.

The fame of the deceased and regret for his loss were increased by the horror of the times which followed, since all believed, with good reason, that the cruelty of Tiberius, which soon burst forth, had been held in check through his respect and awe for Germanicus. (*Suet.Calig.*6)

Some believed it was Caligula's destiny to become emperor: "Verses which were in circulation after he became emperor indicated that he was begotten in the winter quarters of the legions: 'He who was born in the camp and reared 'mid the arms of his country, gave at the outset a sign that he was fated to rule'" (Suet.Calig.*8*).

He was the mascot of the military troops.

His surname Caligula he derived from a joke of the troops, because he was brought up in their midst in the dress of a common soldier. To what extent he won their love and devotion by being reared in fellowship with them is especially evident from the fact that they threatened mutiny after the death of Augustus and were ready for any act of madness, the mere sight of Gaius unquestionably calmed them down. For they did not become quiet until they saw that he was being spirited away because of the danger from their outbreak and taken for protection to the nearest town. Then at last they became contrite, and laying hold of the carriage and stopping it, begged to be spared the disgrace which was put on them. (*Suet.Calig.*9)

Romans believed they were off to a new start with Caligula. Caligula's accession was the start of a new age that everyone had expected. He said and did the right things and won over the hearts of all. The celebrations were so great that thousands of animals were killed for the celebrations. When Caligula was ill, Romans were anxious and nervous. Some offered their lives out of concern for his health. Even foreign rulers sought out Caligula.

By thus gaining the throne he fulfilled the highest hopes of the Roman people, or I may say of all mankind, since he was the prince most earnestly desired by the great part of the provincials and the soldiers, many who had known him in his infancy, as well as by the whole body of the city populace . . . and he was met by a dense and joyful throng, who called him, besides other propitious names, their "star," their "chick," their "babe," and their "nursling."

When he entered the city, full and absolute power were at once put into his hands by the unanimous consent of the Senate and of the mob, which forced its way into the House, and no attention was paid to the wishes of Tiberius, who in his will had named his other grandson, still a boy, joint heir with Caligula. So great was the public rejoicing, that within the next three months, or less than that, more than a hundred and sixty thousand victims are said to have been slain in sacrifice.

A few days after this, when he crossed the islands near Campania, vows were put up for his safe return, while no one let slip even the slightest chance of giving testimony to his anxiety and regard for his safety. But when he fell ill, they all spent the whole night about the Palace; some even vowed to fight as gladiators, and others posted placards offering their lives, if the ailing prince were spared. To this unbounded love of his citizens was added marked devotion from foreigners. Artabanus, for example, king of the Parthians, who was always outspoken in his hatred and contempt for Tiberius, voluntarily sought Caligula's friendship and came to a conference with the consular governor; then crossing the Euphrates, he paid homage to the Roman eagles and to standards and to the statues of the Caesars. (*Suet. Calig.* 13–14)

Caligula gained much favor and adulation from people by doing the right things. He gave the eulogy for Tiberius, and brought back his family's ashes to be properly interred during a storm. He also honored his uncle Claudius and the son of Tiberius.

Gaius himself tried to rouse men's devotion by courting popularity in every way. After eulogizing Tiberius with many tears before the assembled people and giving him a magnificent funeral, he at once posted off to Pandateria and the Pontian Islands, to remove the ashes of his mother and brother to Rome; and in stormy weather too, to make his filial piety more conspicuous. He approached them with reverence and placed them in the urn with his own hands. With no less theatrical effect he brought them to Ostia in a bireme with a banner set in the stern, and from there up the Tiber to Rome, where he had them carried to the Mausoleum on two biers by the most distinguished men of the order of knights, in the middle of the day, when the streets were crowded. He appointed funeral sacrifices too, to be offered each year with due ceremony, as well as games in the Circus in honor of his mother, providing a carriage to carry her image in the procession. But in memory of his father he gave to the month of September the name of Germanicus. After this, by a Decree of the Senate, he heaped upon his grandmother whatever honors Livia Augusta had ever enjoyed; he took his uncle Claudius, who up to the time had been a Roman knight, as his colleague in the consulship; adopted his brother Tiberius on the day he assumed the gown of manhood, and gave him the title of Chief of the Youth. He caused the names of his sisters to be included in all oaths: "And

I will not hold myself and my children dearer than I do Gaius and his sisters": as well as the propositions of the consuls: "Favor and good fortune attend Gaius Caesar and his sisters." *(Suet.Calig.*15*)*

Furthermore, Caligula gained favor by having banned writings made available. "The writings of Titus Labienus, Cremutius Cordus, and Cassius Severus, which had been suppressed by decrees of the Senate, he allowed to be hunted up, circulated and read, saying that it was wholly to his interest that everything which happened be handed down to posterity. He published the accounts of the empire, which had regularly been made public by Augustus, a practice discontinued by Tiberius" *(*Suet.Calig.*16.1)*.

Caligula supported public entertainment and the arts, unlike the cheapskate Tiberius.

He gave several gladiatorial shows, some in the amphitheater of Taurus and some in the Saepta, in which he introduced pairs of African and Campanian boxers, the pick of both regions. He did not always preside at the games in person, but sometimes assigned the honor to magistrates or to friends. He exhibited stage-plays continually, of various kinds and in many different places. *(Suet.Calig.*18*)*

Caligula was also concerned with the infrastructure of the city of Rome as well as around the empire.

He completed the public works which had been half-finished under Tiberius, namely the temple of Augustus and the theater of Pompey. He likewise began an aqueduct in the region near Tibur and an amphitheater beside the Saepta, the former finished by his successor Claudius, while the latter was abandoned. At Syracuse he repaired the city walls, which had fallen into ruin through lapse of time, and the temples of the gods. He had planned, besides, to rebuild the palace of Polycrates of Samos, to finish the temple of Didymaean Apollo at Ephesus, to found a city high up in the Alps, but above all, to dig a canal through the Isthmus in Greece, and he had already sent a chief centurion to survey the work. *(Suet.Calig.*21*)*

Caligula was not blessed with the good looks and personality of his father Germanicus. He was described as follows. He may have been made fun of by others.

He was very tall and extremely pale, with an unshapely body, but very thin neck and legs. His eyes and temples were hollow, his forehead broad and trim, his hair thin and entirely gone on the top of his head, though his body was hairy. Because of this to look upon him from a higher place as he passed by, or for any reason whatsoever to mention a goat, was treated as a capital offence. While his face was naturally forbidding and ugly, he purposely made it even more savage, practicing all kinds of terrible and fearsome expressions before a mirror. (*Suet.Calig.*50)

*Caligula had many fine qualities but also possessed an extremely sarcastic sense of humor. Seneca notes, "Gaius Caesar, among the other vices with which he overflowed, was possessed by a strange, insolent passion for marking everyone with some note of ridicule" (*Sen.Dial.218.1*).*

Suetonius did not like Caligula or the imperial system. The Roman nobility was outraged that it no longer was in power and was subject to the whims of the emperors.

Caligula loved his horse and pampered it just as many pet owners do today. The sources are clear that Caligula's horse was never made a consul. Suetonius merely mentions that he proposed the idea.

He used to send his soldiers on the day before the games and order silence in the neighborhood, to prevent the horse, Incitatus, from being disturbed. Besides a stall of marble, a manger of ivory, purple blankets and a collar of precious stones, he even gave this horse a house, a troop of slaves and furniture, for the more elegant entertainment of the guests invited in his name; and it is also said that he planned to make him consul. (*Suet.Calig.*55.3)

Caligula was a big fan of gladiatorial games and horse racing, something considered scandalous by the upper classes. Even more absurd was the arrogance of Caligula to name the track after himself. Dio Cassius stresses Caligula's lavishness and wastefulness in this quote. His statements appear to be deliberately composed to make the emperor look bad.

Hence even today the place where he used to practice driving the chariots is called the Gaianum after him. One of the horses, which he named Incitatus, he used to invite to dinner, where he would offer him gold barley and drink his health in wine from golden goblets; he swore by the animal's life and fortune and even promised to appoint him consul, a promise that he would certainly have carried out if he had lived. (*Dio.Cass.*59.14.7)

Caligula's interaction with Philo is full of his sarcastic humor. There appears to be no malicious intent.

First, Caligula asks, "why don't you guys eat pork?" And when we made answer that, "different nations have different laws, and there are some things the use of which is forbidden both to us and to our adversaries"; and when someone said, "there are also many people who do not eat lamb's flesh, which is the most tender of all meat," he laughed and said, "they are quite right, for it is not nice." Being joked with and trifled with and ridiculed in this manner, we were in great perplexity. (*Philo.Leg.*45. 362–363)

However, Caligula's humor could be very cruel. Many people were executed as criminals in the arena.

The following are special instances of his innate brutality. When cattle to feed the wild beasts which he had provided for a gladiatorial show were rather costly, he selected criminals to be devoured, and reviewing the line of prisoners without examining their charges, but merely taking his place in the middle of a colonnade, he bade them be led away from bald head to bald head. A man who had made a vow to fight in the arena, if the emperor recovered, he compelled to keep his word, watched him as he fought sword in hand, and would not let him go until he was victorious, and then only after many entreaties. Another who had offered his life for the same reason, but delayed to kill himself, he turned over to his slaves, with orders to drive him through the streets decked with sacred boughs and fillet, calling for the fulfillment of his vow, and finally hurl him from the embankment. (*Suet.Calig.* 27.1–3)

Caligula played another prank.

Publius Afranius Potius, a plebeian, perished, because in a burst of foolhardy servility, he had promised not only of his own free will but also under oath that he would give his life if only Gaius should recover; and likewise, a certain Atanius Secundus, a knight, because he had announced that in the same event he would fight as a gladiator. These men, instead of the money which they hoped to receive from him [Caligula] in return for offering to give their lives in exchange for his, were compelled to keep their promises, so as not to be guilty of perjury. (*Dio.Cass.*59.8.3)

Seneca, a contemporary of Caligula, holds overall a hostile view, but does not mention incest. In fact, he said that Caligula was devastated by the loss of his sister.

On losing his sister Drusilla, Gaius Caesar, a man who could neither mourn nor rejoice as becomes a prince, shrank from seeing and speaking to his countrymen, was not present at his sister's funeral, did not pay her the conventional tribute of respect, but tried to forget the sorrows caused by this most distressing death by playing at dice in his Alban villa, and by sitting on the judgment-seat, and the like customary engagements. What a disgrace to the Empire! A Roman emperor solaced himself by gambling for his grief at the loss of his sister! This same Gaius, with frantic levity, at one time let his beard and hair grow long, at another wandered aimlessly along the coast of Italy and Sicily. (*Sen.Polyb.*17)

It was not unusual for emperors to grant honors to family members. Augustus did this with his sister, Octavia, and his wife, Livia. Caligula honored his sister in the same manner as Livia, who was considered the paragon of Roman womanhood.

When her death occurred at this time, her husband delivered the eulogy and her brother accorded her a public funeral. The Praetorians with their commander and the equestrian order by itself ran about the pyre and the boys of noble birth performed the equestrian exercise called "Troy" about her tomb. All the honors that had been bestowed upon Livia were voted to her, and it was further decreed that she should be deified, that a golden effigy of her should be set up in the Senate House and that in the temple of Venus in the Forum a statue of her should be built for her, that she should have twenty priests, women as well as men; women, whenever they offered testimony, should swear by her name, and on her birthday a festival equal to the Ludi Megalenses should be celebrated, and the Senate and knights should be given a banquet. She accordingly now received the name Panthea and was declared worthy of divine honors in all the cities. (*Dio.Cass.*59.11.1–3)

Caligula mercilessly tormented the head of the Praetorians, Chaerea. It was one thing to humiliate the Senate, but it was foolish to make fun of the military, as it was the real power behind the throne.

Gaius used to taunt him, a man already well on in years, with voluptuousness and effeminacy by every form of insult. When he asked for the watchword, Gaius would give him "Priapus" or "Venus," and when Chaerea had occasion to thank him for anything, he [Caligula] would hold out his hand to kiss, forming and moving it in an obscene fashion. (*Suet.Calig.*56.2)

Eventually Chaerea had enough and killed Caligula. Josephus writes: "We ought, then, in the first place, to decree the greatest honors we are able to those that have taken off the tyrant, especially to Chaerea Cassius; for this one man, with the assistance of the gods, hath by his counsel and by his actions, been the procurer of our liberty" (Jos.AJ.19.2.2).

Dio Cassius happily reports, "Thus Gaius, after doing three years, nine months, and twenty-eight days all that has been related, learned by actual experience that he was not a god" (Dio.Cass.59.30).

Further Reading

Anonymous, "Two: Caligula with Mary Beard," *BBC*. March 12, 2018. https://www.bbc.co.uk/programmes/b037w0qh

Barrett, Anthony A., *Caligula: The Abuse of Power. Roman Imperial Biographies*. Routledge, London and New York, 2015.

Barrett, Anthony A., *Caligula: The Corruption of Power*. Yale University Press, New Haven and London, 1989.

Beard, Mary, *Caligula*, YouTube Documentary, 2013.

Bissler, Joseph, *Caligula Unmasked: An Investigation of the Historiography of Rome's Most Notorious Emperor*. MA Thesis, Kent State, 2013. https://etd.ohiolink.edu/!etd.send_file?accession=kent1374749172&disposition=inline

Fagan, Garrett G., *Gaius (Caligula) 37–41 AD, De Imperitoribus Romanis. An Online Encyclopedia of Roman Emperors*. Pennsylvania State University, 2004. https://www.roman-emperors.org/gaius.htm

"Gaius," *Oxford Classical Dictionary*. Edited by Simon Hornblower and Anthony Spawforth (3rd ed.). Oxford University Press, New York, 1996, pp. 619–620.

O'Donovan, Gerard, "Mary Beard Takes on Caligula, the Emperor with the Worst Reputation in History," *The Telegraph*. July 26, 2013. https://www.telegraph.co.uk/culture/tvandradio/10199155/Mary-Beard-takes-on-Caligula-the-emperor-with-the-worst-reputation-in-history.html

6

Nero Fiddled While Rome Burned

What People Think Happened

Nero is often thought of as the impatient and tyrannical emperor who terrorized Rome from 54 to 68 CE. He fiddled, literally and figuratively, while Rome burned. He brutally persecuted innocent Christians, whom he blamed for the fire.

Nero was born in 37 CE and became emperor because his mother convinced Emperor Claudius to marry her and to adopt Nero as his heir. Then Nero's mother poisoned Claudius, and so Nero came to the throne at age seventeen. He got off to a good start, but there were early indications of his cruelty. Nero roamed nocturnally and beat up strangers. He eventually murdered his mother, advisors, and family members when he no longer needed them. His cruelty had no limits.

The city of Rome was a vast melting pot of more than one million inhabitants from all over its empire. As emperor, Nero's main duty was to protect the Empire and to keep its citizens safe.

Fire, particularly in the slums, was not unusual in ancient Rome because of the extreme heat in summer. However, the blaze that started on July 19, 64 CE, was unlike any other. Small sparks in shops where flammable goods were stored in an area near the Circus Maximus, the chariot-racing stadium, fanned out of control as strong summer winds caused the flames to spread quickly through the twisted, narrow streets. It raged for six days, consuming the homes of rich and poor alike. After it was brought under control, it reignited and burned for another three days. More than 70 percent of the city was destroyed, and only four of

Rome's fourteen districts survived. Most of Rome's palaces, temples, and public buildings were gone, and 500,000 people were homeless.

Nero was away when the inferno broke out. He returned to the city to assist victims. However, people suspected that the emperor or his thugs set the fire. Nero blamed members of a Jewish millennial sect called Christians, who believed that the world was coming to an end. He had them arrested, tortured, and killed in horrible ways, such as being torn apart by dogs or being used as tiki lights for his garden parties. Many believed he scapegoated this religious minority to hide the fact that he actually started the blaze in order to clear land for his lavish plans for a new Rome in his image. In the aftermath of the fire, Nero built the sumptuous Golden Palace, a magnificent series of villas, landscaped parks, and an artificial lake where homes once stood. He also decorated the palace with numerous statues of himself.

This extravagant spending brought the empire to financial ruin. Nero increased taxes and devalued the currency, which was not popular. He cruelly forced senators to make wills naming him as their heir. Once the will was signed, Nero forced the senators to commit suicide.

This emperor was more interested in performing on stage than in governing the empire. When Nero performed, the doors of the theater were locked so no one could leave. Instead of tending to business in Rome, he went on a yearlong (66/67 CE) tour of Greece. Nero won all the competitions he entered, some of which he did not finish! Even the Olympic games of 67 CE were rescheduled just for him.

Eventually, Nero alienated the elite and, by declaration, became an enemy of the state. He committed suicide in 68 CE to escape capture and execution.

How the Story Became Popular

Nero was not an arsonist. Stories regarding his actions during the Great Fire of 64 CE are shrouded in myth and clouded with misinformation. Upper-class Romans constructed a negative image of Nero and used the rumor of the fire to vilify him because of his public performances. Later, Christian writers crafted the fire story to their own purposes. By Shakespeare's day, Nero's reputation was firmly established as the archvillain who played an instrument while his city burned.

Although efforts to destroy his name began shortly after he died, his death also prompted tremendous outpourings of grief. Flowers decorated his tomb long after his death. Nero's successor, Otho, renamed himself Otho Nero

(*Suet.Otho*.7.1), while Vitellius, the next emperor, performed funeral rites for Nero to gain popular favor (*Suet.Vit*.11.2). Sightings of Nero imposters led to the belief that he would return to the people, who loved him. Dio Chrysostom, a Greek historian, reported that "even now everybody wishes [Nero] were still alive. And the great majority do believe that he still is, and believe the Senate is hiding him" (*Dio.Chrys.Disc*.21.8.10).

People liked Nero at the beginning. He issued pardons and abolished secret trials. Tacitus and Suetonius report that Nero was popular with many of the urban plebs and mingled with actors and chariot racers. Unlike the upper classes, he did not despise the masses. Commoners considered him kind and generous, as he provided them with grain and recreational opportunities. He also avoided wars.

Conversely, Nero angered the wealthy and powerful class. He forced members of the elite to compete onstage and in the arena, thus blurring the division between upper- and lower-class persons. In fact, the nobility really hated Nero for this and for his artistic exploits, which they found humiliating. In ancient Rome, performing onstage was a job for slaves and the lower classes. Actors also had a reputation for immorality. Therefore, the nobility thought such activity was highly undignified and improper for an emperor. Roman biographers are all united in condemning Nero's stage antics. They were more disgusted by this activity than by his brutal murders.

Pliny mocked Nero as an "actor-emperor" (*Plin.Pan*.46.4). Likewise, Juvenal scorned the "lyre-player emperor" (*Juv*.8.198). Tacitus disparaged his "repulsive ambition to appear on the stage" (*Tac.Ann*.14.14). Critics also ridiculed Nero's talent. For example, Suetonius described Nero's voice as weak and husky (*Suet.Ner*.20.1), while Juvenal complained that Nero's singing voice was horrid (*Juv*.8.225).

Senators were also angry with Nero because he seized the land in the forum where their homes once stood. They literally lost their seats, power, and prestige because of the fire.

No primary accounts of the fire survive, and most information comes from secondary sources by Tacitus, Suetonius, and Dio Cassius. Probably the fact that the fire reignited and that two parts of the city were burning started the arson story, and Nero's political enemies then found it easy to blame him for the crime. None of the three historians liked Nero, and each mentioned the story of the fire and then retold it in his own way.

Tacitus (c. 56–120 CE) reported that a rumor spread through the city that Nero stood on his private stage and sang the "Sack of Ilium" (*Tac.Ann*. 15.39), comparing Rome's present misfortune to that of Troy. Tacitus dismissed the tale as a popular rumor rather than fact but also noted that "no one knows whether Rome burned from arson or by chance" (*Tac. Ann.*15.38.1). He further implied that the fire was purposely set when he linked the date of the Great Fire with the anniversary of the Gauls' destruction of Rome in 390 BCE (*Tac.Ann.*15.41).

Suetonius (c. 70–122 CE) was a contemporary of Tacitus, born into a wealthy family. He took Tacitus's statement literally, and he gladly blamed Nero for the fire. According to him, Nero was so overjoyed "by the beauty of the flame" (*Suet.Ner.*38.2) while watching the blaze from the Tower of Maecenas that he dressed in theatrical costume and recited the "Capture of Ilium." He wrote as if the story were a fact. Suetonius reported that Nero wanted to rebuild Rome and call it Neropolis (*Suet.Ner.*55). He suggested that the fire was deliberately set to bring about the destruction of the city because of Nero's disgust with its winding streets and squalor (*Suet.Ner.*38.1).

Dio Cassius, writing 150 years after the catastrophic event, mentioned that Nero, in order to get the best seat in the house, ascended to the roof of the palace in his *cithara*-playing outfit and sang "The Fall of Illium." Dio stressed Nero's singing; his mention of the costume implies the presence of the *cithara* (*Dio.Cass.*62.18).

Suetonius and Dio Cassius recounted additional anecdotes insinuating Nero's guilt. For example, Suetonius wrote that a man said to Nero, "When I am dead, may the earth be consumed by fire." Nero replied, "No, rather while I live."

Dio claimed Nero regarded Priam as fortunate because he lived to see the destruction of Troy. In other words, by Nero wishing to suffer the fate of Priam, he identified himself with Priam and wanted to see the destruction of his Troy, that is, Rome (*Dio.Cass.*62.18). Thus, he implied that Nero set fire to Rome in order that he might play while it burned, comparing, as Tacitus said, "present misfortunes with those of the past" (*Tac.Ann.*15.39).

Additional hearsay that may have added fuel to the flames of this theory included the completion of Nero's magnificent Golden Palace soon after the disaster. At its dedication, Suetonius reported that Nero said, "Good, now I can finally begin to live like a human" (*Suet.Ner.*31.2). His hostile portrayal of Nero has greatly influenced the portrait of the emperor in the literary sources that blame Nero for the fire and assert his playing of an instrument.

Christian writers disliked Nero because he persecuted Christians for the fire. Suetonius's view was incorporated into the description of Nero in the fifth century's *Seven Books of History* by Paulus Orosius, who reported, "The emperor himself viewed the conflagration from the lofty tower of Maecenas, it is said he declaimed the Iliad in a tragedian's costume" (*Oros.*7.7.6). He did not mention anything about Nero's musical skills.

Only with Shakespeare in Henry VI, Pt. I, Act I, Scene 4, does Nero appear as a musician who plays the lute:

Plantaginet, I will; and like thee Nero,
Play on the lute, beholding the towns burn.

Over time the lute became the fiddle, as in George Daniel's long poem *Trinarchordia*, 1649:

Let Nero fiddle out Rome's Obsequies
And force the farre-spent world with Tyrannies.

Since then, Nero has fascinated writers and filmmakers as the epitome of excess, cruelty, and depravity. In the eighteenth century, Marquis de Sade raised Nero from the dead, while in the nineteenth century, Nero appeared in Germaine de Staël's novel, *Corinne*. Later works have also immortalized this imagery, such as the film *Quo Vadis*.

The notion that Nero played an instrument and sang while Rome burned or neglected his duties is the result of anti-Nero propaganda and an attempt to tarnish his name. Regardless of his other deeds, the fiddling story is simply a dramatic fiction.

PRIMARY DOCUMENTS

Nero was a cruel monster who murdered his way to the top. Suetonius uses innuendo here. He is accused of parricide in the death of Claudius. He removed Britannicus out of sheer jealousy.

He began his career of parricide and murder with Claudius, for even if he was not the instigator of the emperor's death, he was at least privy to it, as he openly admitted; for he used afterwards to laud mushrooms, the vehicle in which the poison was administered to Claudius, as "food of the gods," as the Greek proverb has it. At any rate, after Claudius's death he vented on him every kind of insult, in act and word, charging him now with folly and now with cruelty; for it was a favorite joke of his to say that Claudius had "ceased to play the fool" among mortals, lengthening the first symbol of the word *morari*, and he disregarded many of his decrees and acts as the work of a madman and a dotard. Finally, he neglected to enclose the place where his body was burned except with a low and mean wall.

He attempted the life of Britannicus by poison, not less from jealousy of his voice (for it was more agreeable than his own) than from fear that he might sometime win a higher place than himself in the people's regard because of the memory of his father. He procured the poison from an arch-poisoner, Locusta, and when the effect was slower than he anticipated merely physicking Britannicus, he called the woman to him and flogged her with his own hand, charging that she had administered a medicine instead of a poison; and when she said in excuse she had given a smaller dose to shield him from the odium of the crime, he replied: "It's likely that I am afraid of the Julian law," and he forced her to mix as swift and instant a potion as she knew how in his own room before his very eyes. Then he tried it on a kid, and as the animal lingered for five hours, had the mixture steeped again and again and threw some before a pig. The beast instantly fell dead, whereupon he ordered that the poison be taken to the dining room and given to Britannicus. The boy dropped dead at the very first taste, but Nero lied to his guest and declared that he was seized with the falling sickness, to which he was subject, and the next day had him hastily and unceremoniously buried in a pouring rain. He rewarded Locusta with her eminent services with a full pardon and large estates in the country, and actually sent her pupils. (*Suet.Ner.*33)

The emperor and his mother, Agrippina the Younger, had a falling out. He disliked her criticism and interference in his reign. Assassins were sent to kill her.

Then [Nero] ordered that [Agrippina's] "freedman be seized and bound, on the charge of being hired to kill the emperor; that his mother be put to death, and the pretense made that she had escaped the consequences of her detected guilt by suicide." (*Suet.Ner.*34.3)

Tacitus describes Agrippina's demise. Nero rigged her boat to sink. She survived and returned to her villa.

The executioners surrounded the couch, and the trierarch began by striking her on the head with a club. The centurion was drawing his sword to make an end, when she proffered her womb to the blow. "Strike here," she exclaimed, and was dispatched with repeated wounds. (*Tac.Ann.*14.8)

Suetonius condemns Nero for his passion for games as well as the arts. Such activities were unbecoming of an emperor. Even worse was that the activities were rigged. Nero played an instrument, went on tour, and encouraged the nobility to do so. Worse yet, Nero refused to return back to the city of Rome at the request of his freedman. People faked death, and children were born at his venues because the doors were locked.

From his earliest years he had a special passion for horses and talked constantly about the games in the Circus, though he was forbidden to do so. Once when he was lamenting with his fellow pupils the fate of a charioteer of the "Greens," who was dragged by his horses, and his preceptor scolded him, he told him a lie and pretended that he was talking of Hector. At the beginning of his reign he used to play every day with ivory chariots on a board, and he came from the country to all the games, even the most insignificant, at first secretly, and then so openly that no one doubted that he would be in Rome on that particular day. He made no secret of his wish to have the number of prizes increased, and in consequence more races were added and the performance was continued to a late hour, while managers of the troupes no longer thought it was worthwhile to produce their drivers at all except for a full day's racing. He soon longed to drive a chariot himself and even to show himself frequently to the public; so after a trial exhibition in his gardens before his slaves and the dregs of the populace, he gave all an opportunity of seeing him in the Circus Maximus, one of his freedmen dropping the napkin from the place usually occupied by the magistrates.

Not content with showing his proficiency in these arts at Rome, he went to Achaeia [Greece], as I have said, influenced especially by the following consideration. The cities in which it was the custom to hold contests in music had adopted the rule of sending all the lyric prizes to him. These he received with the greatest delight, not only giving audience before all others to the envoys who brought them, but even inviting them to his private table. When some of them begged him to sing after dinner and greeted his performance with an extravagant applause, he declared that "the Greeks were the only ones who had an ear for music and that they alone were worthy of his efforts." So, he took ship without delay and immediately on arriving at Cassiope made a preliminary appearance as a singer at the altar of Jupiter Cassius, and then went the round to the contests.

To make this possible, he gave orders that even those which were widely separated in time should be brought together in a single year, so that some had even to be given twice, and he introduced a musical competition at

Olympia also, contrary to custom. To avoid being distracted or hindered in any way while busy with these contests, he replied to his freedman Helius, who reminded him that the affairs of the city required his presence, in these words: "However much it may be your advice and your wish that I should return speedily, yet you ought rather to counsel me and to hope that I may return worthy of Nero."

While he was singing no one was allowed to leave the theater even for the most urgent reasons. And so, it is said that some women gave birth to children there, while many others who were worn out with listening and applauding, secretly leaped from the wall, since the gates of the entrance were closed, or feigned death and were carried out for burial. The trepidation and anxiety with which he took part in the contests, his keen rivalry of his opponents, and his awe of the judges, can hardly be credited. As if his rivals were of quite the same station as himself, he used to show respect to them and tried to gain their favor, while he slandered them behind their backs, sometimes assailed them with abuse when he met them, and even bribed those who were proficient.

Before beginning, he would address the judges in the most deferential terms, saying that he had done all that could be done, but the issue was in the hands of Fortune; they however, being men of wisdom and experience, ought to exclude what was fortuitous. When they bade him take heart, he withdrew with greater confidence, but not even then without anxiety, interpreting the silence and modesty of some as sullenness and ill-nature, and declaring that he had his suspicions of them. (*Suet.Ner.22–23*)

*Suetonius relates how the future emperor Vespasian had to endure Nero's awful performances. "On tour through Greece, among the companions of Nero, he [Vespasian] bitterly offed the emperor by either going out often while Nero was singing or falling asleep, if he remained" (*Suet.Vesp.4.4*).*

*In this passage Juvenal ridicules Nero's lack of talent. "These were the deeds, these the graces of our high-born Prince, whose delight it was to prostitute himself by unseemly singing upon a foreign stage, and to earn a chaplet of Greek parsley!" (*Juv.8.211–230*).*

Tacitus avoids a direct accusation of a crime. Instead, he uses innuendo.

There followed a disaster, whether due to chance or to the malice of the sovereign is uncertain—for each version has its sponsors but graver and more terrible than any other which has befallen this city by ravages of fire. It took rise in the part of the Circus touching the Palatine and Caelian

Hills; where among the shops packed with inflammable goods, the conflagration broke out. (*Tac.Ann.*15.38)

*Here "authority" brings Nero to mind. "None ventured to combat the fire, as there were reiterated threats from a large number of persons who forbade extinction, and others were openly throwing firebrands and shouting that 'they had their authority'—possibly in order to have a freer hand in looting, possibly from orders received" (*Tac.Ann.*15.38).*

*Tacitus mentions a rumor that Nero sang while Rome burned. "Yet his measures, popular as their character might be, failed of their effect; for the report had spread that, at the very moment that Rome was aflame, he had mounted his private stage, and typifying the ills of the present by the calamities of the past, had sung the destruction of Troy" (*Tac.Ann.*15.39).*

Tacitus leaves no doubt as to why the fire was set.

Only on the sixth day was the conflagration brought to an end at the foot of the Esquiline, by demolishing the buildings over a vast area and opposing to the unabated fury of the flames a clear tract of ground and an open horizon. But fear had not yet been laid aside, nor had hope yet returned to the people, when the fire resumed its ravages in the less congested parts of the city, however; so that, while the toll of human life was not so great, the destruction of temples and porticoes dedicated to pleasure was on a wider scale. The second fire produced the greater scandal of the two, as it had broken out on Aemilian property of Tigellinus and appearances suggested that Nero was seeking the glory of founding a new capital and endowing it with his own name. Rome, in fact, is divided into fourteen regions, of which four remain intact, while three were laid level on the ground: in the other seven nothing survived but a few dilapidated and half-burned relics of houses. (*Tac.Ann.*15.40)

Tacitus alludes the cause of the blaze was arson by connecting it to the inferno that destroyed the city in 390 BCE.

So that despite the striking beauty of the rearisen city, the older generation recollects much that it proved impossible to replace. There were those who noted that the first outbreak of the fire took place on the nineteenth of July, the anniversary of the capture and burning of Rome by the Senones: others have pushed their researches so far as to resolve the interval between the two fires into equal numbers of years, of months, and of days. (*Tac.Ann.*15.41)

Suetonius fans the flames by claiming that Rome was burned so that the emperor could rebuild it for his own purposes.

But he showed no greater mercy to the people or the walls of his capital. When someone in a general conversation said: "When I am dead, be earth consumed by fire," he rejoined, "Nay, rather while I live," and his action was wholly in accord. For under the cover of displeasure at the ugliness of the old buildings and the narrow, crooked streets, he set fire to the city so openly that several ex-consuls did not venture to lay hands on his chamberlains although they caught them on their estates with tow and fire-brands, while some granaries near the Golden House, whose room he particularly desired, were demolished by engines of war and set on fire, because their walls were of stone. For six days and seven nights destruction raged, while the people were driven for shelter to monuments and tombs. At that time, besides an immense number of buildings, the houses of the leaders of old were burned, still adorned with the trophies of victory, and the temples of the gods vowed and dedicated by the kings and later in the Punic and Gallic wars, and whatever else interesting and noteworthy had survived from antiquity. Viewing the conflagration from the Tower of Maecenas and exulting, as he said, in "the beauty of the flames" he sang the whole of the "Sack of Ilium" in his regular stage costume. Furthermore, to gain from this calamity too all the spoil and booty possible, while promising the removal of debris and dead bodies free of cost he allowed no one to approach the ruins of his own property; and from the contributions which he not only received, but even demanded, he nearly bankrupted the provinces and exhausted the resources of individuals. (*Suet.Ner.*38.1–3)

Dio Cassius says Nero burned the city because he was evil.

After this Nero set his heart on accomplishing what had doubtless always been his desire, namely to make an end of the whole city and realm during his lifetime. At all events, he, like others before him, used to call Priam wonderfully fortunate in that he had seen his country and throne destroyed together. Accordingly, he secretly sent out men who pretended to be drunk or engaged in other kinds of mischief, and caused them at first to set fire to one or two or even several buildings in different parts of the city. (*Dio.Cass.*62.16.1–2)

Dio reminds readers that Nero wanted to experience the fate of Priam. He uses vivid descriptions of the fire to emphasize that Nero leveled the city for his own selfish needs. The image of chaos and out of control blazes stresses Nero's incompetence as emperor.

So that people were at their wits' end, not being able to find any beginning of the trouble nor to put an end to it, though they constantly were aware of many strange sights and sounds. For there was naught to be seen but many mires, as in a camp, and naught to be heard from the talk of the people except such exclamations as, "This or that is afire," "Where?" "How did it happen?" "Who kindled it?" "Help?" Extraordinary excitement laid hold on all the citizens in all parts of the city, and they ran about, some in one direction, and some in another, as if distracted. Some men in the midst of assisting their neighbors would learn that their own premises were on fire. Others received the first intimation of their own possessions being aflame when informed that they were destroyed. Those who were inside their houses would run out into the narrow streets thinking that they could save them from the outside, while people in the streets would rush into the dwellings in the hope of accomplishing something inside. There was shouting and wailing without end, of children, women, men, and the aged all together, so that no one could see [a] thing or understand what was said by reason of the smoke and the shouting; and for this reason, some might be seen standing speechless, as if they were dumb. Meanwhile many who were carrying out their goods, and many, too, who were stealing the property of others, kept running into one another and falling over their burdens. It was not possible to go forward nor yet to stand still, but people pushed and were pushed in turn, upset others and were themselves upset. Many were suffocated, many were trampled underfoot; in a word, no evil that can possibly happen to people in such a crisis failed to befall them. They could not even escape anywhere easily; and if anybody did save himself from the immediate danger, he would fall into another and perish.

Now this did not take place on a single day, but lasted for several days and nights alike. Many houses were destroyed for want of anyone to help save them, and many others were set on fire by the same men who came to lend assistance; for the soldiers, including the night watch, having an eye to plunder, instead of putting out fires, kindled new ones. While such scenes were occurring at various points, a wind caught up the flames and carried them indiscriminately against all the buildings that were left. Consequently no one concerned himself any longer about goods or houses, but all the survivors, standing where they thought they were safe, gazed upon what appeared to be a number of scattered islands on fire or many cities burning at the same time. There was no longer any grieving over personal losses, but they lamented the public calamity, recalling how once before most of the city had been thus laid waste by the Gauls.

While the whole population was in this state of mind and many, crazed by the disaster, were leaping into the very flames, Nero ascended to the roof of the palace, from which there was the best general view of the greater part of the conflagration, and assuming the lyre-player's garb, he sang the "Capture of Troy," as he styled the song to himself, though to the enemies of the spectators it was the Capture of Rome. (*Dio.Cass.*62.16.2–18)

What Really Happened

Nero was not responsible for the Great Fire of Rome in 64 CE. The inferno was probably an accident, but if it were arson, it is possible that one of the many Christians who believed Rome would be destroyed by fire actually set the blaze (PBS, *Great Fire of Rome*, 2014).

Nero himself was not in Rome at the time; rather, he was staying thirty-five miles away in Antium. Neither did his henchmen start the fire. In fact, Nero rushed back as soon as he got word of it. Once he returned to the city, he took personal control of relief efforts. He ordered buildings torn down to act as a firewall to impede the movement of the blaze. He also opened public buildings and his gardens, providing shelter and food for the victims. He ordered food from neighboring Ostia, reduced the price of corn, and used his own funds to build porticos for shelters (*Tac. Ann.*15.39). After the fire Nero rebuilt and redesigned the city to be more fire-safe by making homes out of fireproof stone, widening streets, and restricting home height to prevent fires from spreading so quickly. These are hardly the actions of an arsonist (*Tac.Ann.*15.43). On the contrary, Nero was the only person to provide leadership during the disaster recovery. And he certainly didn't fiddle.

Nero could not have played the fiddle because it was not invented until the eleventh century. He did play a *cithera* (a Greek musical instrument similar to a lyre) but not during the blaze. In Nero's haste to reach the city by horse after the fire, it is doubtful he packed his lyre or other musical instruments, costume, and props. Roman historians disagree as to where he sang about the fall of Troy. Tacitus said it was in his domestic stage, Dio claimed he sang on the roof of the palace, and Suetonius said it was from the Tower of Maecenas. Nero's private theater was probably in his palace at the *Domus Transitoria*, which was burned. The Tower of Maecenas was located in the Garden of Maecenas, both linked to the buildings on the Palatine by the *Domus Transitoria*, which was right in the path of the fire. One explanation for his singing is that Nero, moved to tears by the sight of his city burning, may have been moved to recite either those lines of Homer that describe the burning of Troy, or some other poem that he reportedly had written. In other words, Nero honored Rome by comparing her destruction with the devastation of Troy, which was the ancestral home of the founders of Rome, Romulus and Remus, and his own Julio-Claudian family.

In 64 CE Nero was literally the king of the world (*Suet.Ner.*10–11). The empire was prosperous. The borders were secure and even expanded under his reign. Nero was interested in and promoted the arts. No signs of public discontent were evident. Nero would have had too much to lose to set his city ablaze. Why do it? First of all, his palace, the *Domus Transitoria* was destroyed. It is unlikely that Nero would destroy this palace, as he salvaged much of the artwork and precious stones. Additionally, the paintings and wall decorations at the Golden Palace were similar to those that burned.

Second, the fire, which Tacitus reported had no eyewitnesses, started in the slums and burned the homes of the poorest Romans, those whom he courted with games, spectaculars, and handouts. It seems unlikely he would destroy their homes in order to exact punishment on the upper classes. Nero would not risk losing the favor of the commoners. Arson itself seems an unlikely cause at all, by Nero or by anyone else. The fire occurred during a full moon on a Roman summer night. The moon's brightness would have made visibility almost like daytime and thus too risky for most arsonists, who don't want exposure while they work.

Fires occurred frequently in ancient Rome, which before the fire of 64 CE was not that elegant (*Suet.Aug.*28.3, *Tac.Ann.*6.45). A huge poor section housed people who lived in crowded tenements—easy tinderboxes for a simple spark. Flammable items often sat on the first floor, such as furniture or junk. Multistory buildings had timber joints separating the floors. On any given day, there may have been one hundred minor fires. More than likely, flammable materials in shops near the Circus Maximus caused the fire. Rome had two additional major fires in 80 and 191 CE. Fire was a constant threat.

The fire's aftermath had a huge impact on Nero's reputation. In the ancient world, people blamed disasters on the wrath of an angry god. Nero knew he would be blamed for somehow angering the gods, and so he made a series of sacrifices and ceremonies to regain the favor of the gods. Thus, his public image was another countervailing argument against his having set the fire himself.

Tacitus reports that to get rid of the rumor, "Nero fastened the guilt and inflicted the most exquisite tortures on a class hated for their abominations, called 'Christians,' by the populace" (*Tac.Ann.*15.44). Tacitus described the religion as a "deadly superstition," while Suetonius called them a "class of persons given to a new and mischievous superstition." In 64 CE, no distinction existed between Christians and Jews. After the modification of the Jewish Tax in 96 CE, practicing Jews paid the tax, but Christians did not. Roman disgust for the new religion continued after the two religions went their separate ways. In a letter to the emperor Trajan, Pliny the Younger refers to Christianity as a "debased superstition carried to extravagant lengths" (*Plin.10.Ep.*96). The term he used for a degenerate cult is "superstition."

Nero may have had good reason to blame Christians: they believed that Rome would soon be destroyed. Christians propagated writings prophesying and emphasizing the destruction of Rome during Christ's return. Early Christians had a motive (e.g., making their prophecies come true) or could have added fuel to the flame of desire to destroy the city. After all, Rome was a place of excessive wealth and moral corruption to them. Tacitus mentioned that at least some Christians made what might be interpreted as a confession (*Tac.Hist.*15.44).

Whether it was accidental or the result of terrorism, the Great Fire of Rome had a negative effect on Nero, eventually leading to his downfall and death in 68 CE.

PRIMARY DOCUMENTS

Nero was not in the city when the fire broke out but rushed back and opened shelters for his people.

Nero, who at the time was staying in Antium, did not return to the capital until the fire was nearing the house by which he had connected the Palatine with the Gardens of Maecenas. It proved impossible, however, to stop it from engulfing both the Palatine and the house and all their surroundings. Still, as a relief to the homeless and fugitive populace, he opened the Campus Martius, the buildings of Agrippa, even his own Gardens, and threw up a number of extemporized shelters to accommodate the helpless multitude. The necessities of life were brought up from Ostia and the neighboring municipalities, and the price of grain was lowered to three sesterces. (*Tac.Ann.*15.39)

There was always the danger of fire in ancient Rome. Fires tended to take place in the same areas. Each fire was said to have completely destroyed the city. At the time of the Gallic blaze of 390 BCE, most houses were small and made of flammable materials.

The houses of the plebeians were barricaded, the halls of the patricians stood open, but they felt greater hesitation about entering the open houses than those which were closed. They gazed with feelings of real veneration upon the men who were seated in the porticoes of their mansions, not only because of the superhuman magnificence of their apparel and their whole bearing and demeanor, but also because of the majestic expression of their countenances, wearing the very aspect of gods. So, they stood, gazing at them as if they were statues, till, as it is asserted, one of the patricians, M. Papirius, roused the passion of a Gaul, who began to stroke his beard—which in those days was universally worn long—by smiting him on the head with his ivory staff. He was the first to be killed, the others were butchered in their chairs. After this slaughter of the magnates, no living being was thenceforth spared; the houses were rifled, and then set on fire. (*Livy.Ab.Urbe.Cond.*5.41.7–10)

The Temple of Vesta was burned in the Gallic conflagration in 390 BCE. It was destroyed a second time by fire in 241 BCE.

Alas, how alarmed the Senate was when the Temple of Vesta caught fire, and the goddess was almost buried under her own roof! Holy fires blazed, fed by wicked fires, and a profane flame was blent with a pious flame. Amazed the priestesses wept with streaming hair; fear had bereft them of bodily strength. Metellus rushed into their midst and in a loud voice cried, "Haste ye to the rescue! There is no help in weeping. Take up in your virgin hands the pledges given by fate; it is not by prayers but by deed that they can be saved. Woe's me, do ye hesitate?" He saw that they hesitated and sank trembling on their knees. He took up water, and lifting up his hands, "Pardon me, ye sacred things," said he, "I, a man will enter a place where no man should set foot. If it is a crime, let the punishment of the deed fall on me! May I pay with my head the penalty, so Rome go free!" With these words he burst in. The goddess whom he carried off approved the deed and was saved by the devotion to her pontiff. (*Ov.Fast.*6.437–454)

Ancient Roman fires had similar causes in most cases and occurred in particular quarters of the city, such as the Circus Maximus, the Roman Forum, the Sacra Via, and the Campus Marius, where the hazard of fires was great. Augustus did all he could to try to fireproof his Capital.

Since the city was not adorned as the dignity of the empire demanded, and was exposed to flood and fire, he [Augustus] so beautified it that he could boast that he had found it built of brick and left it in marble. He made it safe too for the future, so far as human foresight could provide for this. (*Suet.Aug.*28.3)

Augustus took measures to reduce the threat of fire. He used nighttime security guards in stations. He also made sacrifices to the gods for protection from fire.

He divided the area of the city into regions and wards, arranging that the former should be under the charge of magistrates selected each year by lot, and the latter under 'masters' elected by the inhabitants of the respective neighborhoods. To guard against fires, he devised a system of stations of night watchmen, and to control the floods he widened and cleared out the channel of the Tiber, which had for some time been filled with rubbish and narrowed by jutting buildings. Further, to make the approach to the city easier from every direction, he personally undertook to rebuild the Flaminian Road all the way to Arminum, and assigned the rest of the highways to others who had been honored with triumphs, asking them to use their prize money in paving them.

He restored sacred edifices which had gone to ruin through lapse of time or had been destroyed by fire, and adorned both these and the other temples with the most lavish gifts, depositing in the shrine of Jupiter Capitolinus as a single offering sixteen thousand pounds of gold, besides pearls and other precious stones to the value of fifty million sesterces. (*Suet.Aug.*30.1–2)

Five fires occurred during the reign of Tiberius. Two were very serious. Tiberius himself made good for the losses of owners of blocks of houses.

The same year saw the capital visited by a serious fire, the part of the Circus adjoining the Aventine being burnt down along with the Aventine itself: a disaster which the Caesar converted to his own glory by paying the full value of the mansions and tenement blocks destroyed. One hundred million sesterces were invested in this act of munificence. (*Tac.Ann.*6.45)

There was also a major inferno during the time of Claudius. It burned a day and two nights. The emperor's slaves assisted the firefighters because the flames were so bad. Commoners were called upon to deal with the fire.

He always gave scrupulous attention to the care of the city and the supply of grain. On the occasion of a stubborn fire in the Aemiliana, he remained in the Diribitorium (a public voting hall on the campus Martius) for two nights, and when a body of soldiers and his own slaves could not give sufficient help, he summoned the commons from all parts of the city through the magistrates, and placing bags full of money before them, urged them to the rescue, paying each man on the spot a suitable reward for his services. (*Suet.Claud.*18.1)

Nero did not set the blaze. Winds helped fuel the great fire of 64 CE. Overcrowding, flammable material, and no impediments along with winds caused the fire to spread quickly despite relief efforts.

The conflagration broke out, gathered strength in the same moment, and, impelled by the wind, swept the full length of the Circus: for there were neither mansions screened by boundary walls, nor temples surrounded by stone enclosures, nor obstructions of any description, to bar its progress. The flames, which in full career overran the level districts first, then shot up to the heights, and sank again to harry the lower parts, kept ahead of all remedial measures, the mischief traveling fast, and the town being an easy prey owing to the narrow, twisting lanes and formless streets typical of old Rome. In addition, shrieking and terrified women; fugitives stricken or immature in years; men consulting their own safety or the safety of others, as they dragged the infirm along or paused to wait for them, combined by their dilatoriness or their haste to impede everything. Often, while they glanced back to the rear, they were attacked on the flanks or in the front; or, if they had made their escape into a neighboring quarter, that also was involved in the flames, and even districts they had believed remote from danger were found to be in the same plight. At last, irresolute what to avoid or what to seek, they crowded onto the roads or threw themselves down in the field: some who had lost the whole of their means—their daily bread included—chose to die, although the way of escape was open, and were followed by others, through love for the relatives whom they proved unable to rescue. (*Tac.Ann.*15.38)

Nero took great measures to make Rome fireproof.

In the capital, however, the districts spared by the palace were rebuilt, not, as after the Gallic fire, indiscriminately and piecemeal, but in measured lines of streets, with broad thoroughfares, buildings of restricted height and open spaces, while colonnades were added as a protection to the front of the tenement blocks. These colonnades Nero offered to erect at his own expense, and also to hand over the building sites, clear of rubbish, to the owners. He made a further offer of rewards, proportioned to the rank and resources of the various claimants, and fixed a term within which houses or blocks of tenement must be completed, if the bounty was to be secured. As the receptacle of the refuse he settled upon the Ostian Marshes, and gave orders that vessels which had carried grain up the Tiber must run down stream laden with debris. The buildings themselves, to an extent definitely specified, were to be solid, untimbered structures of Gabine or Alban stone, that particular stone being proof against fire. Again, there was to be a guard to ensure that the water supply—intercepted by private lawlessness—should be available for public purposes in greater quantities and at more points; appliances for checking fires were to be kept by everyone in the open; there were to be no joint partitions between buildings, but each was to be surrounded by its own walls. These reforms, welcomed for their utility, were also beneficial to the appearance of the new capital. (*Tac.Ann.*15.43)

Nero's name was destroyed despite his good efforts.

But neither human help, nor imperial munificence, nor all the modes of placating Heaven could stifle scandal or dispel the belief that the fire had taken place by order. Therefore, to scotch the rumor, Nero substituted as culprits, and punished with the utmost refinements of cruelty, a class of men, loathed for their vices, whom the crowd styled Christians. Christus, the founder of the name, had undergone the death penalty in the reign of Tiberius, by sentence of the procurator Pontius Pilatus, and the pernicious superstition was checked for a moment, only to break out once more, not merely in Judea, the home of the disease, but in the Capital itself, where all things horrible or shameful in the world collect and find a vogue. First, then, the confessed members of the sect were arrested; next on their disclosures, vast numbers were convicted, not so much on the count of arson as for the hatred of the human race. And derision accompanied their end: they were covered with wild beasts' skins and torn to death by dogs; or they were fastened on crosses, and when daylight failed were burned to serve as lamps by night. Nero had offered his Gardens for the spectacle, and gave an exhibition in his Circus, mixing with the crowd in the habit of a Charioteer, or mounted on his car. Hence, in spite of a guilt which had earned the most exemplary punishment, there arose a sentiment of pity, due to the impression that they were being sacrificed not for the welfare of the state but to the ferocity of a single man. (*Tac. Ann.*15.44)

Nero was very popular when he became emperor. He honored Claudius and he sponsored entertainment like most emperors. He was very modest and generous to impoverished nobility as well to his adoring masses. Suetonius mentions upper classes participating in games in order to discredit Nero. However, many elite men and women performed freely.

At his formal introduction into public life he announced a largess to the people and a gift of money to the soldiers, ordered a drill of the praetorians and headed them shield in hand; and thereafter returned thanks to his father in the senate. In the latter's consulship he pleaded the cause of the people of Bononia before him in Latin, and those of Rhodes and Ilium in Greek. His first appearance as a judge was when he was prefect of the city during the Latin Festival, when the most celebrated pleaders vied with one another in bringing before him, not trifling and brief cases according to the usual custom, but many of the highest importance, though this had been forbidden by Claudius. Shortly afterwards he took Octavia to wife and gave games and a beast-baiting in the Circus, that health might be vouchsafed Claudius.

When the death of Claudius was made public, Nero, who was seventeen years old, went forth to the watch between the sixth and the seventh hour, since no earlier time for the formal beginning of his reign seemed suitable because of bad omens throughout the day. Hailed emperor on the steps of the Palace, he was carried in a litter to the praetorian camp, and after a brief address to the soldiers was taken from there to the House, which he did not leave until evening, of the unbounded honors that were heaped upon him but one, the Father of His Country, and that because of his youth.

Then beginning with a display of filial piety, he gave Claudius a magnificent funeral, spoke his eulogy and deified him. He paid the highest honors to the memory of his father Domitius. He left to his mother the management of all public and private business. Indeed, on the first day of his rule he gave to the tribune on guard the watchword 'The Best of Mothers,' and afterwards he often rode with her through the streets in her litter. He established a colony at Antium, enrolling the veterans of the praetorian guard and joining with them the wealthiest of the chief centurions, whom he compelled to change their residence; and he also made a harbor there at great expense.

To make his good intentions still more evident, he declared that he would rule according to the principles of Augustus, and he let slip no opportunity for acts of generosity and mercy, or even displaying his affability. The more oppressive sources of revenue he either abolished or moderated. He reduced the rewards paid to informers against violators of the Papian law to one fourth of their former amount. He distributed four hundred sesterces to each man of the people, and granted to the most distinguished of the senators who were without means of an annual salary, to some as much as five hundred thousand sesterces; and to the praetorian cohorts he gave a monthly allowance of grain free of cost. When he was asked according to custom to sign the death warrant for the execution of a man who had been condemned to death, he said: "How I wish I had never learned to write!" He greeted men of all orders off-hand and from memory. When the Senate returned thanks to him, he replied, "When I shall have deserved them." He admitted even to the commons to witness his exercises in the Campus, and often declaimed in public. He read his poems too, not only at home but in the theater as well, so greatly to the delight of all that a thanksgiving was voted because of his recital, while that part of his poems was inscribed in letters of gold and dedicated to Jupiter of the Capitol.

He gave many entertainments of different kinds: the Juvenales, chariot races in the Circus, and a gladiatorial show. At the first mentioned he had even old men of consular rank and aged matrons take part. For the games of the Circus, he assigned places to the knights apart from the rest, and even matched chariots drawn by four camels. At the plays which he gave for the "Eternity of the Empire," which by his order were called the *Ludi Maximi*, parts were taken by several men and women of both the orders; a well-known Roman knight mounted an elephant and rode down a rope. A Roman play of Afranius, too, was staged, entitled, "The Fire," and the actors were allowed to carry off the furniture of the burning house and keep it. Every day all kinds of presents were thrown at the people; these included a thousand birds of every kind each day, various kinds of food, tickets for grain, clothing, gold, silver, precious stones, pearls, painting, slaves, beasts of burden, and even trained wild animals; finally, ships, blocks of houses, and farms. (*Suet.Ner.*7.2–11)

Philostratus of Athens (170–c. 247 CE) was the author of The Life of Apollonius, *a narrative on Apollonius of Tyana, an enigmatic wise man and miracle worker of the first century who is often compared to Jesus of Nazareth. "Since then you have discovered in Vitellius, an image and ape of Nero, and are turning your arms against him, persist in the policy you have embraced, for it too is a noble one, only let its sequel be noble too" (*Philost. VA.5.33*).*

Despite the elite's disapproval of Nero, the emperor remained beloved as reported by Suetonius:

Yet there were some who for a long time decorated his tomb with spring and summer flowers, and now produced his statues on the rostra in the fringed toga, and now his edicts, as if he were still alive and would shortly return and deal destruction to his enemies. Nay, more, Vologaesu, king of the Parthians, when he sent envoys to the senate to renew his alliance, earnestly begged this too, that honor be paid to the memory of Nero. In fact, twenty years later, when I was a young man, a person of obscure origin appeared, who gave out that he was Nero, and the name was still in such favor with the Parthians that they supported him vigorously and surrendered him with great reluctance. (*Suet.Ner.*57)

Further Reading

Barrett, Anthony, Elaine Fantham, and John C. Yardley, *The Emperor Nero: A Guide to the Ancient Sources*. Princeton University Press, Princeton, NJ, 2016.

Champlin, Edward, *Nero*. Harvard University Press, Cambridge, MA, and London, 2003.

Dando-Collins, Stephen, *The Great Fire of Rome: The Fall of the Emperor Nero and His City*. Da Capo Press (A Member of the Perseus Books Group), Cambridge, MA, 2010.

Draper, Robert, "Rethinking Nero," *National Geographic*. 2014. https://www.nationalgeographic.com/magazine/2014/09/emperor-nero/

Griffin, Miriam T., *Nero: The End of a Dynasty*. Yale University Press, New Haven and London, 1984.

Gyles, Mary Francis, "Nero Fiddled While Rome Burned," *The Classical Journal*, Vol. 42, No. 4 (January 1947). http://penelope.uchicago.edu/Thayer/E/Journals/CJ/42/4/Nero_Fiddled*.html

National Geographic, "July 19, 64 CE: Great Fire of Rome," Resource Library 1, *This Day in Geographic History*. https://www.nationalgeographic.org/thisday/jul19/great-fire-rome

PBS, "The Great Fire of Rome," *Secrets of the Dead*. June 4, 2014. https://www.pbs.org/wnet/secrets/great-fire-rome-interactive/1588/

PBS, "The Nero Files," *Secrets of the Dead*. February 20, 2019. https://www.pbs.org/wnet/secrets/the-nero-files-about-the-film/4004/

7

Romans Vomited in Vomitoria

What People Think Happened

Ancient Roman dinner parties are synonymous with gluttony, decadence, and waste. Rome began its decline when wealthy Romans became greedy and obsessed with luxury and food. Diners feasted until sunrise, with plenty of music, dancing, and prostitutes. A unique Roman feature of feasting, called a "vomitorium," was a special room adjacent to the dining area so that guests could purge themselves to make room for the next round of sumptuous delicacies. The vomitorium is the ultimate symbol of Roman decadence and debauchery.

Ancient Rome was infamous for its entertainment. Suetonius said that feasting was a very important part of Roman social life. Elite Romans were great hosts, with plenty of exotic food to gorge on! Meals were extremely decadent and were made expressly to impress certain guests. Trimalchio's feast included "dormice sprinkled with honey and poppy seed" (*Petron.Sat.*31). Apicius suggested that people ate "stuffed pig's stomach" (*Apic.*2.258,7.368). Occasionally, Elgabalus was said to serve ostrich (*SHA.Heliogab.*22,28.4). Furthermore, "in imitation of Apicius he frequently ate camels' heels and also cocks-combs taken from the living birds, and the tongues of peacocks and nightingales" (*SHA.Heliogab.* 20.4).

Such eating orgies lasted from sundown until the sun rose. In fact, Romans enjoyed eating so much that they would binge on food and drink. Many people point to Seneca's words, "they vomit that they may eat and eat that they may vomit" (*Sen.Helv.*10).

Popular belief has it that once they were sated, rich Romans asked a slave to tickle the backs of their throats with a feather so that they could vomit and continue eating and drinking all night long. Roman dining rooms included built-in cement couches with cushions. Seating was based on status and relation to the host: "I was there at the head, next to me Viscus Thurinus" (*Hor.Sat.*2.8).

Guests ate and dropped refuse on the floor for slaves to pick up. Even more disgusting, many guests did not reach the vomitorium in time. Seneca also reported that Romans vomited in special bowls or even on the floor. "When we recline at a banquet, one [slave] wipes away the disgorged food; another crouches beneath the table and gathers up the leftovers of the tipsy guests" (*Sen.Lucil.*47.5).

Julius Caesar also used to vomit after a good meal. Cicero describes how Caesar was nearly murdered at a dinner party because he felt the urge to purge after gorging on food. "When you [Caesar] said you wanted to vomit after dinner, they started to take you to the bathroom: because that's where the ambush was. But your perpetual good luck saved you, because you said you'd rather be in your bedroom" (*Cic.Deiot.*21).

Cicero tells of another dinner occasion when Caesar ate explicitly for the purpose of throwing it up. "On 19 December, himself [Caesar] was with Phillippus until the 7th hour. He didn't see anyone—accounts with Balbus, I think. Afterwards he walked on the beach. A bath after the 8th hour. Then he heard about Mamurra—he didn't change his expression. He got oiled, he reclined (to eat). He was on a regime of emetics, so he ate and drank unreservedly and cheerfully, a very sumptuous and well-prepared meal" (*Cic.Att.*13.52).

So, the popular assumption goes, Ancient Roman diners drank and ate to excess. After purging in the vomitorium, they would return to the table to start the process all over again. Suetonius, therefore, was correct: gluttony led to the decline of the Roman way of life. Not surprisingly, vomitoria and the decline of the Empire coincided with all the excess and waste.

How the Story Became Popular

The prevalent belief is that ancient Roman diners used to purge food in the vomitorium in order to continue feasting throughout the night. Newspapers, travel guides, and even historians have helped to spread the misperception that the vomitorium is the epitome of waste and decadence.

For example, a story in the *Western Mail* (Cardiff, Wales) from January 5, 1871, is the first known mention of the legend. Frenchman Félix

Pyat described an English Yule as, "the Protestant Carnival—Anglo-Saxon gala—a gross, pagan, monstrous orgie—a Roman feast, in which the vomitorium is not wanting."

In *Walks in Rome,* 1875, Augustus Hare mentions that "beyond the Triclinium is a disgusting memorial of Roman imperial life, in the vomitorium, with its basin, whither the feasters retired to tickle their throats with feathers and come back with renewed appetite to the banquet."

Moreover, the *Chronicle* of Kansas City, Kansas, said, "We may smile with contempt upon the practice of the Romans in their degenerate days of providing a 'vomitorium' adjoining the dining room where guests who had surfeited until their stomachs could retain no more, could retire and empty them by emetic" (Thursday, Aug. 28, 1890).

In 1926, the *Windsor Star* contained an article reporting the must-see attraction of the vomitorium "behind the banquet hall of the Caesars." Here diners would "throw up everything they had eaten" (March 26, 1926).

Even the famous author Aldous Huxley contributed to the establishment of the myth in his 1923 comic novel, *Antic Hay*. Petronius also brings to mind the antics of the gluttonous Trimalchio from the *Satyricon*: "there strode in, like a Goth into the elegant marble vomitorium of Petronius Arbiter, a haggard and disheveled person."

Macrobius is another source who inadvertently played a part in the creation of the legend. He is the author of the *Saturnalia* and uses vomitoria to describe entries/exits in amphitheaters that spewed people in/out of seating. Vomiting was mentioned in connection with feasting in some texts.

Roman writers who critiqued ancient Rome, such as Seneca, no doubt influenced modern stories and mentions of the vomitorium. Seneca wrote, "They vomit so they can eat, and they eat so that they can vomit. They don't even consider the dishes which they have assembled from across the Earth worthy of digestion."

Historians who failed to check their sources also had a hand in promoting the legend. Will Durant's February 28, 1928, article in the *LA Times* reported, "Delicacies adorn the tables, and men and women, reclining comfortably as they eat, consume as much as they can, and then, if they are graduate Epicureans, go out to the vomitorium and free themselves for more."

Sociologist Lewis Mumford is a major source for spreading and legitimizing the misperception. His book, *The City in History* (1961), described the vomitorium as a place where insatiable diners could purge in order to eat more food.

Critiques of the moral excess of Romans were a frequent topic of ancient writers. Marcus Gavius Apicius was a Roman who loved luxury so much that he became the subject of a lost work, *On the Luxury of Apicius*, by the Greek writer Apion. Apicius authored a cookbook on exotic dishes for upper-class Romans. Pliny the Elder reported, Apicius "was born to enjoy every extravagant luxury that could be contrived." Apicius recommended that it was best "to let the mullet die in the pickle known as 'the garum of the allies'" (*Plin.HN*.9.30). Apicius was so outrageous that he dined on exotic food such as flamingo tongue, which he described as having an "especially fine flavor" (*Plin.HN*.10.133). His pigs were fed dried figs and killed with an overdose of honey wine (*Apic*.8.259). Apicius loved luxury so much that when he learned he had spent most of his fortune on luxury, he committed suicide rather than die in poverty.

Ancient Roman stories of excessive dining have also promoted the idea of a room to purge oneself after a night of excessive feasting. Plutarch's story of Lucullus's lust for food contributed to the folklore. Lucullus once admonished his slave for commenting that there would be no guests for dinner. Lucullus remarked, "What, did you not know then, that today Lucullus dines with Lucullus?" (*Plut.Vit.Luc*.41.1–6).

Petronius's *Satyricon* added to the misperception with its outrageous images of eating and drinking at Trimalchio's dinner (*Petron.Sat*.26.6–78.8). Trimalchio was a wealthy freedman who served exotic dishes such as live birds sewn inside a pig, live birds inside fake eggs, a rabbit with wings attached so that it looked like Pegasus, and a huge boar surrounded by suckling pigs, which the guests could take away like party favors. Such displays of gluttony and excess were shocking and no doubt have had a massive impact on the modern perception of the common use of a vomitorium. Modern sensibilities perceive that little can be more wasteful and disgusting than eating food in order to vomit and consume more.

Roman moralists have shaped the pop-cultural belief of the vomitorium with stories of extravagance. Tacitus criticized the exotic menu of the Romans in comparison to the simple meals of the Germans (*Tac.Ger*.23).

Suetonius described Claudius as gorging on food and guzzling wine. He stayed at the banquet until he could eat no more. However, a feather down his throat relieved him, and he was able to return to eating. "He gave frequent and grand dinner parties, as a rule in spacious places, where six hundred guests were often entertained at one time" (*Suet.Claud*.32). Suetonius noted that Claudius was unable to remain in the courtroom because of the smell of the food being prepared in an adjacent temple (*Suet.Claud*.31).

Dio Cassius depicted Vitellius as idle, gluttonous and incompetent, "nourished by the mere passage of food" (*Dio.Cass.*64.2). Tacitus implied that this gluttony, idle pleasures, and sumptuous banquets were a threat to morality and traditional values (*Tac.Ann.*1.62). Suetonius expressed disgust because Vitellius reportedly feasted four times a day and threw up in between meals (*Suet.Vit.*13). He was so decadent that he had food brought from all over the Empire to appease his unquenchable need to eat (*Suet.Vit.*7).

Elgabalus surpassed his predecessors in debauchery. "He himself declared that his models were Apicius among commoners, and among emperors, Otho and Vitellius" (*SHA.Heliogab.*2.18.4). "In imitation of Apicius he frequently ate camels' heels and also cocks-combs taken from the living birds, and the tongues of peacocks and nightingales." Elgabalus also served "huge platters heaped up with the viscera of mullets, and flamingo brains, partridge eggs, thrush brains, and the heads of parrots, pheasants and peacocks" (*SHA.Heliogab.*2.20.4).

The legend of the vomitorium has been shaped by political critics who used descriptions of decadent emperors and overindulgent elites as evidence of moral laxity. On this basis, confused writers from the nineteenth century created and embellished the myth of the vomitorium.

PRIMARY DOCUMENTS

A Frenchman showed his contempt regarding the celebration of Christmas in England in the oldest known mention of the vomitorium myth. Barbaric gorging and guzzling bouts were to be expected of the decadent Romans, but not of a Christmas celebration.

M. Félix Pyat gives the following account of Christmas in England: "Christmas is the great English fête—the Protestant Carnival—an Anglo-Saxon gala—a gross, pagan, monstrous orgie—a Roman feast, in which the vomitorium is not wanting. And the eaters of 'bif' laugh at us for eating frogs! Singular nation! The most Biblical and most material of Europe—the best Christians and the greatest gluttons. They cannot celebrate a religious fête without eating. On Holy Friday they eat buns, and for this reason they call it Good Friday. Good, indeed, for them, if not for God. They pronounce messe, mass and boudin, pudding. This pudding is made of suet, sugar, currants and tea. The mess is boiled for 15 days, sometimes for six months; then it is considered delicious. No pudding, no Christmas. The repast is sacred, and the English meditate over it for six months in advance—they are the only people who put money in a savings bank for a dinner. Each poor family economizes for months and takes a shilling to a publican every Saturday for a year, in return for which on Christmas Day they gorge themselves and are sick for a week after. This is their religion—thus they adore their God." (*Western Mail*, Cardiff, South Glamorgan, Wales, Janu. 5, 1871, p. 2)

The vomitorium was a popular topic in the early nineteenth century. Helen L. Manning reported the following based on a lecture by John Harvey Kellogg, M.D., in the Chronicle *of Kansas City, Kansas, in 1890 at the Battle Creek Sanitarium. He railed against lavish food preparation and lack of restraint. Dr. Kellogg mentions Nero and "vomitorium" to get the readers' attention.*

But what we taste is swallowed into the stomach, and what has given us brief pleasure through the gratification of the palate, must make work in the alimentary canal for fourteen hours before it is finally disposed of.

We may smile with contempt upon the practice of the Romans in their degenerate days of providing a "vomitorium" adjoining the dining room where guests who had surfeited until their stomachs could retain no more, could retire, and empty by emetic. But after all it was better than the practice of continual eating for the sake of gratifying the sense of taste and keeping the stomach constantly at work upon all sorts of indigestible things. Feasters of the present day are on a level with those who gathered around Nero's table.

Many people treat their stomach as if it were a pocket; in truth, they put things into it that they would be shy of putting in their pockets—limburger cheese, for instance. But no one has a right to eat or drink except to meet the demands of the body, and wholesome, nutritious unseasoned food can always be prepared so as to be palatable to an un-perverted taste.

Of course, it takes more skill to cook simple foods so that natural flavors shall be preserved, than it does to rob them of natural flavors by poor cookery and supply the deficiency by using a plentiful amount of condiments. So, it behooves everyone who has these important matters of health and temperance at heart, to learn scientific cookery. We have senses through which we may seek enjoyment, and which will lead us to a higher plane, but using the sense of taste for personal gratification can never be too debasing to young or old. (*Chronicle*, Kansas City, Kansas, Aug. 28, 1890, p. 7)

The next example also equates Nero and vomitoria with debauched behavior, which no doubt helped spread the idea that Romans had a special room in which to empty the stomach and return to the table for more. It was published under the "General News" column on page 1. It ends on a sarcastic note on the progress of society.

In the days of Nero, hard by the banqueting hall, a room known as a vomitorium was maintained in which a servant tickled the throat of the revelers with a feather, thereby causing the overloaded stomach to be relieved. In modern times, less modesty is manifested and the sidewalk is too often used for like purposes. Thus, does civilization progress. (*Waterloo Press*, Waterloo, Indiana, Dec. 2, 1897, p. 1)

The Windsor Star *reported that a Roman banquet was not a real feast unless each guest was supplied with a whole bullock (bull) for the meat course alone. The article is full of the clichés associated with this special room. The mention of the Italian guide serves to legitimate the writer's claims.*

There is one peculiar place that is always shown to visitors to the Palatine at Rome. It is just behind what used to be the banquet hall in the palace of the Caesars. The guide says it is the "vomitorium."

Naturally more information is requested and so the Italian, who is intimate with every nook and cranny of the place, goes on to explain. His story is interesting. It reveals a particular side light on the life of the early Roman nobility.

In the days of the Caesars celebrations were always accompanied by elaborate banquets. Sometimes these would last for days at a time. It was not considered a real banquet unless each guest was supplied with a whole bullock for the meat course alone.

On the face of it that sounds preposterous. It would be impossible for an ordinary human being to attempt to eat a whole animal during the course of the banquet. Even for the giant, athletic Romans it would be absurd to consider them capable of sitting down to a meat dish of a whole bullock.

But that is just where the "vomitorium" played its part. And it was a part of no mean importance.

The emperor and his guests would sit and gorge themselves until it became impossible to swallow another morsel. Then they would go out to the "vomitorium" and throw up everything they had eaten. After that exercise they would return to the banquet hall and start the feast all over again.

For those guests who found difficulty in losing their food little feathers were supplied. These were used to tickle the backs of throats of the diners. The feathers also brought the desired result, and the meal would be successfully lost.

That is how the early Romans would eat so much at a sitting. The "vomitorium" on the Palatine remains as mute evidence of the banquet gorges. It is interesting because it throws such a unique side-light on the life of the Caesars. (*Windsor Star*, March 26, 1926, p. 4)

Roman literature is rife with stories of individuals whose eating and drinking habits suggested the need to purge in order to continue feasting. Seneca's Consolation to Helvia was written to console his mother, who had experienced a series of tragic losses throughout her entire life. Seneca wrote the letter while he was exiled for an alleged extramarital affair with Caligula's sister, Julia Livilla. Originally, he was condemned to death but was subsequently pardoned by Caligula. Claudius sent him to Corsica. Seneca mentions Apicius, who committed suicide after realizing he wasted all his fortune on eating. The famous saying, "They eat so they may vomit and vomit so they may eat," suggests the existence of a special room where Romans could purge.

Marcellus, then, nobly endured his exile, and his change of place made no change in his mind, even though it was accompanied by poverty, in which every man who has not fallen into the madness of avarice and luxury, which upset all our ideas, sees no harm. Indeed, how very little is required to keep a man alive? and who, that has any virtue whatever, will find this fail him? As for myself, I do not feel that I have lost my wealth, but my occupation: the wants of the body are few: it wants protection from the cold, and the means of allaying hunger and thirst: all desires beyond these are vices, not necessities. There is no need for prying into all the depths of the sea, for loading one's stomach with heaps of slaughtered animals, or for tearing up shell-fish from the unknown shore of the furthest sea: may the gods and goddesses bring ruin upon those whose luxury transcends the bounds of an empire which is already perilously wide. They want to have their ostentatious kitchens supplied with game from the other side of the Phasis, and though Rome has not yet obtained satisfaction from the Parthians, they are not ashamed to obtain birds from them: they bring together from all regions everything, known or unknown, to tempt their fastidious palate: food, which their stomach, worn out with delicacies, can scarcely retain, is brought from the most distant ocean: they vomit that they may eat, and eat that they may vomit, and do not even deign to digest the banquets which they ransack the globe to obtain. If a man despises these things, what harm can poverty do him? If he desires them, then poverty even does him good, for he is cured in spite of himself, and though he will not receive remedies even upon compulsion, yet while he is unable to fulfill his wishes he is as though he had them not. Gaius Caesar, whom in my opinion Nature produced in order to show what unlimited vice we would be capable of when combined with unlimited power, dined one day at a cost of ten millions of sesterces: and though in this he had the assistance of the intelligence of all his subjects, yet he could hardly find how to make one dinner out of the tribute-money of three provinces. How unhappy are they whose appetite can only be aroused by costly food! and the costliness of food depends not upon its delightful flavor and sweetness of taste, but upon its rarity and the difficulty of procuring it: otherwise, if they chose to return to their sound senses, what need would they have of so many arts which minister to the stomach? of so great a commerce? of such ravaging of forests? of such ransacking of the depths of the sea? Food is to be found everywhere, and has been placed by Nature in every part the world, but they pass it by as though they were blind, and wander through all countries, cross the seas, and excite at a great cost the hunger which they might allay at a small one. One would like to say, "Why do you launch ships? why do you arm your hands for battle both with men and wild beasts? why do you run so riotously hither and thither? why do you amass fortune after fortune? Are you unwilling to remember how small our bodies are? is it not frenzy and the wildest insanity to wish for so much when you can contain so little?" Though you may increase your income, and extend the boundaries of your property, yet you never can enlarge your own bodies: when your business transactions have turned out well, when you have made a successful campaign, when you have collected the food for which you have hunted through all lands, you will have no place in which to bestow all these superfluities. Why do you strive to obtain so much? Do you think that our ancestors, whose virtue supports our vices even to the present day, were unhappy, though they dressed their food with their own hands, though the earth was their bed, though their roofs did not yet glitter with gold, nor their temples with precious stones? and so they used then to swear with scrupulous honesty by earthenware gods; those who called these gods to witness would go back to the enemy for certain death rather than break their word? Do you suppose that our dictator who granted an audience to the ambassadors of the Samnites, while he roasted the commonest food before the fire himself with that very hand with which he had so often smitten the enemy, and with which he had placed his laurel wreath upon the lap of Capitolian Jove, enjoyed life less than the Apicius who lived in our own days, whose habits tainted the entire century, who set himself up as a professor of gastronomy in that very city from which philosophers once were banished as corrupters of youth? It is worthwhile to know his end. After he had spent a hundred million of sesterces on his kitchen, and had wasted on each single banquet a sum equal to so many presents from the reigning emperors, and the vast revenue which he drew from the Capitol being overburdened with debt, he then for the first time was forced to examine his accounts: he calculated that he would have ten millions left of his fortune, and, as though he would live a life of mere starvation on ten millions, put an end to his life by poison. How great must the luxury of that man have been, to whom ten millions signified want? Can you think after this that the amount of money necessary to make a fortune depends upon its actual extent rather than on the mind of the owner? Here was a man who shuddered at the thought of a fortune of ten million sesterces, and escaped by poison from a prospect which other men pray for.

Nothing is sufficient for covetous desire, but Nature can be satisfied even with scant measure. The poverty of an exile, therefore, causes no inconvenience, for no place of exile is so barren as not to produce what is abundantly sufficient to support a man.

Yet, for a mind so diseased, that last draft of his was the most wholesome: he was really eating and drinking poisons when he was not only enjoying, but boasting of his enormous banquets, when he was flaunting his vices, when he was causing his country to follow his example, when he was inviting youths to imitate him, albeit youth is quick to learn evil, without being provided with a model to copy. This is what befalls those who do not use their wealth according to reason, which has fixed limits, but according to vicious fashion, whose caprices are boundless and immeasurable.

Nothing is sufficient for covetous desire, but Nature can be satisfied even with scant measure. The poverty of an exile, therefore, causes no inconvenience, for no place of exile is so barren as not to produce what is abundantly sufficient to support a man. (*Sen.Helv.*11.10)

Trimalchio was desperate to show off his wealth as well as how Roman he was. Worse yet were the singing and dancing servers who recited Trimalchio's bad poetry. This rather vulgar display of lavish dishes implied the need for a room where guests could void the previous meal in order to make room for more exotic courses that followed.

We were in the dining room, the slave for whom we had pleaded ran up, and to our astonishment, rained kisses on us, and thanked us for our mercy. One word, he said, you will know in a minute who owes you a debt of gratitude. "The master's wine is in the butler's gift." ...

At last then we sat down, and boys from Alexandria poured water cooled with snow over our hands. Others followed and knelt down at our feet, and proceeded with great skill to pare our hangnails. Even this unpleasant duty did not silence them, but they kept singing at their work. I wanted to find out whether the whole household could sing, so I asked for a drink. A ready slave repeated my order in a chant, not less a shrill. They all did the same if they were asked to hand anything. It was more like an actor's dance than a gentleman's dining room. But some rich and tasty whets for the appetite were brought on; for everyone had now sat down except Trimalchio, who had the first place kept for him in their new style. A donkey in Corinthian bronze stood on the side-board, with panniers holding olives, white in one side, black in another. Two dishes hid one donkey; Trimalchio's name and their weight in silver was engraved on their edges. There were also dormice rolled in honey and poppy-seed, and supported on little bridges soldered to the plate. Then there were hot sausages laid on a silver grill, and under the grill damsons [plums] and seeds of pomegranates. (*Petron.Sat.*33)

Suetonius's description of Claudius's eating habits leaves no doubt about the existence of the vomitorium. However, his accusations against the emperor are slanderous.

He was eager for food and drink at all times and all places. Once, when he was holding court in the Forum of Augustus and had caught the savor of a meal which was preparing for the *Salii* [priests] in the temple of Mars hard by, he left the tribunal, went up to where the priests were, and took his place at their table. He hardly ever left the dining room until he was stuffed and soaked; then he went to sleep at once, lying on his back with his mouth open, and a feather was put down his throat to relieve his stomach. (*Suet.Claud.*33)

Suetonius also presented Vitellius in a negative light, as a despicable glutton devoted to excess, in order to show his unfitness to rule.

But his besetting sins were luxury and cruelty. He divided his feasts into three, sometimes into four a day: breakfast, luncheon, dinner, and a drinking bout; and he was readily able to do justice to all of them through his habit of taking emetics. Moreover, he had himself invited to each of these meals by different men on the same day, and the materials for any one of them never cost less than four hundred thousand sesterces. Most notorious of all was the dinner given by his brother to celebrate the emperor's arrival in Rome, at which two thousand of the choicest fishes and seven thousand birds are said to have been served. He himself eclipsed even this at the dedication of a platter, which on account of its enormous size he called the "Shield of Minerva, Defender of the City." In this he mingled the livers of pike, the brains of pheasants and peacocks, the tongues of flamingoes and the milk of lampreys, brought by his captains and triremes from the whole Empire, from Parthia to the Hispanic straits. Being besides a man of an appetite that was not only boundless, but also regardless of time or decency, he could never refrain, even when he was sacrificing or making a journey, from snatching bits of meat and cakes amid the altars, almost from the very fire, and devouring them on the spot; and in the cook shops along the road, viands smoking hot or even those left over from the day before and partly consumed. (*Suet.Vit.*13)

What Really Happened

The legend of the vomitorium has been shaped by descriptions of decadent emperors and elites whose overindulgence was a sign of moral laxity. The myth of the vomitorium has perpetuated because it fits in with the cultural trope of Roman banqueting as decadent, immoral and lavish. The vomitorium serves as a disgusting metaphor of Roman wealth and waste.

Yet no ancient writer mentions such a room. Vomitoria were corridors in an amphitheater (*Macrob.Sat.*6.4.3). Furthermore, the usual Roman dinner consisted of three courses and was the main meal of the day. It was not extravagant or wasteful. Cicero says, "I used to dine with these companions—in an altogether moderate way" (*Cic.Sen.*13.45).

Customarily, Romans ate a simple breakfast and a light snack for lunch. Frugality was considered to be virtuous. When Rome became an empire, however, more foods were available, so Roman moralists perceived the luxurious dishes as decadent and destructive to the Roman way of life.

Roman authors gave vivid details of imperial purging in order to advance the notion that Roman emperors gorged on food to the point of needing to void the contents of their bellies in the vomitorium. Suetonius, Dio

Cassius, and the *Augustan History* used descriptions of gluttony and excess to tarnish the reputations of Claudius and Vitellius and the imperial system in general. These texts have been taken literally and misinterpreted.

Suetonius presented Claudius as a wasteful, bungling, and weak buffoon who was unfit to lead. Claudius's outrageous eating and love of taverns figured prominently among his moral deficiencies. An emperor is supposed to be modest (*Suet.Aug.*72). Claudius craved food when he heard a reference to "butchers and vintners," "prompting him to cry out in the Senate, 'Now, pray, who can live without a snack?'" (*Suet.Claud.*40).

Likewise, Suetonius's account of Vitellius's dining habits provoke true disgust. Vitellius is fat and lazy because of his uncontainable indulging.

"He divided his feasts into three, sometimes into four a day: breakfast, luncheon, dinner and a drinking bout" (*Suet.Vit.*13). Similarly, in order to create an unsavory image in the minds of readers, Dio Cassius reports that "he was insatiate to gorging himself, and was constantly vomiting up what he ate, being nourished by the mere passage of food" (*Dio.Cass.*64.2) in order create an unsavory image in the minds of readers.

Vitellius's enormous appetite emphasized his ungovernable devotion to his "bottomless gullet [that] might be filled with the resources of the province" (*Suet.Vit.*7).

"Delicacies were carted all the way from Rome and Italy to tickle his palate" (*Tac.Hist.*2.62). Tacitus stressed the scandalous behavior, which "[led] members of the various cities [to find] the provision of sumptuous banquets a heavy drain on their pockets, and the very cities were reduced to beggary" (*Tac. Hist.*2.62).

These stories of luxury and excess don't prove that Claudius and Vitellius used a vomitorium. Although each was condemned for reckless lavishness, such charges were meant to show that the emperors were corrupt, incompetent, and therefore unqualified to govern.

These narratives demonstrate, rather, a set of contrasting values. Luxury was a sign of decadence; austerity was a mark of virtue. The traditional simplicity of Augustus is obvious in the plainness of his dining habits. Tiberius was so mindful of not being wasteful that "to encourage general frugality by his personal example, he often served at formal dinners meats left over from the day before and partly consumed, or the half of a boar, declaring that it had all the qualities of a whole one" (*Suet.Tib.*34).

Feasts were not large affairs. Banquets were an important part of Roman social life that centered on status. The host would impress his guests with food and entertainment such as acrobats, gladiators, or poetry recitals. Guests were seated according to status but were to be treated as equals. They dined and conversed in a reclining position. Pliny the Younger defines *triclinia* as an area appropriate for a small gathering of intimates (*Plin.Ep*.1.3.1). Generally, Romans were modest and reserved in their eating and drinking. For example, Pliny the Younger described a dinner with Trajan to Cornelianus: "Every day we were summoned to dine with the Emperor, and modest dinners they were for one of his imperial position" (*Plin.Ep*.6.31.13).

As further evidence, Juvenal praised the modesty of the past and the frugality of Manius Curius Dentatus, the incorruptible and modest noble of old, who grew vegetables in his small garden.

> Such were the banquets of our Senate in days of old, when already grown luxurious; when Curius, with his own hands, would lay upon his modest hearth the simple herbs he had gathered in his little garden—herbs scoffed at nowadays by the dirty ditcher who works in chains, and remembers the savor of tripe in the reeking cook-shop. For Feast days, in olden times, they would keep a side of dried pork, hanging from an open rack, or put before the relations a flitch of birthday bacon, with the addition of some fresh meat, if there happened to be a sacrifice to supply it. A kinsman who had thrice been hailed as Consul, who had commanded armies, and filled the office of Dictator, would come home earlier than was his wont for such a feast, shouldering the spade with which he had been subduing the hillside. For when men quailed before a Fabius or a stern Cato, before a Scaurus or a Fabricius—when even a censor might dread the severe verdict of his colleague—no one deemed it a matter of grave and serious concern what kind of tortoise shell was swimming in the waves of Ocean to form a headrest for our Troy born grandees. Couches in those days were small, their sides unadorned: a simple headpiece of bronze would display the head of a begarlanded ass, beside which would romp in play the children of the village. Thus house and furniture were all in keeping with the fare. (*Juv*.11.56–89)

Pliny the Younger once admonished a promising youth for being "mean and extravagant" because the young man "thought he combined elegance with economy, but who appeared to me both mean and lavish, for he set the best dishes before himself and a few others and treated the rest to cheap and scrappy food" (*Plin.Ep*.2.2.6).

Seneca is cited out of context. In his letter to his mother, Seneca does not imply that purging after eating was a Roman custom Instead, he admonishes those who immorally waste and display their wealth: "They vomit so they can eat, and they eat so that they can vomit. They don't even consider the dishes which they have assembled from across the Earth worthy of digestion" (*Sen.Helv*.11.10).

The following excerpt from Cicero's *On Behalf of King Deiotarus* is commonly cited as evidence that Romans regularly overindulged at banquets and threw up in order to continue feasting, but it is similarly taken out of context: "When you (Caesar) said you wanted to vomit after dinner, they started to take you to the bathroom: because that's where the ambush was. But your perpetual good luck saved you, because you said you'd rather be in your bedroom" (*Cic.Deiot*.21).

Purging often had a medicinal purpose. Celsus recommended vomiting for medical reasons but warned that purging should not become a daily practice: "Accordingly I allow that vomiting should not be practiced for the sake of luxury" (*Cels.Med*.1.3.21–22).

Caesar's medicinal purging was well known. Cicero informed Atticus that Caesar "got oiled, he reclined (for dinner). He was on a regime of emetics, so he ate and drank unreservedly and cheerfully, a very sumptuous and well-prepared meal" (*Cic.Att*.13.52).

Cicero also used vomiting to relieve a medical condition: "I have put away and got rid of it. What the reason was I discovered the day after I left you; it was undiluted bile. I got rid of it all that night" (*Cic.Fam*.14.7).

Trimalchio's dinner is not the epitome of Roman waste and debauchery. Instead, Petronius is poking fun at the extravagance and excessive show of wealth. Trimalchio and his guests are nouveau riche. Despite their prosperity and lavish banquet, they are a bunch of wannabe Romans. They don't succeed because of their ignorance.

Stories of Roman binging and purging are greatly exaggerated. In actuality, Roman banquets were mostly modest affairs. No special room existed to allow guests to vomit in order to continue feasting. Vomitoria did exist, but they were architectural features (such as passageways below or behind a row of seats) found in amphitheaters.

PRIMARY DOCUMENTS

Suetonius emphasizes Augustus's restraint and modest eating habits. The emperor's dinners were not too lavish. He was a good entertainer and saw to the needs of his guests.

The simplicity of his furniture and household goods may be seen from couches and tables still in existence, many of which are scarcely fine enough for a private citizen. They say he always slept on a low and plainly furnished bed. Except on special occasions he wore common clothes of the house, made by his sister, wife, daughter or granddaughters; his togas were neither close nor full, his purple stripe neither narrow nor broad, and his shoes somewhat high-soled, to make him taller than he really was. But he always kept shoes and clothing to wear in public ready in his room for sudden and unexpected occasions.

He gave dinner parties constantly and always formally with great regard to the rank and personality of his guests. Valerius Messala writes that he never invited a freedman to dinner with the exception of Menas, and then only when he had been enrolled among the freeborn after betraying the fleet of Sextus Pompey. Augustus himself writes that he once entertained a man at whose villa he used to stop, who had been one of his bodyguard. He would sometimes come to the table late on these occasions and leave early, allowing his guests to dine before he took his place and keep their places after he went out. He served dinner of three courses or six when he was more lavish, without needless extravagance but with the greatest good-fellowship. For he drew into the general conversation those who were silent or chatted under their breath, and introduced music and actors, or even strolling players from the circus, especially story-tellers.

Festivals and holidays he celebrated lavishly as a rule, but sometimes only in a spirit of fun. On the Saturnalia, and at any other time when he took it into his head, he would now give gifts of clothing or gold and silver; again, coins of every device, including old pieces of the kings and foreign money; another time nothing but hair cloth, sponges, pokers and tongs, and other such things under misleading names of double meaning. He used also at a dinner party to put up auction lottery-tickets for articles of most unequal value, and paintings of which only the back was shown, thus by the caprice of fortune disappointing or filling to the full expectations of the purchasers, requiring however that all the guests should take part in the bidding and share loss or gain.

He was a light eater (for I would not omit even this detail) and as a rule ate of plain food. He particularly liked coarse bread, small fishes, handmade moist cheese, and green figs of the second crop; and he would eat even before dinner, wherever and whenever he felt hungry. I quote word for word from some of his letters: "I ate a little bread and some dates in my carriage." And again: "As I was on my homeward way from the *Regia* in my litter, I devoured an ounce of bread and a few berries from a cluster of hard-fleshed grapes." Once more: "Not even a Jew, my dear Tiberius, fasts so scrupulously on his sabbaths as I have today; for it was not until after the first hour of the night that I ate two mouthfuls of bread in the bath before I began to be anointed." Because of this irregularity he sometimes ate alone either before a dinner party began or after it was over, touching nothing while it was in progress.

He was by nature most sparing also in his use of wine. Cornelius Nepos writes that in camp before Mutina it was his habit to drink not more than three times at dinner. Afterwards, when he indulged most freely he never exceeded a pint; or if he did, he used to throw it up. He liked Raetian wine best, but rarely drank before dinner. Instead he would take a bit of bread soaked in cold water, a slice of cucumber, a sprig of young lettuce, or an apple with a tart flavor, either fresh or dried.

After his midday meal he used to rest for a while just as he was, without taking off his clothes or shoes, with feet uncovered and his hand to his eyes. After dinner he went to a couch in his study, where he remained too late at night, until he had attended to what was left of the day's business, either wholly or in great part. Then he went to bed and slept not more than seven hours at most, and not even that length of time without a break, but waking three or four times. If he could not resume his sleep when it was interrupted, as would happen, he sent for readers or story tellers, when sleep came to him he often prolonged it until after daylight. He would never lie awake in the dark without having someone sit at his side. He detested early rising and when he had to get up earlier than usual because of some official or religious duty, to avoid inconveniencing himself he spent the night in the room of one of his friends near the appointed place. Even so, he often suffered from want of sleep, and he would drop off while he was being carried through the streets and when his litter was set down because of some delay. (*Suet.Aug.*73–78)

Diners of different rank were supposed to be treated as equals at a Roman banquet. Pliny the Younger comments on friendship in a letter to Avitus, whom he mentored. He offers his personal experience as a role model for his young friend. Feasting was an assembly of equals. Roman feasts and seating reflected the social hierarchy. Pliny comments on the differences in quality offered to the guests, who are treated according to their status, and not equally.

It would be a long story—and it is of no importance—to tell how I came to be dining—for I am no particular friend of his—with a man who thought he combined elegance with economy, but who appeared to me to be both mean and lavish, for he set the best dishes before himself and a few others and treated the rest to cheap and scrappy food. He had apportioned the wine in small decanters of three different kinds, not in order to give his guests their choice but that they might not refuse. He had one kind for himself and us, and another for his less distinguished friends—for he is a man who classifies his acquaintances—and a third for his own freedmen and those of his guests. The man who sat next to me noticed this and asked me if I approved of it. I said no. "Then how do you arrange matters?" he asked. "I set the same before all," I answered, "for I invited my friends to dine not to grade them one above the other, and those whom I have set at equal places at my board and my couches I treat as equals in every respect." "What! even the freedmen," he said. "Yes," I replied, "for then I regard them as my guests at the table, not as freedmen." He went on: "It must cost you a lot." "Not at all," said I. "Then how do you manage it?" "It's easily done; because my freedmen do not drink the same wine as I do, but I drink the same that they do." And, by Jove, the fact is that if you keep off gluttony it is not at all ruinously expensive to entertain a number of people to the fare you have yourself. It is this gluttony which is to be put down, to be reduced as it were to the ranks, if you wish to cut down expenses, and you will find it better to consult with your own moderate living than to care about the nasty things people may say of you. What then is my point? Just this, that I don't want you, who are a young man of great promise, to be taken in by the extravagance with which some people load their tables under the guise of economy. Whenever such a concrete instance comes in my way it becomes the affection I bear you to warn you of what you ought to avoid by giving you this example. So, remember that there is nothing you should eschew more than this association of extravagance and meanness; they are abominable qualities when separated and single, and still more so when you get a combination of them. Farewell. (*Plin.Ep.*2.2.6)

Petronius (27–80 CE) was a famous satirist who lived during the Julio-Claudian Dynasty and into the Flavian period. In Trimalchio's dinner, Petronius lampoons the would be "Roman" and his vulgar guests for their stupidity and complete ignorance of Roman table manners. Trimalchio is the stereotypical gluttonous, and overweight wannabe Roman. He picks his teeth at the table, and wears an ostentatious amount of jewelry. He is self-made and the wealthiest man in his area. His dinner party is rather small, but he makes and wastes enough food to feed the Roman army. Trimalchio uses the entire affair to display his power and resources.

We were engaged with these delicacies, Trimalchio was conducted in to a sound of music, propped on the tiniest of pillows. A laugh escaped the unwary. His head was shaven and peered out of a scarlet cloak, and over the heavy clothes on his neck he had put on a napkin with a broad stripe and fringes hanging from it all around. On the little finger of his left hand he had an enormous gilt ring, and on the top joint of the next finger a small ring which appeared to me to be entirely gold, but was really set all around with iron cut out in little stars. Not content with this display of wealth, he bared his right arm, where a golden bracelet shone, and an ivory bangle clasped with a plate of bright metal. Then he said, as he picked his teeth with a silver quill, it was not convenient for me to come to dinner yet, my friends, but I gave up all my own pleasure; I did not like to stay away any longer and keep you waiting. But you will not mind if I finish my game? A boy followed him with a table of terebinth wood and crystal pieces, and I noticed the prettiest thing possible. Instead of black and white counters they used gold and silver coins. Trimalchio kept passing every kind of remark as he played, and we were still busy with the hors d'oeuvres, when a tray was brought in with a basket on it, in which there was a hen made of wood, spreading out her wings as they do when they are sitting. The music grew loud; two slaves at once came up and began to hunt in the straw. Peahen's eggs were pulled out and handed to the guests. Trimalchio turned his head to look, and said, "I gave orders, my friends, that peahen's eggs should be put under a common hen. And upon my oath I am afraid they are hard-set by now. But we will try whether they are still fresh enough to suck." We took our spoons, half a pound in weight at least, and hammered at the eggs, which were balls of fine meal. I was on the point of throwing away my portion. I thought a peachick had already formed. But hearing a practiced diner say, "what treasure we have here?"

I poked through the shell with my finger, and I found a fat becafico [the figpecker, a small bird] rolled up in spiced yolk of egg. Trimalchio had now stopped his game, and asked for all the same dishes, and in a loud voice invited any of us who wished, to take a second glass of mead. Suddenly the music gave the sign, and the light dishes were swept away by a troop of singing servants. An entrée dish happened to fall in the rush, and a boy picked it up from the ground. Trimalchio saw him, and directed that he should be punished by a box on the ear, and made to throw down the dish again. A chairman followed and began to sweep out the silver with a broom among the other rubbish. Then two long haired Ethiopians with little wineskins, just like the men who scatter sand in an amphitheater, came in and gave us wine to wash our hands in, for no one offered us water. We complimented our host on his arrangements. "Mars loves a fair field," said he, "and so I gave orders that everyone should have a separate table. In that way these filthy slaves will not make us hot by crowding past us."

Just then some glass jars carefully fastened with gypsum were brought on, with labels tried to their necks, inscribed, "Falernian of Opimius's vintage. 100 years in a bottle." As we were poring over the labels Trimalchio clapped his hands and cried, "Ah me, so wine lives longer than a miserable man. So, let us be merry." (Petron.Sat.32–34)

Seneca's letter is not evidence for the existence of the vomitorium. Instead, Seneca condemns those who are not modest but instead devoted to excess and waste.

The second section of the following quote has been taken out of context. Seneca the Younger is commenting on how slaves are maltreated, not complaining about how decadent Romans are. "Disgorged food" is not a synonym for vomit.

I am glad to learn, through those who come from you, that you live on friendly terms with your slaves. This befits a sensible and well-educated man like yourself. "They are slaves," people declare. Nay, rather they are men. "Slaves!" No, comrades. "Slaves!" No, they are unpretentious friends. "Slaves!" No, they are our fellow-slaves, if one reflects that Fortune has equal rights over slaves and free men alike.

That is why I smile at those who think it degrading for a man to dine with his slave. But why should they think it degrading? It is only because purse-proud etiquette surrounds a householder at his dinner with a mob of standing slaves. The master eats more than he can hold, and with monstrous greed loads his belly until it is stretched and at length ceases to do the work of a belly; so that he is at greater pains to discharge all the food than he was to stuff it down. All this time the poor slaves may not move their lips, even to speak. The slightest murmur is repressed by the rod; even a chance sound—a cough, a sneeze, or a hiccup—is visited with the lash. There is a grievous penalty for the slightest breach of silence. All night long they must stand about, hungry and dumb.

The result of it all is that these slaves, who may not talk in their master's presence, talk about their master. But the slaves of former days, who were permitted to converse not only in their master's presence, but actually with him, whose mouths were not stitched up tight, were ready to bare their necks for their master, to bring upon their own heads any danger that threatened him; they spoke at the feast, but kept silence during torture. Finally, the saying, in allusion to this same high-handed treatment, becomes current: "As many enemies as you have slaves." They are not enemies when we acquire them; we make them enemies.

I shall pass over other cruel and inhuman conduct toward them; for we maltreat them, not as if they were men, but as if they were beasts of burden. When we recline at a banquet, one slave mops up the disgorged food, another crouches beneath the table and gathers up the left-overs of the tipsy guests. Another carves the priceless game birds; with unerring strokes and skilled hand he cuts choice morsels along the breast or the rump. Hapless fellow, to live only for the purpose of cutting fat capons correctly—unless, indeed, the other man is still more unhappy than he, who teaches this art for pleasure's sake, rather than he who learns it because he must. Another, who serves the wine, must dress like a woman and wrestle with his advancing years; he cannot get away from his boyhood; he is dragged back to it; and though he has already acquired a soldier's figure, he is kept beardless by having his hair smoothed away or plucked out by the roots, and he must remain awake throughout the night, dividing his time between his master's drunkenness and his lust; in the chamber he must be a man, at the feast a boy. Another, whose duty it is to put a valuation on the guests, must stick to his task, poor fellow, and watch to see whose flattery and whose immodesty, whether of appetite or of language, is to get them an invitation for tomorrow. Think also of the poor purveyors of food, who note their masters' tastes with delicate skill, who know what special flavors will sharpen their appetite, what will please their eyes, what new combinations will rouse their cloyed stomachs, what food will excite their loathing through sheer satiety, and what will stir them to hunger on that particular day. With slaves like these the master cannot bear to dine; he would think it beneath his dignity to associate with his slave at the same table! Heaven forfend! (*Sen.Lucil.*47.1–8)

Further Reading

Butler, Stephanie, "Vomitoriums: Fact or Fiction?" *History*. November 20, 2012. https://www.history.com/news/vomitoriums-fact-or-fiction

Davenport, C., and Shushma Malik, "Mythbusting Ancient Rome—The Truth about the Vomitorium," *The Conversation*. January 19, 2017. https://theconversation.com/mythbusting-ancient-rome-the-truth-about-the-vomitorium-71068

Dove, Laurie L., "Did Romans Really Purge Their Bellies in Vomitoria?" *howstuffworks. Culture*. https://history.howstuffworks.com/history-vs-myth/did-romans-purge-bellies-in-vomitoriums.htm

Gainsford, Peter, "Vomiting Romans: Or Were the Romans Happy Chuckers?" *Kiwi Hellenist.* June 13, 2016. http://kiwihellenist.blogspot.com/2016/06/vomiting-romans-or-were-romans-happy.html

Law, Emma, "What Goes in Must Come Out: The Truth behind Ancient Rome's Vomitoriums," *Culture Trip.* November 13, 2017. https://theculturetrip.com/europe/italy/articles/what-goes-in-must-come-out-the-truth-behind-ancient-romes-vomitoriums/

Pappas, Stephanie, "Purging the Myth of the Vomitorium," *Scientific American.* August 28, 2016. https://www.scientificamerican.com/article/purging-the-myth-of-the-vomitorium/

Radin, Alice P., *"Fictitious Facts": The Case of the Vomitorium*, APA Classics, American Philological Association, January 8, 2003. https://web.archive.org/web/20030320192257/http://www.apaclassics.org/AnnualMeeting/03mtg/abstracts/radin.html

8

The City of Rome Was Very Hygienic

What People Think Happened

When most people think of ancient Rome, they picture a city unparalleled for its cleanliness, sanitation system, public health consciousness, and waterworks. Rome is commonly assumed to have attained a quality of life in this regard that went unmatched until nineteenth-century Europe. For example, the city is often believed to have had an ample and high-quality water supply and to have boasted one of the first public health systems created for all citizens, regardless of social class. Therefore, Romans must have known that bad water and waste cause bad health. As a result, the Romans built sewers, aqueducts, public fountains, baths, and toilets that, according to popular assumptions, helped people stay clean and healthy and stopped the spread of disease.

Many people thus believe that the most impressive contribution toward this end was the famous network of aqueducts. Local water was undrinkable, as the Tiber was polluted. So, initially, most people got their water from public wells and from springs. As the population grew to approximately one million people, so did the need for a more reliable source of water. Thus, the Romans built a system of aqueducts, which flowed via gravity and brought fresh water daily to various cities in the Roman Empire, including the nine that serviced Rome itself. Some of the aqueducts are still used in local agriculture and water fountains today.

As the aqueducts delivered the water, the sewage system removed the contaminated liquid and concomitant waste. Sewers were originally built to drain lower-lying areas and rainwater but expanded to include this sanitation function, prompting Pliny the Elder to note in his *Natural History* that the "sewers are the most noteworthy things of all that the Romans have accomplished" (*Plin.HN*.36.24.4). The Cloaca Maxima ("greatest sewer"), wide enough to drive a wagon through, was the largest and emptied into the Tiber. If not for the sewers, the streets of Rome would have been covered in waste and rotting garbage.

Clean water from aqueducts was also essential for the public baths, which are popularly believed to place Roman hygiene on par with our modern standards of cleanliness. Originally, baths were an indulgence for those with discriminating taste. Eventually, public bathing became a common activity for rich and poor alike, because most homes did not have bathing facilities. Romans loved going to the baths because they were huge complexes similar to a modern fitness club. Some of the fun activities that Romans looked forward to included working out, playing dice, poetry readings, music, or meeting friends to learn the latest gossip. Bathhouses had a changing room and separate provisions for men and women. Any Roman, regardless of social class, could enjoy the hot, warm, and cold pools and even get a massage from a slave if one had the resources. Celsus extolled the therapeutic virtues of the baths after a small meal (*Cels.Med*.3.22.6). Romans recycled public bath waste by using it to flush toilets, which were commonly found in the context of the bathhouses.

Thus, another feature of the ancient Roman water system that people also equate with modern standards of public health was the public toilets, or *forica*, that were flushed by running water. Roman toilets, which could accommodate between ten and twenty visitors at a time, were in the shape of stone or wooden benches that were very close together. Togas provided some privacy, and men and women used the same facilities. Water ran continuously through a drainage canal below the seats and removed the waste. Visitors would clean themselves with a sponge on a stick that may have been dipped in wine or vinegar to keep it clean, and they washed their hands in a basin. Private toilets owned by the very wealthy could be connected to the sewer system, although this was rare. Even without this, Romans could dispose of excrement with, in a few cases, a latrine in the home, or a chamber pot.

All these factors led to the common assumption that public health and civic cleanliness were major concerns in ancient Rome.

How the Story Became Popular

Rome was the most sophisticated empire the Western world had known, due in part to the city of Rome's continual supply of fresh water and its sanitation system, unprecedented and not seen again in Europe until the Industrial Revolution. This seemingly Western and modern engineering accomplishment is interpreted by some as a serious ancient Roman preoccupation with health and cleanliness. People believe that the Romans were "ahead of their time" because of their use of public latrines. Romans stressed a "healthy body and healthy mind" and perceived that daily bathing had preventative value, also taken by many as evidence of an especially hygienic culture.

Furthermore, Roman doctors emphasized the preservation of health. Galen recommended a health regime whereby a paunch Roman male elite was the epitome of physical perfection. Even the satirist Juvenal emphasized a "healthy body and a healthy mind" (*Juv.*10.356). People thus assumed that the need to stay healthy led Romans to develop the world's first sanitation system, including sewers, aqueducts, public baths, and toilets.

Romans were aware that bad water and sewage caused bad health. They believed Rome was in a healthful site: "Not without good reason did gods and men choose this spot as the site of a City, with its bracing hills" (*Livy. Ab.Urbe.Cond.*5.54).

Further evidence that perpetuated the assumption of a hygienic culture was the Roman concern with waste disposal. The Cloaca Maxima initially was built by Tarquin to drain the forum. It was eventually covered and used to move water and to remove waste. It also was greatly admired because it was one of the oldest constructions in the city. The notion of sanitation and sewer are closely connected in Frontinus's *De Aquaeductu*, which brags about the improved health of the city resulting from the overflow from the fountains and public basins (*Frontin.Aq.*1.111). Strabo was thoroughly impressed by the sewer system's abilities to move great amounts of water (*Strab.Geog.*5.3.8). Pliny the Elder hinted at the efficiency of the sewers when he said that of all the things the Romans had accomplished, the sewers were "the most noteworthy achievements of all" (*Plin.HN.*36.24). Managing the sewers was very important, as evidenced by the fact that Romans had legislation regarding the sewers. Whenever the sewers were clogged, censors had them cleaned (*Dion.Hal.Ant.Rom.*3.67.5). The *Digest* mentions that a praetor's edict required that sewers had to be kept clean and in good condition (*Dig.*43.23.1–2). Agrippa traveled by boat to inspect the Cloaca during his term as aedile (a Roman official whose duties included managing the sewer system, street cleaning and supervision of the baths) to inspect and renovate the system in 19 BCE (*Dio.Cass.* 49.43.1). Still functioning today, the Cloaca Maxima served as a storm drain and mechanism for waste removal.

Aqueducts are also regarded as a superlative feat of the ancient Romans. The fresh water supply they brought and the conscientious emphasis on water quality were considered as further evidence of the Romans' concern for health and hygiene. Water quality was determined by the appearance, smell, temperature, and taste of the water. The poorest water was used for agriculture, and the best was used for drinking. The Aqua Virgo was used only for drinking because it had the highest quality water. Cassiodorus reported, "The Aqua Virgo runs with delightful purity, for while other waters during excessive rains are invaded by earthy matter, the Virgo's current runs pure as a never-clouded sky" (*Cassiod.Var.*7.6). Bad-tasting water required the use of an artificial lake that served as a settling basin to improve the quality of the water. These basins slowed down the water, thus removing impurities. Pliny the Elder recommended chemical treatments such as herbs for treating water. Water was collected in cisterns and flowed to fountains and public baths. The physician Galen remarked that Rome's water was high quality: "In Rome, just as there are many other advantages in the city, also there is the goodness and abundance of fountains and the water of none of them is smelly, muddy, toxic or hard" (*Hipp.*6.4, *Hipp.Epid.*4.10.17B.159K).

From the time of Augustus, inhabitants of Rome received an ample *supply* of water as well. The commissioner of water was responsible for the upkeep and maintenance of Rome's aqueducts, which required the use of many slaves (Aquarians, maintenance workers). Aqueduct repair was more important than the repair of roads because neglect would "cause people to die of thirst" (*Dig.*43.21.4). By the third century CE, the city had eleven aqueducts. Aqueducts became a common feature of other cities throughout the empire, along with public baths.

Romans perceived that bathing had a preventative value, but few homes had the luxury of running water. Subsequently, the existence of so many public baths preserved the notion that Romans were hygiene people. Romans visited the baths for health and social reasons, and almost all Romans could enjoy this basic feature of Roman life.

Romans exercised and soaked in a series of warm, hot, and cold pools to develop a sound body. Martial recommended bathing at the eighth hour (2 p.m.) because "this hour tempers the warm baths the hour before emits heat too great, and the sixth is hot with the excessive heat of Nero's baths" (*Epigram*.10.48). Bathing was to be avoided at night, probably because the sick would use the baths at that time.

Toilets were commonly found in the public baths. By the fourth century, there were 144 CE public latrines throughout Rome, again assuring the continuation of the idea that hygiene was paramount in Roman culture.

Rome also provided flushing toilets to dispose of waste for its citizens, often cited as a hallmark of an advanced civilization. Some homes of the wealthy had indoor plumbing connected directly to the sewer systems. Others had small latrines located in or near the kitchen. Even without those conveniences, people had access to large public toilet facilities, as noted above. The Roman zeal for providing adequate toilet facilities helped extend the assumption that Roman life was hygienic by contemporary standards.

Although the Roman Empire ended, its physical remains, such as the sewer system, endured, leading subsequent admiring generations to surmise that Rome's water supply system was built to the same standards of cleanliness as are used in the modern world.

PRIMARY DOCUMENTS

The sewers and sanitation system of ancient Rome were great undertakings. Many of the sewers were as large as modern-day sewers. Ancient authors viewed these constructions as a testament to Rome's origins and greatness. Marcus Agrippa was aedile under Augustus and viewed the sewers by boat.

Pliny the Elder brags of the wonders of Rome and its sewage system.

But it is now time to pass on to the marvels in building displayed by our own City, and to make some enquiry into the resources and experience that we have gained in the lapse of eight hundred years; and so prove that here, as well, the rest of the world has been outdone by us: a thing which will appear, in fact, to have occurred almost as many times as the marvels are in number which I shall have to enumerate. If, indeed, all the buildings of our City are considered in the aggregate, and supposing them, so to say, all thrown together in one vast mass, the united grandeur of them would lead one to suppose that we were describing another world, accumulated in a single spot.

Not to mention among our great works, the Circus Maximus, that was constructed by the Dictator Caesar, one stadium in width and three in length, and occupying, with the adjacent buildings, no less than four judges with room for two hundred and sixty thousand spectators seated; am I not to include in the number of our magnificent constructions, the Basilica of Paulus, with its admirable Phrygian columns; the Forum of the late Emperor Augustus; the Temple of Peace, erected by the Emperor Vespasianus Augustus—some of the finest works that the world has ever beheld—the roofing, too, of the Vote Office, that was built by Agrippa? not to forget that, before his time, Valerius of Ostia, the architect, had covered in a theater at Rome, at the time of the public Games celebrated by Libo?

We behold with admiration pyramids that were built by kings, when the very ground alone, that was purchased by the Dictator Caesar, for the construction of his Forum, cost one hundred million of sesterces! If, too, an enormous expenditure has its attractions for anyone whose mind is influenced by monetary considerations, be it known to him that the house in which Clodius dwelt, who was slain by Milo, was purchased by him at the price of fourteen million eight hundred thousand sesterces! a thing that, for my part, I look upon as no less astounding than the monstrous follies that have been displayed by kings. And then, as to Milo himself, the sums in which he was indebted, amounted to no less than seventy millions of sesterces; a state of things, to be considered, in my opinion, as one of the most portentous phenomena in the history of the human mind. But it was in those days, too, that old men still spoke in admiration of the vast proportions of the Agger, and of the enormous foundations of the Capitol; of the public sewers, too, a work more stupendous than any; as mountains had to be pierced for construction, and, like the hanging city which we recently mentioned, navigation had to be carried on beneath Rome; an event which happened in the aedileship of M. Agrippa, after he filled the office of consul.

For this purpose, there are seven rivers, made, by artificial channels, to flow beneath the city. Rushing onward, like so many impetuous torrents, they are compelled to carry off and sweep away all the sewerage; and swollen as they are by the vast accession of the pluvial waters, they reverberate against the sides and bottom of their channels. Occasionally, too, the Tiber, overflowing, is thrown backward in its course, and discharges itself by these outlets: obstinate is the contest that ensues within between the meeting tides, but so firm and solid is the masonry, that it is enabled to offer an effectual resistance. Enormous as are the accumulations that are carried along above, the work of the channels never gives way. Houses falling spontaneously to ruins, or levelled with the ground by conflagrations, are continually battering against them; the ground, too, is shaken by earthquakes every now and then; and yet, built as they were in the days of Tarquinius Priscus, seven hundred years ago, these constructions have survived, all but unharmed. We must not omit, too, to mention one remarkable circumstance, and all the more remarkable from the fact that the most celebrated historians have omitted to mention it. (*Plin.HN.*36.24)

Here Pliny proudly sings the praises of the Roman aqueducts.

But let us now turn our attention to some marvels which, justly appreciated, may be truthfully pronounced to remain unsurpassed. Q. Marcius Rex, upon being commanded by the Senate to repair the Appian Aqueduct, and those of the Anio and Tepula, constructed during his praetorship a new aqueduct, which bore his name, and was brought hither by a channel pierced through the sides of mountains. Agrippa, in his aedileship, united the Marcian with the Virgin Aqueduct, and repaired and strengthened the channels of the others. He also formed seven hundred wells, in addition to five hundred fountains, and one hundred and thirty reservoirs, many of them magnificently adorned. Upon these works, too, he erected three hundred statues of marble or bronze, and four hundred marble columns; and all this in the space of a single year! In the work which he has written in commemoration of his aedileship, he also informs us that public games were celebrated for the space of fifty-nine days, and that one hundred and seventy gratuitous baths were opened. The number of these last at Rome has increased to an infinite extent since his time.

The preceding aqueducts, however, have all been surpassed by the costly work which was more recently commenced by the Emperor Caius [Caligula], and completed by Claudius. Under these princes, the Curtian and Caerulean Waters, with the New Anio, were brought from a distance of forty miles, and at so high a level that all the hills were supplied with water, on which the City is built. The sum expended on these works was three hundred and fifty millions of sesterces. If we only take into consideration the abundant supply of water to the public, for baths, ponds, canals, household purposes, gardens, places in the suburbs, and country-houses; and then reflect upon the distances that are traversed, the arches that have been constructed, the mountains that have been pierced, the valleys that have been levelled, we must of necessity admit that there is nothing to be found more worthy of our admiration throughout the whole universe. (*Plin.HN.*36.24)

Pliny was not alone. Strabo also raved about the aqueducts that brought fresh water to Rome, citing their size and monumental appearance. He was greatly impressed by the ability of the Romans to furnish water to all citizens, but he did not indicate any concern for health. He also mentions the sewers being wide enough for wagons to drive through.

But the Roman prudence was more particularly employed on matters which had received but little attention from the Greeks, such as paving their roads, constructing aqueducts, and sewers, to convey the sewage of the city into the Tiber. In fact, they have paved the roads, cut through hills, and filled up valleys, so that the merchandise may be conveyed by carriage from the ports. The sewers, arched over with hewn stones, are large enough in some parts for wagons loaded with hay to pass through; while so plentiful is the supply of water from the aqueducts, that rivers may be said to flow through the city and the sewers, and almost every house is furnished with water-pipes and copious fountains—with which Marcus Agrippa concerned himself most, though he also adorned the city with many other structures. (*Strab.Geog.*5.3.8)

Dionysius of Halicarnassus was a Greek critic, historian, and teacher of rhetoric. His twenty-volume work, Roman Antiquities, *is one of most important works on the history of Rome.*
Likewise, in the next passage, the greatness of Rome is indicated by its monuments, such as the sewers, built by Tarquin. Dionysius is impressed by the antiquity of the monument and the role that it played in creating a new city center. The Cloaca was one of the success stories that made Rome great.

Tarquinius also adorned the Forum, where justice is administered, the assemblies of the people held, and other civil matters transacted, by surrounding it with shops and porticos. And he was the first to build the walls of the city, which previously had been temporary and of careless construction, with huge stones regularly squared. He also began the digging of the sewers, through which all the water that collects from the streets is conveyed into the Tiber—a wonderful work exceeding all description. Indeed, in my opinion the three most magnificent works of Rome, in which the greatness of her empire is seen, are the aqueducts, the paved roads and the construction of the sewers. I say this with respect not only to the usefulness of the work (concerning which I shall speak in the proper place), but also to the magnitude of the cost, of which one may judge by a single circumstance, if one takes as his authority Gaius Acilius [he wrote a history of Rome in Greek during the second century BCE], who says that once, when the sewers had been neglected and no longer passable for the waters, the censors let out the cleaning and repairing of them at a thousand talents. (*Dion.Hal.Ant.Rom.*3.67)

Likewise, Livy boasts of the ability of the sewers to move water.

The low-lying parts of the City round the Forum, and the other valleys between the hills, where the water could not escape, were drained by conduits which emptied into the Tiber. He built up with masonry a level space on the Capitol as a site for the Temple of Jupiter which he had vowed during the Sabine War, and the magnitude of the work revealed his prophetic anticipation of the future greatness of the place. (*Livy.Ab.Urbe .Cond.*1.38.6)

According to Livy nothing surpassed the greatness of the Cloaca Maxima.

Still they [plebeians] felt it less of a hardship to build the temples of the gods with their own hands, than they did afterwards when they were transferred to other tasks less imposing, but involving greater toil—the construction of the "ford" in the Circus and that of the Cloaca Maxima, a subterranean tunnel to receive all the sewage of the City. The magnificence of these two works could hardly be equaled by anything in the present day. (*Livy.Ab.Urbe.Cond.*1.56.2)

Vitruvius (first century BCE) explains how water is distributed to its various destinations. He wished to make sure that the water supply was sufficient.

There are three methods of conducting water, in channels through masonry conduits, or in lead pipes, or in pipes of baked clay. If in conduits, let the masonry be as solid as possible, and let the bed of the channel have a gradient of not less than a quarter of an inch for every hundred feet, and let the masonry structure be arched over, so that the sun may not strike the water at all. When it has reached the city, build a reservoir with a distribution tank in three compartments connected with the reservoir to receive the water, and let the reservoir have three pipes, one for each of the connecting tanks, so that when the water runs over from the tanks at the ends, it may run into one of them.

From this central tank, pipes will be laid to all the basins and fountains; from the second tank, to baths, so that they may yield an annual income to the State; and from the third to private houses, so that water for public use will not run short; for people will be unable to divert it if they have only their own supplies from headquarters. This is the reason why I have made these divisions, and also in order that individuals who take water into their houses may by their taxes help to maintain the conducting of water by the contractors. (*Vitr.de.Arch.*8.61–62)

Frontinus provides more information on the water supply system. He was a well-connected member of the senatorial class. His major works are Strategemata (Stratagems) *and* De Aquaeductu urbis Romae (The Aqueducts of Rome), *which is the most valuable source of information on the water system. Appointed consul three times, he also became water commissioner at the behest of Emperor Nerva in 96 CE. He was not an engineer; however, Frontinus personally inspected the entire water system before writing his report,* The Aqueducts of Rome, *a history and description of the city's aqueducts and the laws pertaining to them. He also worked hard to deal with corruption and waste. Frontinus took his job and duties seriously, as indicated in the introduction of his book.*

Inasmuch as every task assigned by the Emperor demands special attention; and inasmuch as I am excited, not merely to diligence, but also to devotion, when any matter is entrusted to me, be it as a consequence of my natural sense of responsibility or of my fidelity; and inasmuch as Nerva Augustus (an emperor of whom I am at a loss to say whether he devotes more industry or love to the State) has laid me the duties of water commissioner, an office that concerns not merely convenience but also the health and safety of the City, and which has always been administered by the most eminent men of our State; therefore I deem it of the first and greatest importance to familiarize myself with the business I have undertaken, a policy which I have always made a principle in other affairs. (*Frontin.Aq.*1.1)

Frontinus was very proud of the aqueducts, and he disparages other public works and monuments that he considered useless when he writes: "With such an array of indispensable structures carrying so many waters, compare, if you will, the idle Pyramids or the useless, though famous, works of the Greeks!" *(*Frontin.Aq.*1.16).*

Frontinus equates the cleansing of the gutters with well-being. Romans were concerned about the quality of their water.

I desire that no one shall draw "lapsed" water except those who have permission to do so by grants from me or preceding sovereigns; for there must necessarily be some overflow from the reservoirs, this being proper not only for the health of our City, but also for use in the flushing of the sewers. (*Frontin.Aq*.111)

Frontinus stresses the importance of keeping the gutters clean in order to keep up with the increase in people using water. He also looked into the illegal tapping of the system. The Aqua Marcia supplied Romans with vast quantities of good water. Maintenance of the system was so important that Marcius's tenure in office was lengthened until the project was finished.

One hundred and twenty seven years later, that is, in the six hundred and eighth year from the founding of the City, in the consulship of Servius Sulpicius Galba and Lucius Aurelius Cotta, when the conduits of Appia and Old Anion had become leaky by reason of their age, and water was also being diverted from them unlawfully by individuals, the Senate commissioned Marcius, who at that time administered the law as praetor between citizens, to reclaim and repair these conduits; and since the growth of the City was seen to demand a more bountiful supply of water, the same man was charged by the Senate to bring into the City other waters so far as he could. He restored the old channels and brought in a third supply, more wholesome than these, which is called Marcia after the man who introduced it. We read in Fenestella that 180,000,000 sesterces were granted to Marcius for these works, and since the term of his praetorship was not sufficient for the completion of the enterprise, it was extended for a second year. At that time the Decemvirs, on consulting the Sibylline Books for another purpose, are said to have discovered that it was not right for the Marcian water, or rather the Anio (for tradition more regularly mentions this) to be brought to the Capital. The matter is said to have been debated in the Senate, in the consulship of Appius Claudius and Quintus Caecilius, Marcus Lepidus acting as spokesman for the Board of Decemvirs; and three years later the matter is said to have been brought up again by Lucius Lentulus, in the consulship of Gaius Laelius and Quintus Servilius, but on both occasions the influence of Marcius Rex carried the day; and thus, water was brought to the Capital. (*Frontin.Aq*.1.7)

Seneca the Younger tells Lucilius about the conditions of the bath of Scipio, the conqueror of Carthage. Unlike the baths of his day, bathers had no one to pour water over them, and neither did they have the luxury of clean, hot water from fresh sources.

I have inspected the house, which is constructed of hewn stone; the wall which encloses a forest; the towers also, buttressed out on both sides for the purpose of defending the house; the well, concealed among buildings and shrubbery, large enough to keep a whole army supplied; and the small bath, buried in darkness according to the old style, for our ancestors did not think that one could have a hot bath except in darkness. It was therefore a great pleasure to me to contrast Scipio's ways with our own. Think, in this tiny recess the "terror of Carthage," to whom Rome should offer thanks because she was not captured more than once, used to bathe a body wearied with work in the fields! For he was accustomed to keep himself busy and to cultivate the soil with his own hands, as the good old Romans were wont to do. Beneath this dingy roof he stood; and this floor, mean as it is, bore his weight.

But who in these days could bear to bathe in such a fashion? We think ourselves poor and mean if our walls are not resplendent with large and costly mirrors; if our marbles from Alexandria are not set off by mosaics of Numidian stone, if their borders are not faced over on all sides with difficult patterns, arranged in many colors like paintings; if our vaulted ceilings are not buried in glass; if our swimming-pools are not lined with Thasian marble, once a rare and wonderful sight in any temple pools into which we let down our bodies after they have been drained weak by abundant perspiration; and finally, if the water has not poured from silver spigots. I have so far been speaking of the ordinary bathing-establishments; what shall I say when I come to those of the freedmen? What a vast number of statues, of columns that support nothing, but are built for decoration, merely in order to spend money! And what masses of water that fall crashing from level to level! We have become so luxurious that we will have nothing but precious stones to walk upon.

In this bath of Scipio's there are tiny chinks—you cannot call them windows—cut out of the stone wall in such a way as to admit light without weakening the fortifications; nowadays, however, people regard baths as fit only for moths if they have not been so arranged that they receive the sun all day long through the widest of windows, if men cannot bathe and get a coat of tan at the same time, and if they cannot look out from their bath-tubs over stretches of land and sea. So it goes; the establishments which had drawn crowds and had won admiration when they were first opened are avoided and put back in the category of venerable antiques as soon as luxury has worked out some new device, to her own ultimate undoing. In the early days, however, there were few baths, and they were not fitted out with any display. For why should men elaborately fit out that which costs a penny only, and was invented for use, not merely for delight? The bathers of those days did not have water poured over them, nor did it always run fresh as if from a hot spring. *(Sen.Lucil.86.4–9)*

*Ancient writers such as Celsus also thought highly of bathing: "It is well also at times to go to the baths to make use of cold waters" (*Cels.Med.*1.2).*

*Celsus also noted: "The bath also is sometimes beneficial, but only after a scanty meal" (*Cels.Med.*3.22).*

Celsus recommended the baths as a treatment for many types of ailments and illnesses such as diarrhea:

If it stops of itself, the patient should make use of the bath, and take a little food; if it persists, he should abstain, not only from food, but even from drink. If on the day following, in spite of all, the stool is still liquid, he should rest as before and take a little astringent food. On the third day he should go to the bath. (*Cels.Med.*4.26)

What Really Happened

Roman writers justifiably admired the Cloaca Maxima as an engineering marvel. Yet, despite the Romans' ability to create and maintain an elaborate and outstanding water system to remove waste, its effectiveness on health and hygiene has been overestimated. Because the ancient Roman sanitation system was not hygienic in the modern sense of the word and did not reflect an understanding of the connection between bacteria and illness, it had limited efficacy in terms of public health.

True, it did remove stagnant water and other refuse from the streets, resulting in decreased stench and fewer mosquitos. Yet the sewers had flaws, such as being uncovered, which allowed animals such as rats and other vermin access to houses. Aelian illustrated this danger in an extremely colorful manner in the tale of an octopus swimming into a house to eat pickled fish (*Ael.NA.*13.6). In addition, sewers were not self-cleaning and tended to build up slime and sludge, which in turn could cause an unpleasant odor, create methane gas, and cause explosions. The Tiber flooded annually, causing the Cloaca to become inundated with water that would back up into homes. Another hazard was its slippery surface. Suetonius reported that Crates of Mallos (*Suet.Gram.Et.Rhet.*2) broke his leg after falling into the sewer. Trajan ordered Pliny to cover the "river" at Amastris because it was clogged with waste (*Plin.Ep*.10.98–99). Trajan suggested that prisoners and slaves perform routine cleanings to alleviate these problems. A bigger danger to public health was the disposal of corpses into the sewers. According to the *Historia Augusta*, Elgabalus was dumped into the sewer after being assassinated (*SHA.Heliogab*.17.1.3). Suetonius reported that Nero "would attack men on their way home from dinner, stab them if they offered resistance, and then drop them into the sewer" (*Suet.Ner*.26.1). People disposed of corpses despite stone markers warning against dumping sewage and corpses in defined areas. Disposing of the dead in the sewers or the Tiber was customary, however, and certainly did nothing to improve hygiene.

Public sewers like the Cloaca were State maintained. Private owners were liable for private ones as well as storefronts. Although ancient Romans tried to keep the streets clean, the absence of official street cleaning made this difficult. Instead, dogs disposed of excrement, street refuse, and corpses. These same dogs, however, defecated in the streets and were disease carriers.

A dog carrying a human hand in its mouth, which it placed under the table, interrupted Vespasian's repast (*Suet.Vesp*.1.5.4). Martial described the last moments of a dying beggar as he flapped his rags at birds while listening to dogs howling in anticipation of their next meal (*Epigram*. 10.5.11).

Most tenements and private homes had cesspits near the kitchen. Cesspits were malodorous and subject to major infections, despite regular manual cleansing. The contents were mixed with animal excrement to fertilize fields. However, the use of human excrement as fertilizer also increased the risk of food and water contamination without proper composting. In addition, many people lived in poorly built and minimally maintained apartments. These dwellings might have had a communal toilet. Tenants could risk their lives using the public toilets (*Juv*.3.299–305) or use chamber pots that they emptied in large pots on the street, or directly onto the street. Many people found it easier to throw the contents of these pots out of the windows onto streets below. For the unsuspecting victim, this shower was extremely annoying, according to Juvenal:

> And now regard the different and diverse perils of the night. See what a height it is to that towering roof from which a potsherd comes crack upon my head every time that some broken or leaky vessel is pitched out of the window! See with what a smash it strikes and dints the pavement! There's

death in every open window as you pass along at night; you may well be deemed a fool, improvident of sudden accident, if you go out to dinner without having made your will. You can but hope, and put up a piteous prayer in your heart, that they may be content to pour down on you the contents of their slop-pails! (*Juv*.3.299–305)

Feckless indeed was the law forbidding contamination of the public water supply or the soiling of anyone with dung or filth (*Dig*.47.11.1). Caligula ignored this law when, according to Suetonius, he had Vespasian smeared with muck when he served as an aedile, because Caligula thought Vespasian was not keeping the streets clean (*Suet.Vesp*.5.3).

The lack of street cleanliness led to flies and germs. Flies were rampant, and slaves had to shoo flies from landing on guests' food (*Epigram*. 3.82.12). Rain cleaned the streets somewhat during the winter months, but overall it was not enough to improve the health of the community.

Public toilets may have been convenient, but they also provided no health benefits to the Romans. Dark, dirty, poorly ventilated toilets offered little privacy, as men and women used the same facilities. The biggest danger to health was the use of the Roman equivalent of toilet paper: a sponge on the end of a stick. Although the small water channel at floor level may have been used to rinse the sponge or wash one's hands, reusable sponges were a breeding ground for bacteria. Seneca related the story of the *bestiarius* who committed suicide after years of mistreatment by shoving the latrine sponge down his throat (*Sen.Lucil*.70.20–21). Martial referred to the "luckless sponge on a doomed stick" (*Epigram*.12.48.7).

However, of bigger peril for users was the fear of explosions caused by the buildup of methane gas, which could not escape fast enough from the toilets' tiny windows. Toilets were poorly lit, full of stench, difficult to navigate, and home to small biting creatures. Even more frightening, the Romans believed demons could emerge from the depths of the latrine. Visitors could use an image of the goddess Fortuna to ward them off.

Furthermore, urine collected from the public toilets was placed in terracotta pots set out in the streets for the fullers, akin to a drycleaner, to retrieve the contents, which were used to clean togas. This method of procuring urine was very unhygienic. Many times the porous, unglazed terracotta jars burst and spilled their contents onto the streets.

Unfortunately, visiting the public baths was no remedy, as they posed significant health risks of their own. Because sick people visited the baths for various diseases, bathers had a high risk of being infected with contagious diseases. Bacteria spread in pools with sick people. Hadrian was so concerned about the practice of ill people bathing with the healthy that he passed legislation against it. Hadrian's biographer said the emperor ordained that the sick use the baths before the eighth hour (*SHA.Hadr.* 22.7).

Pools were probably drained and cleaned, but it is not clear how often. Water was contaminated with skin oils, bodily fluids, and waste. Celsus cautioned against the dangers of gangrene if one bathed with open sores (*Cels.Med.*5.26.28). The instrument used to scrape dead skin and dirt and then fling it on the walls was another source of germs. Because of these common conditions, the public baths did not improve hygiene.

The Roman sanitation system did not survive the fall of the Empire. Some aqueducts in former provinces were maintained. Pope Nicholas V renovated others in 1453. Ancient Romans were seriously concerned about sanitation and fresh drinking water in order to prevent illness. However, although sewers, toilets, and baths contributed to an overall improvement in *sanitation*, their presence, as well as that of aqueducts and fountains, did little to improve *health* for the population.

While Romans did not have the same understanding of hygiene as the modern world, thus creating certain public health problems, the ancient Roman sanitation system was a superlative engineering feat.

PRIMARY DOCUMENTS

Rome's sewer system was an ancient marvel. There were laws requiring clean water.

The Praetor placed two interdicts under this title, one of which is prohibitory, and the other restitutory and he first discusses the one which is prohibitory.

By means of these interdicts, the Praetor provides that sewers shall be cleaned and repaired, and both of them have reference to the health and protection of cities; for the filth of the sewers threatens to render the atmosphere pestilential and ruin buildings. The same rule applies even when the sewers are not repaired. (*Dig.*43.23.1–2)

Conduits are opposed to ditches, and are for the purpose of conducting and forcing water from a stream, whether they are of wood, stone, or any other material whatsoever. They were invented for the purpose of containing and conveying water. (*Dig.*43.21.4)

Despite maintenance regulations, there were times "when the sewers had been neglected and were no longer passable for the water, the censors let out the cleaning and repairing of them at a thousand talents" (Dion.Hal.Ant.Rom. 3.67).

A safe sanitation system was easier said than done as indicated by this entertaining account. Uncovered sewers allowed vermin easy access to homes.

Octopuses naturally, with the lapse of time, attain enormous proportions and approach cetaceans and are actually reckoned as such. At any rate, I learn of an octopus at Dicaearchia in Italy which attained to a monstrous bulk and scorned and despised food from the sea and such pasturage as it provided. And so, this creature actually came out onto the land and seized things there. Now it swam up through a subterranean sewer that discharged the refuse of the aforesaid city into the sea and emerged in a house on the shore where some Iberian merchants had their cargo, that is, pickled fish from that country in immense jars: it threw its tentacles round the earthenware vessels and with its grip broke them and feasted on the pickled fish. And when the merchants entered and saw the broken pieces, they realized that a large quantity of their cargo had disappeared; and they were amazed and could not guess who had robbed them: they saw that no attempt had been made upon the doors; the room was undamaged; the walls had not been broken through. They also saw the remains of the pickled fish that had been left behind by the uninvited guest. So, they decided to have their most courageous servant armed and waiting in ambush in the house. Well, during the night the octopus crept up to its accustomed meal and clasping the vessels, as an athlete puts a stranglehold upon his adversary with his might gripping firmly, the robber—if I may so call the octopus—crushed the earthenware with the greatest ease. It was full moon, and the house was full of light, and everything was quite visible. But the servant was not attacking the brute single handed as he was afraid, moreover his adversary was too big for one man, but in the morning, he informed the merchants what had happened. They could not believe their ears. Then some of them remembering how much they had lost, were for risking the danger and were eager to encounter their enemy, while others in their thirst for this singular and incredible spectacle voluntarily shut themselves up with their companions in order to help them. Later in the evening the marauder paid his visit and made for his usual feast. Thereupon some of them closed off the conduit. (*Ael.NA.*13.6)

Open sewers could also cause injury to unsuspecting pedestrians.

In my opinion then, the first to introduce the study of grammar into our city was Crates of Mallos, a contemporary of Aristarchus. He was sent to the Senate by King Attalus between the Second and Third Punic Wars, at about the time when Ennius died; and having fallen into the opening of a sewer in the Palatine quarter and broken his leg. (*Suet.Gram.Et.Rhet.*2)

Uncovered gutters were bad for the public's well-being. Pliny informs Trajan of "a sewer of the foulest kind" (Plin.Ep.*10.98*).

This is not only an eyesore because it is so disgusting to look at, but it is a danger to health from its shocking smells. For these reasons, both for the sake of health and appearance, it ought to be covered over.

Trajan tells him to cover it because "if by remaining uncovered it endangers the public health" (Plin.Ep.*10.98–99*).
　Dumping bodies was another threat to health: "[Nero] used to beat men as they came home from dinner, stabbing any who resisted him and throwing them into the sewers" (Suet.Ner.*26*).
　Dropping corpses into the water system was all too common. The Emperor Elgabalus was killed in a latrine. "But since the sewer chanced to be too small to admit the corpse, they attached a weight to it to keep it from floating, and hurled it from the Aemilian Bridge into the Tiber, in order that it might never be buried" (SHA.Heliogab.*17.1–2*).
　Rotting bodies left on the roads were another harm to one's well-being. Scavenging dogs ate whatever was available. A canine interrupted Vespasian during his morning meal: "Once when he was taking breakfast, a stray dog brought in a human hand from the crossroads and dropped it under the table" (Suet.Vesp.*5.4.1*).
　It was against the law to throw waste into the water system. "An injury is committed against good morals, for instance, where one person throws manure upon another, or smears him with filth, or mud: or defiles water, canals or reservoirs; or fouls anything for the purpose of injuring the public; and upon persons of this kind it is customary to inflict the most condign punishment" (Dig.*47.11.1*).
　Obviously, Gaius Caesar (Caligula) did not get the message: "Later, when Vespasian was aedile, Gaius Caesar, incensed at his neglect of his duty of cleaning the streets, ordered that he be covered with mud, which the soldiers accordingly heaped upon the bosom of his purple bordered toga; this some

*interpreted as an omen that one day in some civil commotion his country, trampled underfoot and forsaken, would come under his protection and as it were into his embrace" (*Suet.Vesp.5.3*).*

Similar to the modern world, ancient Romans of all classes had access to hot baths. Roman bathing complexes contained a series of pools. The frigidarium was unheated, while the second pool used by patrons was the tepidarium (tepid water). Vents were connected to the tepidarium and the caldarium, which was similar to a modern sauna. The hypocaust system, or underfloor heating technique, was very efficient. Seneca comments on the heated pools used in the baths.

Reason did indeed devise all these things, but it was not right reason. It was man, but not the wise man, that discovered them; just as they invented ships, in which we cross rivers and seas—ships fitted with sails for the purpose of catching the force of the winds, ships with rudders added at the stern in order to turn the vessel's course in one direction or another. The model followed was the fish, which steers itself by its tail, and by its slightest motion on this side or on that bends its swift course. "But," says Posidonius, "the wise man did indeed discover all these things; they were, however, too petty for him to deal with himself and so he entrusted them to his meaner assistants." Not so; these early inventions were thought out by no other class of men than those who have them in charge today. We know that certain devices have come to light only within our own memory—such as the use of windows which admit the clear light through transparent tiles, and such as the vaulted baths, with pipes let into their walls for the purpose of diffusing the heat which maintains an even temperature in their lowest as well as in their highest spaces. Why need I mention the marble with which our temples and our private houses are resplendent? Or the rounded and polished masses of stone by means of which we erect colonnades and buildings roomy enough for nations? Or our signs for whole words, which enable us to take down a speech, however rapidly uttered, matching speed of tongue by speed of hand? All this sort of thing has been devised by the lowest grade of slaves. (*Sen.Lucil.*90.24–5)

Vitruvius thought highly of the baths. The floor was raised up to provide an empty space for a furnace. The heating system burned wood that in turn heated the tiles, which retained heat.

First, as warm a spot as possible is to be selected, that is to say, one sheltered from the north and the north-east. The hot and tepid baths are to receive their light from the winter west; but if the nature of the place prevents that, at all events from the south, because the hours of bathing are principally from noon to evening. Care must be taken that the warm baths of the women and the men adjoin, and have the same aspect; in which case the same furnace and vessels will serve both. The cauldrons over the furnaces are to be three in number, one for hot water, another for tepid water, and a third for cold water: and they must be so arranged, that hot water which runs out of the heated vessel, may be replaced by an equal quantity from the tepid vessel, which in like manner is supplied from the cold vessel, and that the arched cavities in which they stand may be heated by one fire. The floors of the hot baths are to be made as follows. First, the bottom is paved with tiles of a foot and a half inclining towards the furnace, so that if a ball be thrown into it, it will not remain there, but roll back to the mouth of the furnace; thus, the flame will better spread out under the floor. Upon this, piers of eight-inch bricks are raised, at such a distance from each other, that two tiles of two-feet in height, are to be laid in clay mixed with hair, on which the above mentioned two-feet tiles are placed, which carry the pavement. (*Vitr.de.Arch.5.10.1–2*)

Martial complains that the baths could be too hot. "Now the warm baths have acquired a proper temperature; at the preceding hour they exhaled an intolerable excess of steam; at the sixth the heat of the baths of Nero is unsupportable" (Epigram.10.48).

Republican Romans were modest farmers who were uncorrupted by the pleasures of the east. Seneca prefers Scipio Africanus's humble bath in his unassuming villa as opposed to the lavishness of his own day.

In the early days, however, there were few baths, and they were not fitted out with any display. For why should men elaborately fit out that which costs a penny only, and was invented for use, not merely for delight? The bathers of those days did not have water poured over them, nor did it always run fresh as if from a hot spring; and they did not believe that it mattered at all how perfectly pure was the water into which they were to leave their dirt. Ye gods, what a pleasure it is to enter that dark bath, covered with a common sort of roof, knowing that therein your hero Cato, as aedile, or Fabius Maximus, or one of the Cornelii, has warmed the water with his own hands! For this also used to be the duty of the noblest aediles—to enter these places to which the populace resorted, and to demand that they be cleaned and warmed to a heat required by considerations of use and health, not the heat that men have recently made fashionable, as great as a conflagration—so much so, indeed, that a slave condemned for some criminal offence now ought to be *bathed* alive! It seems to me that nowadays there is no difference between "the bath is on fire," and "the bath is warm."

How some persons nowadays condemn Scipio as a boor because he did not let daylight into his perspiring-room through wide windows, or because he did not roast in the strong sunlight and dawdle about until he could stew in the hot water! "Poor fool," they say, "he did not know how to live! He did not bathe in filtered water; it was often turbid, and after heavy rains almost muddy!" But it did not matter much to Scipio if he had to bathe in that way; he went there to wash off sweat, not ointment. And how do you suppose certain persons will answer me? They will say: "I don't envy Scipio; that was truly an exile's life – to put up with baths like those!" Friend, if you were wiser, you would know that Scipio did not bathe every day. It is stated by those who have reported to us the old-time ways of Rome that the Romans washed only their arms and legs daily—because those were the members which gathered dirt in their daily toil—and bathed all over only once a week. Here someone will retort: "Yes; pretty dirty fellows they evidently were! How they must have smelled!" But they smelled of the camp, the farm, and heroism. Now that spick-and-span bathing establishments have been devised, men are really fouler than of yore. What says Horatius Flaccus, when he wishes to describe a scoundrel, one who is notorious for his extreme luxury? He says: "Buccillus smells of perfume." Show me a Buccillus in these days; his smell would be the veritable goat-smell—he would take the place of the Gargonius with whom Horace in the same passage contrasted him. It is nowadays not enough to use ointment, unless you put on a fresh coat two or three times a day, to keep it from evaporating on the body. But why should a man boast of this perfume as if it were his own? (*Sen.Lucil.* 86.9–13)

Baths were like the modern health club. You could socialize, get a bath, and sweat while eating sweets or meats. They were also very loud. Poor Seneca lived above a bathhouse.

I have lodgings right over a bathing establishment. So, picture to yourself the assortment of sounds, which are strong enough to make me hate my very powers of hearing! When your strenuous gentleman, for example, is exercising himself by flourishing leaden weights; when he is working hard, or else pretends to be working hard, I can hear him grunt; and whenever he releases his imprisoned breath, I can hear him panting in wheezy and high-pitched tones. Or perhaps I notice some lazy fellow, content with a cheap rubdown, and hear the crack of the pummeling hand on his shoulder, varying in sound according as the hand is laid on flat or hollow. Then, perhaps, a professional comes along, shouting out the score; that is the finishing touch. Add to this the arresting of an occasional roysterer [partyer] or pickpocket, the racket of the man who always likes to hear his own voice in the bathroom, or the enthusiast who plunges into the swimming-tank with unconscionable noise and splashing. Besides all those whose voices, if nothing else, are good, imagine the hair-plucker with his penetrating, shrill voice—for purposes of advertisement—continually giving it vent and never holding his tongue except when he is plucking the armpits and making his victim yell instead. Then the cake-seller with his varied cries, the sausage-man, the confectioner, and all the vendors of food hawking their wares, each with his own distinctive intonation. (*Sen.Lucil.*56.1–2)

Despite the marvels of heated baths, they were not the cleanest places. Marcus Aurelius has his reservations about taking a dip. "Such as bathing appears to thee—oil, sweat, dirt, filthy water, all things disgusting—so is every part of life and every-thing" (M.Aur.Med.*24.8*).

Tiberius Claudius Secondus, a former slave and slave trader, lauds the social aspects of the bathhouses. "Baths, wine, and sex corrupt our bodies, but baths, wine, and sex make life worth living" (Har.CILVI.*15258*).

Two men from Herculaneum enjoyed extracurricular activities. "Two friends were here. While they were, they had bad service in every way from a guy named Epaphroditus. They threw him out and spent 105 and half sestertii most agreeably on whores" (Har.Herc.*10675*).

Roman latrines were another place to gossip, as suggested by Martial. Individuals might be subject to ridicule.

You are afraid, Ligurra, lest I should compose verses on you, some short and pungent epigram, and you wish to be thought a proper object of such rear. But vain is your fear. and vain your desire! Libyan lions rush upon bulls; they do not hurt butterflies. If you aim at getting your name into verse, seek, I advise you, some sort of a poet from some dark den, who writes, with coarse charcoal and crumbling chalk, verses which people read as they ease (relieve) themselves. Your brow is not to be branded with my mark. (*Epigram.*12.61)

Fear of derision is one reason that Tiberius did not allow anyone "to carry a ring or coin stamped with his image into a privy or a brothel, or to criticize any word or act of his" (Suet.Tib.58).

Besides granting him [Julius Caesar] these honors, they made the day on which he had been murdered, a day on which there had always been a regular meeting of the senate, an unlucky day. The room in which he had been murdered they closed for the time being and later transformed into a privy [toilet]. (*Dio.Cass.*47.19)

Further Reading

Koloski-Ostrow, Ann Olga, *The Archaeology of Sanitation in Roman Italy: Toilets, Sewers, and Water Systems. Studies in the History of Greece and Rome.* Edited by Robin Osborne, James Rives, and Richard J. A. Talbert. The University of North Carolina Press, Chapel Hill, 2015.

Koloski-Ostrow, Ann Olga, "Talking Heads: What Toilets and Sewers Tell Us about Ancient Roman Sanitation," *The Conversation.* November 19, 2015. https://theconversation.com/talking-heads-what-toilets-and-sewers-tell-us-about-ancient-roman-sanitation-50045

PBS, *A Day at the Baths.* (The PBS TV program *Nova* has an excellent website discussing the Roman baths. The highlight is a virtual tour of the imperial Roman baths at Caracalla.) www.pbs.org/wgbh/nova/lostempires/roman/day.html

Schram, Wilke, van Opstal, and Passchier, Cees, *Roman Aqueducts.* www.romanaqueducts.info/index.html

Scobie, Alex, "Slums, Sanitation, and Mortality in the Roman World," *KLIO*, Vol. 68 (1986), pp. 399–433.

Wald, Chelsea, "Ancient Rome's Terrorizing Toilets," *Discover Magazine.* July/August 2014. http://discovermagazine.com/2014/julyaug/4-archeological-crap-shoot

Wald, Chelsea, "The Secret History of Ancient Toilets," *Nature.* May 24, 2016. https://www.nature.com/news/the-secret-history-of-ancient-toilets-1.19960

9

Not All Gladiators Were Slaves

What People Think Happened

Gladiatorial games and blood sport are synonymous with ancient Rome. According to popular imagination, slaves fought to the death in order to please the Roman mobs. If they refused to fight, they would be killed. Famously, Spartacus was a slave and gladiator who revolted because of mistreatment. Gladiators were despised. For example, Cicero described them as "either debased men or foreigners" (*Cic.Tusc.*2.41). Tacitus agreed that appearing in the arena was one of the "vices in this city, which seem to me to be practically born in the womb: the obsession with actors and the passion for gladiatorial shows" (*Tac.Agr.*29).

Many people believe that the lot of the gladiator was miserable indeed. He lived in horrible conditions and had a very short life. Gladiators entered the arena knowing that only one of them would survive. Before entering the arena, they passed in front of the emperor and shouted the gladiatorial oath: "*Ave imperator moriuri te salutant*" ("Hail Caesar! those about to die salute you"). After they uttered this cry, the bloodbath began.

In order to remain popular, the emperor usually did what the mob wanted, giving rise to the saying, "The outcome of every fight is death" (*Sen.Lucil.*7.4). When the unruly rabble demanded that a gladiator slaughter his opponent, it yelled, "Kill him or cut his throat." Then, once the fatal blow was struck, the masses screamed, "He's had it!"

Juvenal described the power of the mob: "[T]oday they hold shows of their own and win applause by slaying whomsoever the crowd, with a turn, of the thumb, bids them slay" (*Juv.*3.34–37). The mob, he complained, no longer cared for anything and "now restrains itself and anxiously hopes for just two things: 'bread and circuses'" (*Juv.*10.77–81).

People also generally think that animals and Christians appeared in the arena for sport. Eusebius tells the fate of the martyrs "if they persisted in the profession of Christianity" (*Euseb.Hist.Ecc.*8.2.4). "They were then killed for not worshipping the emperor." Eusebius described the fate of Procopius: "[W]hen he was commanded to offer libations to the four emperors, having quoted a sentence which displeased them, he was immediately beheaded" (*Euseb.Hist.Ecc.*1.1). In addition, churches were destroyed and many people were martyred by the Romans in Phoenicia, Egypt and in Thebais (*Euseb.Hist.Ecc.*6.6).

Christians were to blame for every natural disaster and thus the origin of the despicable utterance: "'The Christians to the lion.' What! So many of them to the lion" (*Tert.Apol.*40). The emperor Nero had many believers torn apart by dogs (*Tac.Ann.*15.44.4). Many were condemned to a particularly gruesome death at the hands of wild beasts. Ignatius wrote, "Suffer me to become food for the wild beasts" (*Ign.Ant.Rom.*4.1).

Another victim, Blandina, was one of many Christians killed in Lyon in 177 CE. She was tied to a stake and set upon by wild animals, scourged, and tossed into the air by a wild bull before being killed. Another victim was Saint Perpetua, a Roman noblewoman, and her slave, Felicity, who were martyred in the arena in Carthage under Septimius Severus at the celebration of the birthday party for his son, "Geta the Caesar."

The final sufferer was St. Telemachus, an Eastern monk who was stoned to death by the angry mob for trying to stop a gladiatorial fight (*Theod. Hist.Ecc.*26). After this happened, the Emperor Honorius banned the games in 404 CE. Thus, many people assume that suffering and slaughter are the bloody legacy of cruel gladiatorial games.

How the Story Became Popular

Despite the fact that movies and television have made gladiators popular, they have also perpetuated a number of misconceptions about them, mostly based on a narrow set of historic documents. For instance, many think gladiators were slaves who fought frequently. Others imagine that all matches led to the death. People believe that emperors sponsored games to pacify the unruly masses, who cheered the slaughter of Christians in the arena. No wonder, then, that most people consider the Romans to be cruel, brutish pagans.

Roman accounts of Spartacus created the view that gladiators were all slaves who fought to the death. Plutarch included him in the *Life of Crassus*, while Appian mentioned Spartacus in his *Civil Wars*. Spartacus was a Thracian sentenced to the arena (*App.B.Civ.*14.116.1). Plutarch said maltreatment caused the revolt of which Spartacus was a part: "[T]hrough no misconduct of theirs, but owing to the injustice of their owner, they were kept in close confinement and reserved for gladiatorial combats" (*Plut.Vit.Crass.*8.1). They fled captivity and their shameful lives as slaves. Plutarch stresses that the slaves exchanged their arms for real weapons: "[T]hey gladly took these in exchange for their own, casting away their gladiatorial weapons as dishonorable and barbarous" (*Plut.Vit.Crass.*9.1). Spartacus "persuaded about seventy of his fellows to risk their lives for freedom rather than for exhibition as a spectacle" (*App.B.Civ.*14.116.1). Initially, the elite did not take the war seriously "as being merely the work of gladiators" (*App.B.Civ.*14.118.1). Crassus was the only volunteer to fight the slaves. Spartacus was killed by the army of Crassus (*App.B.Civ.*14.119, *Plut.Vit.Crass.*11). In the aftermath Crassus crucified six thousand prisoners along the Appian Way from Capua to Rome as punishment (*App.B.Civ.*14.120).

Cicero is another writer who implied that all gladiator matches ended in death. He described them as "debased men or foreigners and consider the blows they endure." Furthermore, as good slaves, "if they have given satisfaction to their masters, they are pleased to fall" (*Cic.Tusc.*2.41).

Seneca's writings also promote the notion that gladiators fought to the death. He commented on the poor quality of life: "Do you regard as more fortunate the fighter who is slain on the last day of the games than one who goes to his death in the middle of the festivities?" (*Sen.Lucil.*93.12). Their lot was so bad: "Do they fight to the death? That is not enough. Are they torn to pieces? That is not enough. Let them be crushed by animals of monstrous bulk" (*Sen.De.Brev.*13.6). And finally, he stated simply, "The outcome of every fight is death" (*Sen.Lucil.*7.4).

Dio Cassius reported that Claudius loved watching gladiators die "so he could watch their faces as they died" (*Suet.Claud.*34.1). Juvenal's much-cited phrase implies how the populace cared only for "Bread and circuses!" (*Juv.*10.77–81). According to Cicero, "such entertainment is demanded by the people, men of right judgment must at least consent to furnish it" (*Cic.Off.*2.58). Juvenal also played a role in spreading the myth that all bouts ended in the death of one gladiator: "[T]oday they hold shows of their own, and win applause by slaying with the turn of the thumb whomsoever the mob bids them slay, seeing that they are of the kind that Fortune raises from the gutter to the mighty places of Earth whenever she wishes to enjoy a laugh" (*Juv.*3).

Suetonius is another source who has led to the notion that gladiators destined to die in the arena screamed the gladiatorial oath: "Hail Caesar! Those who are about to die salute you" (*Suet.Claud.*21.6). The notion that Charon and Mercury dragged off dead gladiators by hooks is based on Tertullian (*Tert.Apol.*15.4).

The myth that Christian martyrs were killed for cruel amusement in the arena stems from Christian sources such as Tertullian, who claimed that Christians were always to blame for any ill: "If the Tiber rises too high for the walls, or the Nile too low for the fields, if the heavens do not open, or the Earth does, if there is a famine, if there is a plague, instantly the howl is 'The Christians to the lion!' What, all of them, to a single lion?" (*Tert.Apol.*40).

Lactantius (250–325 CE) wrote *On the Death of the Persecutors*, which describes the martyrs killed by Nero. This source has led to the misunderstanding that the persecution of Christians by Romans was commonplace. "He [Nero] was who first persecuted the servants of God; he crucified Peter and slew Paul" (*Lact.De.Mort.Pers.*2).

Eusebius described the deaths of Blandina and her companions in his *Ecclesiastical History* as well as in *The Letter from the Churches of Vienna and Lyon to the Churches of Asia and Phrygia*, which has perpetuated the view that Christians were martyred for not worshipping the emperor. Eusebius explicitly describes how Blandina was tortured for several days. She died after "she had been scourged and exposed to the wild beasts, and roasted in the iron chair, she was at last enclosed in a net and cast before a bull. She was tossed by the bull" (*Euseb.Hist.Ecc.*5.1).

The Martyrdom of Perpetua and Felicitas is the prison journal of a young Roman noblewoman and her slave who were killed in 203 CE at Carthage. Its grisly details imply that Perpetua and her companions were killed for their faith. For example, Perpetua was told to offer a sacrifice but said, "I will not." Hilarian, the governor, asked, "Are you a Christian?" And she said, "Yes, I am." Next, "Hilarian passed sentence on all of us: we were condemned to the beasts, and we returned to prison in high spirits" (*August. Perp.*6, *Tert.Mart.*2).

Salvian was a Christian writer who lived in the fifth century. His best-known work is *On the Governances of God*. In it, he reveals the savage cruelty of the Romans: denying innocent Christians a decent burial. Moreover, Christians were ripped to shreds and then devoured by wild animals. He laments the malice and brutality of the martyrs: "In these the greatest pleasure is to have men die, or, what is worse and more cruel than death, to have them torn in pieces, to have the bellies of wild beasts gorged with human flesh" (*Salv.De.Guber.Dei*.6.2.10).

Even artists in subsequent centuries perpetuated the myths of the Roman gladiator. For example, Jean-Léon Gérôme was a highly respected painter known for historically correct art. His painting *Pollice Verso* depicts a gladiator standing over the body of his opponent. The Vestal Virgins give the sign to the victor. As a result, even today people believe "thumbs down" meant death.

Spectacles were popular in Rome, certainly. Gladiators were loathed by the elite for performing in public, yet admitted for bravery. Still, Victorian historical novels, such as *Quo Vadis*, and the Hollywood film industry are mostly to blame for modern society's continued fascination with gladiators as well as for the continuation of the popular misconceptions about them.

PRIMARY DOCUMENTS

Elite Romans despised gladiators because of their low status and because they were forced to fight in the arena. It was a very tough, harsh life. The earliest gladiators were slaves, foreign prisoners of war, or criminals.

Plutarch's account stresses Spartacus's status. Plutarch and most elite Romans looked down on slaves and gladiators. Describing Spartacus as "more Hellenic than Thracian" was a way of saying that Spartacus was smarter and therefore more civilized than the other slaves. At the same time, Plutarch expresses admiration and respect for Spartacus for his bravery and leadership skills. He reports that abuse and confinement of the slave gladiators were the catalysts of the rebellion. The slave revolt shook the Romans and changed the way that Romans dealt with slaves.

The insurrection of the gladiators and their devastation of Italy, which is generally called the War of Spartacus, had its origin as follows. A certain Lentulus Batiatus had a school of gladiators at Capua, most of whom were Gauls and Thracians. Through no misconduct of their own, owing to the injustice of their owner, they were kept in close confinement and reserved for gladiatorial combats. Two-hundred of these planned to make their escape, and when information was laid against them, those who got wind of it and succeeded in getting away, seventy-eight in number, seized cleavers and spits from some kitchen and sallied out. On the road they fell in with wagons conveying gladiators' weapons to another city; these they plundered and armed themselves. They took up a strong position and elected leaders. The first of these was Spartacus, a Thracian of Nomadic stock, possessed not only of great courage and strength, but also in sagacity and culture superior to his fortune, and more Hellenic than Thracian. It is said that when he was first brought to Rome to be sold, a serpent was seen coiled about his face as he slept, and his wife, who was of the same tribe as Spartacus, a prophetess, and subject to visitations of the Dionysiac frenzy, declared it the sign of a great and formidable power which would attend him to a fortunate issue. The woman shared in his escape and was then living with him. (*Plut. Vit. Crass.*8)

Plutarch's Lives *depicts cases of good and bad conduct. To some extent, he respects Spartacus's military skills and considers him an equal to the various generals he was fighting against. However, overall Plutarch is harsh on Spartacus, who was a slave and not one to be emulated. The War of Spartacus was important only in depicting the glorious exploits of the Roman elites. This statement reflects his own biases against slaves and gladiators in general. The Senate had difficulty finding men to fight the rebellion because, as upper-class Romans, it was humiliating to lower themselves to battle the dregs of society.*

To begin with, the gladiators repulsed the soldiers who came against them from Capua, and getting hold of many arms of real warfare, they gladly took these in exchange for their own, casting away their gladiatorial weapons as dishonorable and barbarous. Then Clodius the praetor was sent out from Rome against them with three-thousand soldiers, and laid siege to them on a hill which had but one ascent, and that a narrow and difficult one, which Clodius closely watched; everywhere else there were smooth and precipitous cliffs. But the top of the hill was covered with a wild vine of abundant growth, from which the besieged cut off the serviceable branches, and wove these into strong ladders of such strength and length that when they were fastened at the top they reached along the face of the cliff to the plain below. On these they descended safely, all but one man, who remained above to attend to the arms. When the rest had got down, he began to drop the arms, and after he had thrown them all down, got away himself also last of all in safety. Of all this the Romans were ignorant, and therefore their enemy surrounded them, threw them into consternation by the suddenness of the attack, put them to flight, and took their camp. They were also joined by many of the herdsmen and shepherds of the region, sturdy men and swift of foot, some of whom they armed fully, and employed others as scouts and light infantry.

In the second place, Publius Varinus, the praetor, was sent out against them, whose lieutenant, a certain Furius, with two-thousand soldiers, they first engaged and routed; then Spartacus narrowly watched the movements of Cossinius, who had been sent out with a large force to advise and assist Varinus in the command, and came near seizing him as he was bathing near Salinae. Cossinius barely escaped with much difficulty, and Spartacus at once seized his baggage, pressed hard upon him in pursuit, and took his camp with great slaughter. Cossinius also fell. By defeating the praetor himself in many battles, and finally capturing his lictors and the very horse he rode, Spartacus was soon great and formidable; but he took a proper view of the situation, and since he could not expect to overcome the Roman power, began to lead his army toward the Alps, thinking it necessary for them to cross the mountains and go to their respective homes, some to Thrace, and some to Gaul. But his men were now strong in numbers and full of confidence, and would not listen to him, but went ravaging over Italy.

It was now no longer the indignity and disgrace of the revolt that harassed the Senate, but they were constrained by their fear and peril to send both consuls into the field, as they would to a war of the utmost difficulty and magnitude. Gellius, one of the consuls, fell suddenly upon the Germans, who were so insolent and bold as to separate themselves from the main body of Spartacus, and cut them all to pieces; but when Lentulus, the other consul, had surrounded the enemy with large forces, Spartacus rushed upon them, joined battle, defeated the legates of Lentulus, and seized all their baggage. Then, as he was forcing his way toward the Alps, he was met by Cassius, the governor of Cisalpine Gaul, with an army of ten-thousand men, and in the battle that ensued, Cassius was defeated and lost many men, and escaped himself with difficulty. (*Plut.Vit.Crass.*9)

Appian, too, considers gladiators as the scum of the Earth. Although to him Spartacus is a brave and competent leader, similar to Plutarch, he also views the uprising in negative terms because it was embarrassing to fight slaves. Spartacus, as a gladiator, was a nightmare figure who sought to overturn the established order of things.

Spartacus changed his intention of marching on Rome. He did not consider himself ready as yet for that kind of fight, as his whole force was not suitably armed, for no city had joined him, but only slaves, deserters, and riff-raff. However, he occupied the mountains around Thurii and took the city itself. He prohibited the bringing in of gold or silver by the merchants, and would not allow his own men to acquire any, but he bought largely of iron and brass and did not interfere with those who dealt in these articles. Supplied with abundant material from this source his men provided themselves with plenty of arms and made frequent forays for the time being. When they next came to an engagement with the Romans they were again victorious, and returned laden with spoils. This war, so formidable to the Romans (although ridiculed and despised at the beginning, as being merely the work of gladiators), had now lasted three years. When the election of new praetors came on, fear fell upon all, and nobody offered himself as a candidate until Licinius Crassus, a man distinguished among the Romans for birth and wealth, assumed the praetorship and marched against Spartacus with six new legions. When he arrived at his destination he received also the two legions of the consuls, whom he decimated by lot for their bad conduct in several battles. Some say that Crassus, too, having engaged in battle with his whole army, and having been defeated, decimated the whole army and was not deterred by their numbers, but destroyed about 4,000 of them. Whichever way it was, when he had once demonstrated to them that he was more dangerous to them than the enemy, he overcame immediately 10,000 of the Spartacans, who were encamped somewhere in a detached position, and killed two-thirds of them. He then marched boldly against Spartacus himself, vanquishing him in a brilliant engagement, and pursued his fleeing forces to the sea, where they tried to pass over to Sicily. He overtook them and enclosed them with a line of circumvallation consisting of ditch, wall and paling. (*App.B.Civ*.1.14.117–118)

Cicero expressed a similar hostile view of gladiators by referring to them as "debased men or foreigners and consider the blows they endure!"

Consider how they who have been well-disciplined prefer to accept a blow than ignominiously to avoid it! How often it is made clear that they consider nothing other than the satisfaction of their master or the people! Even when they are covered with wounds they send a messenger to their master to inquire his will. If they have given satisfaction to their masters, they are pleased to fall. What even mediocre gladiator ever groans, ever alters the expression on the face? Which of them acts shamefully, either standing or falling? And which of them, even when he does succumb, ever contracts his neck when ordered to receive the blow? (*Cic.Tusc*.2.41)

NOT ALL GLADIATORS WERE SLAVES

In this quote, Seneca protests fighters perishing in the arena.

Do you regard as more fortunate the fighter who is slain on the last day of the games than one who goes to his death in the middle of the festivities? Do you believe that anyone is so foolishly covetous of life that he would rather have his throat cut in the dressing-room than in the amphitheater? (*Sen.Lucil.* 93.12)

Seneca opposed the games and spoke out against them in this letter. He complains that it is killing just for killing's sake. The mob gets its thrills watching men massacred in a bloodbath.

But nothing is so damaging to good character as the habit of lounging at the games; for then it is that vice steals subtly upon one through the avenue of pleasure. What do you think I mean? I mean that I come home more greedy, more ambitious, more voluptuous, and even more cruel and inhuman, because I have been among human beings. By chance I attended a mid-day exhibition, expecting some fun, wit, and relaxation—an exhibition at which men's eyes have respite from the slaughter of their fellow-men. But it was quite the reverse. The previous combats were the essence of compassion; but now all the trifling is put aside, and it is pure murder. The men have no defensive armor. They are exposed to blows at all points, and no one ever strikes in vain. Many persons prefer this program to the usual pairs and to the bouts "by request." Of course, they do; there is no helmet or shield to deflect the weapon. What is the need of defensive armor, or of skill? All these mean delaying death. In the morning they throw men to the lions and the bears; at noon, they throw them to the spectators. The spectators demand that the slayer shall face the man who is to slay him in his turn; and they always reserve the latest conqueror for another butchering. The outcome of every fight is death, and the means are fire and sword. This sort of thing goes on while the arena is empty. You may retort: "But he was a highway robber; he killed a man!" And what of it? Granted that, as a murderer, he deserved this punishment, what crime have you committed, poor fellow, that you should deserve to sit and see this show? In the morning they cried, "Kill him! Lash him! Burn him! Why does he meet the sword in so cowardly a way? Why does he strike so feebly? Why doesn't he die game? Whip him to meet his wounds! Let them receive blow for blow, with chests bare and exposed to the stroke!" And when the games stop for the intermission, they announce: "A little throat cutting in the meantime, so that there may still be something going on!" (*Sen.Lucil.*7.2–5)

Roman politicians put on entertainment to please the crowds and get elected.

These men once were horn-blowers, who went the round of every provincial show, and whose puffed-out cheeks were known in every village; today they hold shows of their own, and win applause by slaying with a turn of the thumb whomsoever the mob bids them slay; from that they go back to contract for cesspools, and why not for any kind of thing, seeing that they are of the kind that Fortune raises from the gutter to the mighty places of Earth whenever she wishes to enjoy a laugh? (*Juv.*3.34)

"Bread and Circuses" is cited in many books to indicate that the Roman masses were interested only in entertainment such as the gladiatorial games. However, it was written in the context of the death of Sejanus. Juvenal saw power as fleeting and subject to the unpredictability of the finicky mob.

Lead forth a grand chalked bull to the Capital! Sejanus is being dragged along by a hook, as a show and joy to all! What a lip the fellow had! What a face! "Believe me, I never liked the man!" "But on what charge was he condemned? Who informed against him? What was the evidence, who the witnesses, who made the case?" "Nothing of the sort; a great and wordy letter came from Capri."—"Good; I ask no more."

And what does the mob of Remus say? It follows fortune, as it always does, and rails against the condemned. That same rabble, if Nortia had smiled upon the Etruscan, if the aged Emperor had been struck down unawares, would in that very hour have conferred upon Sejanus the title of Augustus. Now that no one buys our votes, the public has long since cast off its cares; the people that once bestowed commands, consulships, legions and all else, now meddles no more and longs eagerly for just two things—Bread and Circuses. (*Juv.*10.56–113)

Tacitus mentions how Nero blamed Christians for the Great Fire of 64 CE and had them killed in various venues for the fun of it.

Therefore, to scotch the rumor, Nero substituted as culprits, and punished with the utmost refinements of cruelty, a class of men, loathed for their vices, whom the crowd styled Christians. Christus, the founder of the name, had undergone the death penalty in the reign of Tiberius, by sentence of the procurator Pontius Pilatus, and the pernicious superstition was checked for a moment, only to break out once more, not merely in Judea, the home of the disease, but in the Capital itself, where all things horrible or shameful in the world collect and find a vogue. First, then, the confessed members of the sect were arrested; next, on their disclosures, vast numbers were convicted, not so much on the count of arson as for the hatred of the human race. And derision accompanied their end: they were covered with wild beasts' skins and torn to death by dogs; or they were fastened on crosses, and when daylight failed were burned to serve as lamps by night. Nero had offered his Gardens for the spectacle, and gave an exhibition in his Circus, mixing with the crowd in the habit of a Charioteer, or mounted on his car. (*Tac.Ann.*15.44)

Lactantius depicts innocents being slain for Christ by the evil emperor Nero.

His apostles were at that time eleven in number, to whom were added Matthias, in the room of the traitor Judas, and afterwards Paul. Then were they dispersed throughout all the Earth to preach the Gospel, as the Lord their Master had commanded them; and during twenty-five years, and until the beginning of the reign of the Emperor Nero, they occupied themselves in laying the foundations of the Church in every province and city. And while Nero reigned, the Apostle Peter came to Rome, and, through the power of God committed unto him, wrought certain miracles, and, by turning many to the true religion, built up a faithful and steadfast temple unto the Lord. When Nero heard of those things, and observed that not only in Rome, but in every other place, a great multitude revolted daily from the worship of idols, and, condemning their old ways, went over to the new religion, he, an execrable and pernicious tyrant, sprung forward to raze the heavenly temple and destroy the true faith. He it was who first persecuted the servants of God; he crucified Peter, and slew Paul: nor did he escape with impunity; for God looked on the affliction of His people; and therefore, the tyrant, bereaved of authority, and precipitated from the height of empire, suddenly disappeared, and even the burial-place of that noxious wild beast was nowhere to be seen. This has led some persons of extravagant imagination to suppose that, having been conveyed to a distant region, he is still reserved alive; and to him they apply the Sibylline verses concerning the fugitive, who slew his own mother, being to come from the uttermost boundaries of the Earth, as if he who was the first should also be the last persecutor, and thus prove the forerunner of Antichrist! (*Lact.De.Mort.Pers.*2)

Salvian saw the Romans as evil and completely depraved. Christians were killed as criminals in the arena. Their bodies were abused and mutilated. However, they were not consumed by animals.

In these the greatest pleasure is to have men die, or what is worse and more cruel than death, to have them torn to pieces, to have the bellies of wild beasts gorged with human flesh; to have men eaten, to the great joy of the bystanders and the delight of the onlookers, so that the victims seem devoured almost as much by the eyes of the audience as by the teeth of the beasts. That such things may take place the whole world is ransacked; great is the care with which the search is carried on and perfected. Hidden retreats are entered, pathless ravines are searched, impenetrable forests traversed, the cloud-bearing Alps are climbed, the depths of valleys plumbed, and in order that the flesh of men be devoured by wild animals, the last secrets of the world of nature are revealed. (*Salv.De.Guber.Dei*.6.2.10)

What Really Happened

Gladiatorial contests became a Roman form of entertainment, and the gladiators were its stars. Although some were captives or criminals, not all gladiators were slaves. In fact, many freemen and women volunteered to fight in the arena. Contrary to the popular view that gladiators were the scum of Roman society, their lives reveal the opposite.

For example, gladiatorial games were originally a funerary obligation. Nicolas of Damascus (*Nic.Dam.Athlet*.4.153, *Ath*.4.49) claimed the games originated in Etruria, while Livy places the starting point in Campania (*Livy.Ab.Urbe.Cond*.9.40). The first Roman bout, which featured three gladiator pairs, took place in 264 BCE in the Forum Boarum (*Livy.Ab.Urbe.Cond.Per*.16.6). Gladiatorial games became very popular and evolved into spectacles that the elite used to acquire favor with the masses (*Livy.Ab.Urbe.Cond*.39.22). For instance, Julius Caesar sponsored games featuring 320 gladiators. "By these means he put the people in such a humor that every man of them was seeking out new offices and new honors with which to requite him" (*Plut.Vit.Caes*.5.8–9). Sponsoring spectacles increased his popularity (*Suet.Caes*.39.3). Eventually, the emperor had to fund these spectacles because they became so expensive, such as the ones that Augustus sponsored featuring 10,000 gladiators (*Aug*.22).

It is true that the earliest gladiators were slaves, prisoners of war, or condemned criminals. As the games increased in popularity, however, volunteers willing to risk death for fame and fortune took the gladiatorial oath. As a result of this celebrity, gladiators began training extensively in schools. They were well cared for, well fed, and received medical treatment. Gladiators fought in pairs. Each was proficient in a specific fighting style. A *retiarius* fought with a net and trident, while his opponent, the *secutor*, was armed with a shield and a sword. Other popular gladiatorial types included the crested-helmeted *murmillo*-class gladiator and the *thraex*-style fighter. All levels of society enjoyed these spectacles. Games began early and were divided into three events during the course of the day. Gladiators fought in the afternoon and were the main attraction.

Moreover, most gladiators fought only a few times a year—and not to the death. Why train a gladiator only to have him killed? These contests were similar to the kind of combat sports that many cultures enjoy today. For example, gladiators were carefully matched in strength and skill. Each fighter tried to subdue his opponent, not kill him. Gladiators fought bravely and put on a good show. Referees made sure each combatant followed the rules. Music helped maintain the crowd's enthusiasm. Many fights ended in a draw. It was the editor or sponsor who took the crowd's reaction into consideration in deciding who won the match.

An enslaved gladiator could gain freedom (*Epigram.*29), but many continued to fight because of the benefits. It was not the deadly sport many people assume it was. The mortality rate was only about 5 percent. If there were a casualty, it generally occurred in a gladiator's first or second fight. The longer a gladiator fought, however, the better his survival rate.

Another false assumption is that "thumbs down" meant death. This popular myth was taken from a painting called *Pollice Verso*, meaning "turn down or press the thumb." Quintilian gave this gesture a negative meaning (*Quin.Inst.*11.3.119); however, Pliny the Elder claimed, "There is even a proverb that bids us turn down our thumbs to show approval" (*Plin.HN.*28.25). The audience made some sort of gesture that may have been a request for mercy. Dead gladiators were removed by stretcher, not dragged off with hooks (*Plin.HN.*37.11.45).

Animal hunting and killings were also popular forms of gladiatorial combat. *Venatores* hunted animals, while *bestiarri* fought for their lives against wild animals. Rare animals from throughout the Empire were slaughtered. This opening act was followed by the execution of criminals at lunchtime.

Most of the mortalities in the arena were doomed criminals, considered enemies of the State. Although these included some Christians, it is a misperception that they were persecuted for refusing to worship the emperor. Christians were unpopular because they did not participate in the social expectations of sacrifice or worshiping the gods. Trajan's response to Pliny the Younger's letter makes it clear that there was not a sustained Roman effort to persecute Christians: "They are not to be sought out" (*Plin.Ep.*10.96–97). Some martyrs existed, but overall, persecutions were sporadic and localized.

Condemned criminals also fought to the death in naval battles called *naumachia*. One took place under Claudius at Lake Fucine in 52 CE. Suetonius describes how Claudius "gave a sham sea-fight first. But when the combatants cried out, 'Hail, emperor, they who are about to die salute thee,' he replied, 'Or not'" (*Suet.Claud.*21.6). No other sources mention the alleged "gladiatorial oath."

Spectacles became so expensive that only emperors could afford to sponsor games. Commodus fought as a gladiator but never faced real opponents. Commodus bound individuals without feet and clubbed them to death (*Dio.Cass.*73.20.3). He was assassinated in 192 CE. The elite found his behavior to be scandalous because "his conduct was hardly becoming for an emperor" (*Hdn.*1.15.7).

Spectacles were popular with all levels of society. Despite what the elite thought of them, the gladiators had no shame and were celebrities and sex symbols. Juvenal reported that "When Eppia, the senator's wife, ran off with a gladiator, to Pharos and the Nile and the ill-famed city of Lagos, Canopus itself cried shame upon the monstrous morals of our town." Juvenal later adds, "What did she see in him to allow herself to be called a she-gladiator?" (*Juv.*6.15).

Women did appear as gladiators. They fought in pairs and were armed similarly to the men. Nicolaus of Damascus reported that like male gladiators, fights between women date back to the origins of Roman civilization (*Nic.Dam.Athlet.*4.153, *Ath.*4.49).

Women gladiators did not fight against dwarves. Although Dio mentioned that Domitian "would pit women and dwarves against each other" (*Dio.Cass.*67.8.4), Statius made it clear that women did not fight dwarves, but rather, each other (*Stat.Silvae.*1.6.53). Suetonius condemned the practice, but also made it explicit that there were "not only combats between men but between women as well" (*Suet.Dom.*4.1).

Women were marketed as descendants of Amazons, such as the two women depicted on a stela from Halicarnassus: Achila and Amazona. Juvenal mocked gladiatrixes because they did not conform to the norms of Roman womanhood. The marble relief indicated the women fought to an honorable draw. The monument shows female gladiators were honored and commemorated.

A statue from Hamburg depicts a woman gladiatrix holding a curved dagger up in the air, a typical victory gesture. She is dressed similarly to women on the Halicarnassus stone.

Tacitus was highly critical because "more women of rank and senators disgraced themselves in the arena" (*Tac.Ann.*15.32). Juvenal considered women gladiators as traitors to their sex: "What modesty can you expect in a woman who wears a helmet, abjures her own sex, and delights in feats of strength?" (*Juv.*6.252). Dio also condemned the appearance of upper-class men and women in the arena (*Dio.Cass.*62.17.3–4).

The senatorial decree of 11 CE forbidding freeborn women under age twenty from appearing in the arena suggests that freeborn women were fighting in the arena. Slave women were allowed to fight as gladiators. Emperor Septimius Severus banned female gladiators in 200 CE. Despite the injunction, an inscription from Ostia from the tombstone of Hostilianus brags that he was the first to allow women to fight in the arena (Vesley 1998). This evidence suggests women still fought as gladiators despite the prohibition.

Men and women fought as gladiators to entertain the crowd. Gladiatorial games were extremely popular, and gladiators were the heroes of the masses. Risking death was part of the attraction. Although despised by the elite as social outcasts, those who succeeded in the arena had the possibility of fame, fortune, or even freedom.

PRIMARY DOCUMENTS

*Gladiatorial contests were originally private and performed as a funerary rite. "To honor his father, Decimus Junius Brutus was the first one to organize gladiatorial games" (*Livy.Ab.Urbe.Cond.Per.*16.6).*

Games were originally a communal display of the status of an elite Roman who warranted a public funeral. Over time these became displays of prestige and status for those putting on the games.

At the time when this intelligence was received from Spain, the "Taurii" Games were celebrated as a special religious observance. These were followed by the games which M. Fulvius had vowed in the Aetolian war and were exhibited for ten days. Many actors from Greece came to do him honor, and athletic contests were witnessed for the first time in Rome. The hunting of lions and panthers formed a novel feature, and the whole spectacle presented almost as much splendor and variety as those of the present day. A shower of stones, lasting three days, fell at Picenum, and fire from the sky was said to have appeared in various places and singed many persons' garments. In consequence of these portents, special religious services were held for nine days. An additional day's service was ordered by the pontiffs owing to the Temple of Ops on the Capitol being struck by lightning. The consuls sacrificed full-grown victims and purified the City. Almost at the same time a report came from Umbria of the discovery of a child there, nine years old, who was a hermaphrodite. Horrified at such a portent the auruspices gave orders for it to be removed from Roman soil as speedily as possible and put to death. (*Livy.Ab.Urbe.Cond.*39.22)

Sources are unclear as to the origins of the gladiatorial games. The games may have been adopted from the Etruscans by way of Campania. Here Livy criticizes the entertainment because of its lavish waste of resources.

The war in Samnium, immediately afterwards, was attended with equal danger and an equally glorious conclusion. The enemy, besides their other warlike preparations, had made their battle-line to glitter with new and splendid arms. There were two corps: the shields of the one were inlaid with gold, of the other with silver. The shape of the shield was this: the upper part, where it protected the breast and shoulders, was rather broad, with a level top; below it was somewhat tapering, to make it easier to handle. They wore a sponge to protect the breast, and the left leg was covered with a greave. Their helmets were crested, to make their stature appear greater. The tunics of the gilded warriors were parti-colored [many colored]; those of the silver ones were linen of a dazzling white. The latter had silver sheaths and silver baldrics: the former gilded sheaths and golden baldrics, and their horses had gold-embroidered saddle-cloths. The right wing was assigned to these: the others took up their post on the left. The Romans had already learned of these splendid accoutrements, and their generals had taught them that a soldier should be rough to look on, not adorned with gold and silver but putting his trust in iron and in courage: indeed those other things were more truly spoil than arms, shining bright before a battle, but losing their beauty in the midst of blood and wounds; manhood they said, was the adornment of a soldier; all those other things went with the victory, and a rich enemy was the prize of the victor, however poor.

Whilst his men were animated by these words, Cursor led them into battle. He took up his own post on the right, and committed the left to the master of the horse from the moment of encountering, there was a mighty struggle with the enemy, and a struggle no less sharp between the dictator and the master of the horse, to decide which wing was to inaugurate the victory. It so happened that Junius was the first to make an impression on the Samnites. With the Roman left he faced the enemy's right, where they had consecrated themselves, as their custom was, and for that reason were resplendent in white coats and equally white armor, declaring that he offered up these men in sacrifice to Orcus, Junius charged, threw their ranks into disorder, and clearly made their line recoil. When the dictator saw this, he cried, "shall the victory begin upon the left? shall the right, the dictator's division, follow the attack of others? shall it not carry off the honors of the victory?" This fired the soldiers with new energy; nor did the cavalry display less valor than the foot, or the lieutenants less enthusiasm than the generals. Marcus Valerius on the right and Publius Decius on the left, both men of consular rank, rode out to the cavalry, which was posted on the wings, and, exhorting them to join with themselves in seizing a share of glory, charged obliquely against the enemy's flanks. Thus, a new and appalling danger enveloped their line on either side, and when the Roman legions, observing the terror of the Samnites, pressed forward with redoubled shouts, the enemy began to flee. The fields were soon heaped with slain and with glittering armor. At first the frightened Samnites found a refuge in their camp, but presently even that had to be abandoned, and ere nightfall it had been taken, sacked, and set on fire.

The dictator, as decreed by the Senate, celebrated a triumph, in which by far the finest show was afforded by the captured armor. so magnificent was its appearance that the shields inlaid with gold were divided up amongst the owners of the moneychangers' booths, to be used in decking out the Forum. From this is said to have come the custom of the aediles adorning the Forum whenever the *tensae*, or covered chariots of the gods, were conducted through it. So, the Romans made use of the splendid armor of their enemies to do honor to the gods; while the Campanians, in consequence of their pride and in hatred of the Samnites, equipped after this fashion the gladiators who furnished them entertainment at their feasts, and bestowed on them the name of Samnites. (*Livy.Ab.Urbe.Cond.*9.40)

No one compared to Julius Caesar when it came to promoting lavish games and spectacles. Ambitious men put on expensive entertainment to get support from the common people. Plutarch describes how Caesar, an up-and-coming politician, ingeniously used spectacle to gain favor with the mob as well as to advance his political career.

He was unsparing in his outlays of money, and was thought to be purchasing a transient and short-lived fame at a great price, though in reality he was buying things of the highest value at a small price. We are told, accordingly, that before he entered upon any public office he was thirteen hundred talents in debt. Again, being appointed curator of the Appian Way, he expended upon it vast sums of his own money; and again, during his aedile-ship, he furnished three hundred and twenty pairs of gladiators, and by lavish provision besides for theatrical performances, processions, and public banquets, he washed away all memory of the ambitious efforts of his predecessors in the office. By these means he put the people in such a humor that every man of them was seeking out new offices and new honors with which to requite him. (*Plut. Vit. Caes.* 5.8–9)

Julius Caesar borrowed extensively and was impoverished most of his life. However, Caesar's extravagant spectacles (with a variety of acts) drew crowds from all over. Moreover, attending the games could be dangerous for spectators.

Combats with wild beasts were presented on five successive days, and last of all there was a battle between opposing armies, in which five hundred foot-soldiers, twenty elephants and thirty horsemen engaged on each side. To make room for this, the goals were taken down and in their place two camps were pitched over against each other. The athletic competitions lasted for three days in a temporary stadium built for the purpose in the region of the Campus Martius. For the naval battle a pool was dug in the lesser Codeta [a district on the right bank of the Tiber River] and there was a contest of ships of two, three and four banks of oars, belonging to the Tyrian and Egyptian fleets, manned by a large force of fighting men. Such a throng flocked to all these shows from every quarter, so that many strangers had to lodge in tents pitched in streets or along the roads, and the press was often such that many were crushed to death, including two senators. (*Suet. Caes.* 39)

Only one description of a gladiatorial bout survives. Priscus and Verus were two gladiators who fought at the opening of the Colosseum in 80 CE. Both men fought so well that each was declared the winner and awarded his freedom.

While Verus and Priscus were prolonging the combat, and the valor of each had been for a long time equal, quarter for the combatants was demanded with great clamor. But Caesar obeyed his own law. The law was to fight with a stated reward in view, till by his thumb one of the pair proclaimed himself vanquished; but as was allowed, he frequently gave them dishes and gifts. An end, however, was found for the well-matched contest: equal they fought, equal they resigned. Caesar sent wands to each, to each the reward of victory. Such was the reward that adroit valor received. Under no other princes save thee, Caesar, has this ever happened, that, when two fought each other, both were victors. (*Epigram*.29)

Pliny the Younger was the governor of the Roman province of Bithynia from 111–113 CE. He and the emperor Trajan had a lively correspondence on provincial matters. This correspondence is the first mention of Christianity as separate from Judaism. In the first letter, Pliny asks the emperor how he should deal with people accused of being Christians. He had never encountered any but sentenced them to execution despite the fact he was generally dismissive of them. The Christians had been given opportunities to recant but refused to do so. The letters show that there was no universal policy of oppression of Christians by the Romans. Most persecutions were limited and infrequent.

To Trajan.

It is my custom, Sir, to refer to you in all cases where I do not feel sure, for who can better direct my doubts or inform my ignorance? I have never been present at any legal examination of the Christians, and I do not know, therefore, what are the usual penalties passed upon them, or the limits of those penalties, or how searching an inquiry should be made. I have hesitated a great deal in considering whether any distinctions should be drawn according to the ages of the accused; whether the weak should be punished as severely as the more robust; whether if they renounce their faith they should be pardoned, or whether the man who has once been a Christian should gain nothing by recanting; whether the name itself, even though otherwise innocent of crime, should be punished, or only the crimes that gather round it.

In the meantime, this is the plan which I have adopted in the case of those Christians who have been brought before me. I ask them whether they are Christians; if they say yes, then I repeat the question a second and a third time, warning them of the penalties it entails, and if they still persist, I order them to be taken away to prison. For I do not doubt that, whatever the character of the crime may be which they confess, their pertinacity and inflexible obstinacy certainly ought to be punished. There were others who showed similar mad folly whom I reserved to be sent to Rome, as they were Roman citizens. Subsequently, as is usually the way, the very fact of my taking up this question led to a great increase of accusations, and a variety of cases were brought before me. A pamphlet was issued anonymously, containing the names of a number of people. Those who denied that they were or had been Christians and called upon the gods in the usual formula, reciting the words after me, those who offered incense and wine before your image, which I had given orders to be brought forward for this purpose, together with the statues of the deities—all such I considered should be discharged, especially as they cursed the name of Christ, which, it is said, those who are really Christians cannot be induced to do. Others, whose names were given me by an informer, first said that they were Christians and afterwards denied it, declaring that they had been but were so no longer, some of them having recanted many years before, and more than one so long as twenty years back. They all worshipped your image and the statues of the deities, and cursed the name of Christ. But they declared that the sum of their guilt or their error only amounted to this, that on a stated day they had been accustomed to meet before daybreak and to recite a hymn among themselves to Christ, as though he were a god, and that so far from binding themselves by oath to commit any crime, their oath was to abstain from theft, robbery, adultery, and from breach of faith, and not to deny trust money placed in their keeping when called upon to deliver it. When this ceremony was concluded, it had been their custom to depart and meet again to take food, but it was of no special character and quite harmless, and they had ceased this practice after the edict in which, in accordance with your orders, I had forbidden all secret societies. I thought it the more necessary, therefore, to find out what truth there was in these statements by submitting two women, who were called deaconesses, to the torture, but I found nothing but a debased superstition carried to great lengths. So, I postponed my examination, and immediately consulted you. The matter seems to me worthy of your consideration, especially as there are so many people involved in the danger. Many persons of all ages, and of both sexes alike, are being brought into peril of their lives by their accusers, and the process will go on. For the contagion of this superstition has spread not only through the free cities, but into the villages and the rural districts, and yet it seems to me that it can be checked and set right. It is beyond doubt that the temples, which have been almost deserted, are beginning again to be thronged with worshippers, that the sacred rites which have for a long time been allowed to lapse are now being renewed, and that the food for the sacrificial victims is once more finding a sale, whereas, up to recently, a buyer was hardly to be found. From this it is easy to infer what vast numbers of people might be reclaimed, if only they were given an opportunity of repentance. (*Plin.Ep.*10.96)

Trajan's response to Pliny shows he had not heard of Christians and that there was no concerted effort by the State to hunt them down.

To Pliny.

You observed proper procedure, my dear Pliny, in sifting the cases of those who had been denounced to you as Christians. For it is not possible to lay down any general rule to serve as a kind of fixed standard. They are not to be sought out; if they are denounced and proved guilty, they are to be punished, with this reservation, that whoever denies that he is a Christian and really proves it—that is, by worshiping our gods—even though he was under suspicion in the past, shall obtain pardon through repentance. But anonymously posted accusations ought to have no place in any prosecution. For this is both a dangerous kind of precedent and out of keeping with the spirit of our age. (*Plin.Ep.*10.97)

Tertullian railed against the gladiatorial games because they were pagan. Star gladiators who fought well but were killed were removed via litters decorated with amber. Being dragged off by hooks was reserved for criminals, whose bodies were abused.

You are, I presume, more religious in the theater, where your gods in the same way dance over human blood, the stains resulting from penalties undergone, and supply the arguments and stories for the criminals, except that the criminals themselves often impersonate your very gods. We have sometimes seen Atys, that god from Pessinus, mutilated; and one burnt alive who had assumed the part of Hercules. We have smiled too, amidst the sportive cruelties of the noon-day combats, at Mercury examining the dead with a branding iron. We have seen the brother of Jupiter dragging off the corpses of the gladiators with his hammer in his hand. (*Tert.Apol.*15.4)

Tacitus complained about women who demeaned themselves by behaving like the lower classes. "The same year witnessed a number of gladiatorial shows, equal in magnificence to their predecessors, though more women of rank and senators disgraced themselves in the arena" (Tac.Ann.*15.32*).

Juvenal condemned women who go against their "natural" role as wife and mother. Appearing in the arena was akin to being a prostitute or a slave.

What modesty can you expect in a woman who wears a helmet, abjures her own sex, and delights in feats of strength? Yet, she would not choose to be a man, knowing the superior joys of womanhood. What a fine thing for a husband, at an auction of his wife's effects, to see her belt and armlets and plumes up for sale, with a gaiter that covers half the left leg or if she fights another sort of battle, how charmed you will be to see your young wife disposing of her greaves! Yet these are the women who find the thinnest of thin robes too hot for them; whose delicate flesh is chafed by the finest of silk tissue. See how she pants as she goes through her prescribed exercises; how she bends under the weight of her helmet; how big and coarse are the bandages which enclose her haunches; and then laugh when she lays down her arms and shows herself to be a woman! Tell us, ye granddaughters of Lepidus, or the blind Metellus or of Fabius Gurges, what gladiator's wife ever assumed accoutrements like these? When did the wife of Asylus ever gasp against a stump? (*Juv.*6.32–33)

Similarly, Dio criticizes the elite women for their behavior. However, he also notes that some were forced to fight.

There was another exhibition that was at once most disgraceful and most shocking, when men and women not only of the equestrian but even of the senatorial order appeared as performers in the orchestra, in the circus, and in the hunting theater, like those who are held in the lowest esteem. Some of them played the flute and danced in pantomimes or acted in tragedies and comedies or sang to the lyre; they drove horses, killed wild beasts and fought as gladiators, some willingly and some sore against their will. (*Dio.Cass.*62.17.3–4)

Further Reading

Andrews, Evan, "10 Things You May Not Know about Roman Gladiators," *History.* March 4, 2014. https://www.history.com/news/10-things-you-may-not-know-about-roman-gladiators

Anonymous, *Spectacles of Blood: Roman Gladiators and Christian Martyrs. Primary Sources for Gladiatorial Games.* Bates College, Lewiston, ME, Fall 2001. http://abacus.bates.edu/~mimber/blood/gladiator.sources.htm#Cicero

Brunet, Stephen, "Women with Swords: Female Gladiators in the Roman World," in *A Companion to Sport and Spectacle in Greek and Roman*

Antiquity. Edited by Paul Christesen and Donald G. Kyle. Wiley-Blackwell, Chichester, 2014, pp. 478–491.

Davies, Dave, "From Gladiator Duels to Caesar's Last Words: The Myths of Ancient Rome," *Fresh Air, NPR*. November 30, 2015. https://www.npr.org/2015/11/30/457319066/from-gladiator-duels-to-caesars-last-words-the-myths-of-ancient-rome

Justice, Faith L., "Busting Gladiator Myths." September 9, 2015. https://faithljustice.com/busting-gladiator-myths

Justice, Faith L., "A Day at the Pompeii Arena." October 5, 2015. https://faithljustice.com/tag/gladiators/

Knapp, Robert, "Fame and Death: Gladiators," in *Invisible Romans*. Harvard University Press, Cambridge, MA, 2011, pp. 265–289.

Kyle, Donald G., *Spectacles of Death in Ancient Rome*. Routledge, New York, 1998.

Low-Chappell, Samuel, "Bravery in the Face of Death: Gladiatorial Games and Those Who Watched Them," *Hirundo*, Vol. 13 (2014–2015). https://www.mcgill.ca/classics/files/classics/2014-15-03.pdf

Manas, Alfonso, "New Evidence of Female Gladiators: The Bronze Statuette at the Museum für Kunst und Gewerbe at Hamburg," *The International Journal of the History of Sport*, Vol. 28, No. 18 (2011), pp. 2726–2752.

McManus, Barbara, "Gladiatorial Games." http://www.vroma.org/~bmcmanus/arena.html

Murray, Steven, "Female Gladiators of the Ancient Roman World," *Journal of Combative Sport*, July 2003. https://ejmas.com/jcs/jcsart_murray_0703.htm

PBS, "Gladiators," *The Roman Empire in the First Century*. https://www.pbs.org/empires/romans/empire/gladiators.html

Ancient Sources

***Acolast.*:** Nicholson, Samuel, *Acolastus, His After-Witte* (1600). *A Poem by Samuel Nicholson. Containing Quotations and Adaptations from Shakespeare and Barnfield, Etc.* Edited with Introduction and Notes and Illustrations by the Rev. Alexander B. Grosart. Printed by Charles E. Simms, Manchester, 1876.

***Ael.NA.*:** Aelian, *On the Nature of Animals*, Vol. 3, Books 12–17. Translated by A. F. Scholfield. Published in the Loeb Classical Library 449. Harvard University Press, Cambridge, MA, 1958. http://www.attalus.org/info/aelian.html

***Apic.*:** Apicius, Marcus Gavius, *De Re Coquinaria* (*Cooking and Dining in Imperial Rome*). A bibliography, critical review and translation of the ancient book known as *Apicius De Re Coquinaria*. Translated by Joseph Dommers Vehling. Project Gutenberg, 1936. https://www.gutenberg.org

***App.B.Civ.*:** Appian of Alexandria, *Belles Civiles* (*The Civil Wars*). Horace White, London, 1899.

***App.Pun.*:** Appian of Alexandria, *The Foreign Wars*. Translated by Horace White. Macmillan, New York, 1899.

***ARI*:** Grayson, Albert Kirk, *Assyrian Royal Inscriptions: From the Beginning to Ashur-resha-ishi I*, Vol. I. Otto Harrassowitz, Wiesbaden, 1972, p. 60.

***August.De.civ.D.*:** "Augustine of Hippo, The Works of Aurelius Augustine." A New Translation. Vol. 1, *The City of God*. Edited by Rev. Marcus Dods. T. & T. Clark, Edinburgh, 1913.

***August.Perp.*:** Augustine of Hippo, *The Passion of St. Perpetua and Felicity*. MM: A new edition and translation of the Latin text, together with the sermons of St. Augustine upon these saints, now translated into English. Translated by W. H. Shewring. Sheed and Ward, London, 1931.

Aur.Vict.Caes.: Victor, Aurelius, *Epitome de Caesaribus* (*A Booklet about the Style of Life and the Manners of the Imperatores*). Translated by Thomas M. Banchich, Canisius College Translated Texts Number 1. Third Edition. Canisius College, Buffalo, NY, 2018. http://www.roman-emperors.org/epitome.htm

CAD.: *The Assyrian Dictionary of the Oriental Institute of the University of Chicago* (Gelb *et al.*) Oriental Institute, Chicago, 1956–2010.

Caes.B.Gall.: Caesar, Julius, *Caesar's Gallic War*. Translated by W. A. McDevitte and W. S. Bohn (1st ed.). Harper & Brothers and Harper's New Classical Library, New York. 1869. http://www.perseus.tufts.edu/hopper/text?doc=Perseus:abo:tlg,0551,017:2:16

Cassiod.Var.: *The Letters of Cassiodorus.* Being a condensed translation of the Variae epistolae of Magnus Aurelius Cassiodorus Senator with an introduction by Thomas Hodgkin. Henry Frowde, London; Horace Hart, Oxford. Printer to the University, 1886.

Cato./Varro.: Cato and Varro, *De Re Rustica* (*On Agriculture*). Translated by W. D. Hooper. Loeb Classical Library, Vol. 283. Harvard University Press, Cambridge, MA, 1934. http://penelope.uchicago.edu/Thayer/E/Roman/Texts/Varro/de_Re_Rustica/1*.html

Cels.Med.: Celsus, *De Medicina* (*On Medicine*), Vol. 1, Books 1–4. Translated by W. G. Spencer. Loeb Classical Library 292. Harvard University Press, Cambridge, MA. 1935. http://penelope.uchicago.edu/Thayer/E/Roman/Texts/Celsus/1*.html

Cic.Agr.: Cicero, *De Legre Agraria* (*On the Agrarian Law*). The orations of Marcus Tullius Cicero, literally translated by C. D. Yonge. Henry G. Bohn, London, 1856. http://perseus.uchicago.edu/perseus-cgi/citequery3.pl?dbname=PerseusLatinTexts&getid=1&query=Cic.%20Agr.%201.fr1

Cic.Att.: Cicero, *Epistulae ad Atticum* (*Letters to Atticus* 1–281), Vols. 22–24. Translated by Eric Otto Winstedt. Loeb Classical Library, 7, 8, 97. Harvard University Press, Cambridge, MA, 1912. Internet Archive. https://archive.org/details/letterstoatticus01ciceuoft/page/n12

Cic.Brut.: Cicero, *Orator ad M. Brutum* (*The Fourteen Orations against Marcus Antonius. Phillipics*). *The Orations of Marcus Tullius Cicero.* Translated by C. C. Young. G. Bell & Sons, London, 1903. http://www.perseus.tufts.edu/hopper/text?doc=urn:cts:latinLit:phi0474.phi035.perseus-eng1:2.38.99

Cic.Fam.: Cicero, *Epistulae ad Familiares (Letters to Friends)*, Vol. 1. Evelyn S. Shuckburgh. *The Letters of Cicero; the Whole Correspondence in Chronological Order, in Four Volumes*. G. Bell & Sons, London, 1908–1909. http://perseus.uchicago.edu/perseus-cgi/citequery3.pl?dbname =PerseusLatinTexts&query=Cic.%20Fam.&getid=

Cic.Fin.: Cicero, *De Finibus Bonorum et Malorum (On the Ends of Good and Evil)*, Vol. 17. Translated by H. Harris Rackham. Loeb Classical Library 40. Harvard University Press, Cambridge, MA, 1914. http://penelope.uchicago.edu/Thayer/E/Roman/Texts/Cicero/de_Finibus/1*.html

Cic.Mil.: Cicero, *Pro Milone. In Pisonem. Pro Scaur. Pro Fonteio. Pro Fabiro Polstumuo. Pro Marcello. Pro Ligaro. Pro Rege Deiotaro*, Vol. 9. Translated by N. H. Watts. Loeb Classical Library, Vol. 252. Harvard University Press, Cambridge, MA, 1932. http://perseus.uchicago.edu /perseus-cgi/citequery3.pl?dbname=LatinAugust2012&getid=1&query =Cic.%20Deiot.%201

Cic.Off.: Cicero, *De Officiis (On Duties)*, Vol. 21. Translated by Walter Miller. Loeb Classical Library 30. Harvard University Press, Cambridge, MA, 1913. http://penelope.uchicago.edu/Thayer/E/Roman/Texts/Cicero/de _Officiis/home.html

Cic.Orat.: Cicero, *Epistulae ad Atticum (Letters to Atticus)*. Evelyn S. Shuckburgh. *The Letters of Cicero; the Whole Extant Correspondence in Chronological Order, in Four Volumes*. G. Bell & Sons, London, 1908–1909.

Cic.Sen.: Cicero, *Cato Maior. De Senectute (Cato the Elder, on Old Age, on Friendship. On Divination)*, Vol. 20. Published in the Loeb Classical Library 154. Harvard University Press, Cambridge, MA, 1923. http://penelope.uchicago.edu/Thayer/E/Roman/Texts/Cicero/Cato_Maior _de_Senectute/text*.html

Cic.Tusc.: Cicero, *Tusculan Disputations; Also, Treatises on the Nature of the Gods, and on the Commonwealth*. Literally translated, chiefly by C. D. Yonge. Harper & Brothers, New York, 1877. http://www.gutenberg.org/files/14988/14988-h/14988-h.htm

Dante's Inferno: Dante Alighieri, *Dante's Inferno*. Translated by Henry Wadsworth Longfellow. Ticknor and Fields, Boston, MA, 1867. https://www.gutenberg.org/files/1001/1001-h/1001-h.htm

Dig.: "Digest," in *The Civil Law, Including the Twelve Tables, The Institutes of Gaius, The Rules of Ulpian, The Opinions of Paulus, The Enactments of Justinian, and The Constitutions of Leo: Translated from the Original Latin, Edited, and Compared with All Accessible Systems of Jurisprudence*

Ancient and Modern. By S. P. Scott, A. M., author of *History of the Moorish Empire in Europe*, translator of the *Visigothic Code in Seventeen Volumes*. The Central Trust Company, Cincinnati, OH, 1932.

Dio.Cass.: Dio Cassius, *Roman History*, Vols. 1–9. Loeb Classical Library, Vols. 32, 37, 53, 66, 82–3, 175–177. Translated by Earnest Cary, Herbert B. Foster. Harvard University Press, Cambridge, MA, 1914–1927. http://penelope.uchicago.edu/Thayer/E/Roman/Texts/Cassius_Dio/home.html

Dio.Chrys.Disc.: Dio Chrysostom, *Discourses 12–30*, Vol. II. Translated by J. W. Cohoon. Loeb Classical Library 339. Harvard University Press, Cambridge, MA, 1939.

Dio.Chrys.Or.: Dio Chrysostom, *Discourses*: 1–11. Translated by J. W. Cohoon. Loeb Classical Library 257, 339, 358, 376, 385. Harvard University Press, Cambridge, MA, 1932–1951. http://penelope.uchicago.edu/Thayer/E/Roman/Texts/Dio_Chrysostom/home.html

Diod.Sic.: Siculus, Diodorus, *Bibliotheca Historica* (*The Library of History*), Books 34/35. (Fragments covering the period 134–105 BCE). Attalus translation is based on: *The Historical Library of Diodorus the Sicilian, in fifteen books. To which are added the Fragments of Diodorus, and those published by H. Valesius, I [sic] Rhodomannus, and F. Ursinius*. Translated by G. Booth. London, 1814 and *Bibliotheque de Diodore de Sicile*, translated by F. Hoefer. L. Hachette, Paris, 1865. http://www.attalus.org/translate/diodorus34.html

Diod.Sic.Frag.: Siculus, Diodorus, *Bibliotheca Historica* (*The Library of History*), *Fragments of Books 21–32*. Translated by C. Bradford Wells. Loeb Classical Library 409. Harvard University Press, Cambridge, MA, 1957. http://penelope.uchicago.edu/Thayer/E/Roman/Texts/Diodorus_Siculus/32*.htm

Dion.Hal.Ant.Rom.: Dionysius of Halicarnassus, *The Roman Antiquities of Dionysius of Halicarnassus*. Translated by Earnest Cary. Vols. 1–7 of the Loeb Classical Library 319, 347, 357, 364, 372, 378, 388, 465–466. Harvard University Press, Cambridge, MA, 1914–1927. http://penelope.uchicago.edu/Thayer/E/Roman/Texts/Dionysius_of_Halicarnassus/home.html

Epigram.: Martial, *Epigrammata* (*Epigrams*) *of Martial Book 3*. Bohn's Classical Library. G. Bell & Sons, London, 1897.

Euseb.Hist.Ecc.: Eusebius, *Ecclesiastical History. Emperors and Persecutions in the Third Century AD*. J. Vanderspoel, Department of Greek, Latin and Ancient History, University of Calgary. http://people.ucalgary.ca/~vandersp/Courses/texts/eusebius/eusehef.html

***Eutr.*:** Eutropius, *Abridgement of Roman History*. Translated, and notes, by the Reverend John Selby Watson. Henry Bohn, London, 1853.

***Flor.Epit.*:** Florus, *The Epitome of Roman History*. Translated by E. S. Forster. Published in the Loeb Classical Library 231. Harvard University Press, Cambridge, MA, 1929. http://penelope.uchicago.edu/Thayer/E/Roman/Texts/Florus/Epitome/1I*.html#XXXI

***Frontin.Aq.*:** Frontinus, *De Aqueductu urbs Romae* (*The Aqueducts of Rome*). *The Stratagems, and the Aqueducts of Rome*. English translation by Charles E. Bennett; the translation of the *Aqueducts* being a revision of that of Clemens Herschel; edited and prepared for the press by Mary B. McElwain. Loeb Classical Library 174. Harvard University Press, Cambridge, MA, 1925. http://penelope.uchicago.edu/Thayer/E/Roman/Texts/Frontinus/De_Aquis/home.html

***Gell.NA.*:** Gellius, *Noctes Atticae* (*Attic Nights*), Vol. 2, Books 6–13. Translated by J. C. Rolfe. Loeb Classical Library 200. Harvard University Press, Cambridge, MA, 1927. http://penelope.uchicago.edu/Thayer/E/Roman/Texts/Gellius/13*.html

***Har.*:** Harvey, Brian, *Graffiti from Pompeii*, Pompeiana. http://www.pompeiana.org/Resources/Ancient/Graffiti%20from%20Pompeii.htm

***Har.CILVI.*:** *Epitaph of Tiberius Claudius Secundus = Corpus Inscriptionum Latinarum VI 1528* (Rome, 1st century C.E., trans. Brian K. Harvey, *Daily Life in Ancient Rome: A Sourcebook*). Hackett Publishing Company, Indianapolis, 2016, p. 256.

***Hdn.*:** Herodian or Herodian of Antioch (c. 170–c. 240). *History of the Roman Empire from the Death of Marcus Aurelius to the Accession of Gordian III*. Translated from the Greek by Edward C. Echols. University of California Press, Berkeley and Los Angeles, 1961. http://www.tertullian.org/fathers/herodian_00_intro.htm

***Hipp.*:** Hippocrates and Galen, *De Elementis Secundum Hippocratem* (*On the Elements According to Hippocrates*). Translated by John Redman Coxe. Lindsay & Blakiston, Philadelphia, PA, 1846. https://oll.libertyfund.org/titles/hippocrates-the-writings-of-hippocrates-and-galen

***Hom.Il.*:** Homer. *The Iliad*. With an English translation by A. T. Murray, 2 vols. Harvard University Press, Cambridge, MA; William Heinemann, London, 1924.

***Hor.Carm.*:** Horace, *Carmina* (*The Odes and Carmen Saeculare of Horace*). Translated by John Conington. G. Bell & Sons, London, 1882. http://www.perseus.tufts.edu/hopper/text?doc=Perseus%3Atext%3A1999.02.0025%3Abook%3D2%3Apoem%3D16

ANCIENT SOURCES

***Hor.Epist.*:** Horace, *The Works of Horace.* Translated Literally into English Prose by Christopher Smart, A.M. of Pembroke College, Cambridge. A New Edition, Revised, with a Copious Selection of Notes. By Theodore Alois Buckley, S.A. of Christ Church. American Book Company, New York, Cincinnati and Chicago, 1883. https://www.gutenberg.org/files/14020/14020-h/14020-h.htm

***Hor.Sat.*:** Horace. *The Works of Horace.* Edited by C. Smart and Theodore Alois Buckley. Harper & Brothers, New York, 1863.

***Ign.Ant.*:** Ignatius, *Ante-Nicene Christian Library/The Translations of the Writings of the Church Fathers Down to AD 325*, Vol. 1. Edited by Alexander Roberts and James Donaldson. Christian Literature Publishing Company, New York, 1867, 1885.

***Ign.Ant.Rom.*:** Ignatius of Antioch, "Epistle to the Romans." Translated by Alexander Roberts and James Donaldson. *From Ante-Nicene Fathers*, Vol. 1. Edited by Alexander Roberts, James Donaldson, and A. Cleveland Coxe. Christian Literature Publishing Company, Buffalo, NY, 1885. Revised and Edited for New Advent by Kevin Knight.

***JC.*:** Shakespeare, William, *The Tragedy of Julius Caesar* (1599). http://shakespeare.mit.edu/julius_caesar/full.html

***Jos.AJ.*:** Josephus, *Antiquities. Antiquitates Judicae* (*Antiquities of the Jews*): *The Genuine Works of Flavius Josephus the Jewish Historian.* Translated from the Original Greek According to Havercamp's Accurate Edition. Containing the Twenty Books of the Jewish Antiquities, with the Appendix or Life of Josephus, Written by Himself: Seven Books of the Jewish War: And Two against APION. http://penelope.uchicago.edu/josephus

***Juv.*:** Juvenal and Perseus, *The Satires of Juvenal.* Translated by George Gilbert Ramsay and William Heneman. G. P. Putnam's Sons, London and New York, 1918.

***Kim.Sloc.Proc.Anitt.*:** Kimball, Sara E., and Jonathan Slocum, *Hittite Online. Lesson 1. The Proclamation of Anittas.* Linguistics Research Center, University of Texas at Austin. https://lrc.la.utexas.edu/eieol/hitol/10

***Lact.De.Mort.Pers.*:** Lactantius, *Of the Manner in Which the Persecutors Died.* Addressed to Donatus. J. Vanderspoel. Department of Greek, Latin and Ancient History, University of Calgary. http://people.ucalgary.ca/~vandersp/Courses/texts/lactant/lactperf.html

***Livy.Ab.Urbe.Cond.*:** Livy, *Ab Urbe Condita* (*The History of Rome*). English translation by. Rev. Canon Roberts. E. P. Dutton and Co., New York, 1912. http://www.perseus.tufts.edu/hopper/text?doc=Perseus:text:1999.02.0026

Livy.Ab.Urbe.Cond.Per.: Livy, *Ab Urbe Condita Periochae* (*The History of Rome. Summaries*). Translated by Jona Lendering. https://www.livius.org/sources/content/livy/livy-periochae-51-55

Luc.Civil Wars: Lucan, *Pharsalia, or, The Civil Wars of Rome, between Pompey the Great, and Julius Caesar. The Whole Ten Books*, Englished by Thomas May, Esquire. Second Edition, corrected, and the Annotations enlarged by the Author. London, 1631.

M.Aur.Med.: Aurelius, Marcus, *The Meditations of the Emperor Marcus Aurelius Antoninus.* Translated by George Long. G. Bell & Sons, London, 1913.

Macrob.Sat.: Macrobius, *The Saturnalia.* The Latin text of the critical edition edited by Ludwig von Jan (Gottfried Bass; Quedlinburg and Leipzig, 1852), web edition by Bill Thayer. *Opera quae supersunt*, 2 vols., Quedlinburgi et Lipsiae, typis et sumptibus Godofredi Bassii, 1848–1852.

Nep.: Nepos, Cornelius, *De Viris Illistribus* (*Lives of Eminent Commanders*). Translated by the Rev. John Selby Watson. Hinds & Noble, New York, 1886, pp. 305–450.

Nic.Dam.: Nicholas of Damascus, *Bios Kaisaros* (*Life of Augustus*). Translated by Clayton M. Hall. G. Banta, Menasha, WI, 1923.

Nic.Dam.Athlet.: Athenaeus. *The Deipnosophists*, Vol. II. With an English translation by Charles Burton Gulick. Loeb Classical Library 208. Harvard University Press, Cambridge, MA; William Heinemann, London, 1927.

Oros.: Orosius, Paulus, *Seven Books of History against the Pagans.* Translated with introduction and notes by Irving Woodworth Raymond. Columbia University Press, New York, 1934.

Ov.Fast.: Ovid, *Fasti*, Vol. 5. Translated by James G. Fraser. Loeb Classical Library 253. Harvard University Press, Cambridge, MA, 1931.

Petron.Sat.: Petronius, *Satyricon, with Seneca the Younger's Apocolocyntosis.* Translated by Michael Heseltine, W. D. Rouses. Revised by E. H. Warmington. Loeb Classical Library 15. Harvard University Press, Cambridge, MA, 1913. http://www.perseus.tufts.edu/hopper/text?doc=Perseus%3Atext%3A2007.01.0027%3Atext%3DSatyricon

Philo.Leg.: Philo of Alexandria, *Legatio ad Gaium. Embassy to Gaius. The Works of Philo Judeaus. The contemporary of Josephus, translated from the Greek. Complete and Unabridged.* Translated by Charles Duke Yonge. H. G. Bohn, London, 1854–1855.

Philost.VA.: Philostratus of Athens, *The Life of Apollonius of Tyana; The Epistles of Philostratus; The Treatise of Eusebius*, Vol. 1, Books 1–5.

English translation by F. C. Conybeare. Loeb Classical Library L016, Cambridge Mass, 1912.

***Pl.Poen.*:** Plautus, T. Maccius, *Poenelus* (*Little Carthaginian*). *The Comedies of Plautus*. Henry Thomas Riley. G. Bell & Sons, London, 1912. http://www.perseus.tufts.edu/hopper/text?doc=Perseus%3Atext%3A1999.02.0106

***Plin.Ep.*:** Pliny the Younger, *Epistulae* (*Letters Book* 10). Translated by J. B. Firth, Letters 61–121. Walter Scott, London, 1900.

***Plin.HN.*:** Pliny the Elder, *Naturalis Historia* (*The Natural History*). Edited by John Bostock. Taylor and Francis, London, 1855. http://www.perseus.tufts.edu/hopper/text?doc=Perseus%3Atext%3A1999.02.0137%3Abook%3D36%3Achapter%3D24

***Plin.Pan.*:** Pliny, *Letters and Panegyricus [of] Pliny*. With an English translation by Betty Radice, 2 vols. Loeb Classical Library 55 and 59. Harvard University Press, Cambridge, MA, 1969.

***Plut.Vit.*:** Plutarch, *Vitae Parallelae* (*The Parallel Lives*), Vols. 7, 8, 9, 10, and 11. Loeb Classical Library 99, 100, 101, 102, 103. Harvard University Press, Cambridge, MA, 1919–1926. http://penelope.uchicago.edu/Thayer/E/Roman/Texts/Plutarch/Lives/home.html

***Plutarch*:** Plutarch, *Shakespeare's Plutarch*. Edited by C. F. Tucker Brooke, Vol. 1 *Containing the Main Sources of Julius Caesar* [1579]. Duffield and Company, New York, London, 1909.

***Polyb.*:** Polybius, *The Histories of Polybius*, Vols. 1 and 2. Translated from the text of F. Hultsch by Eveylyn S. Shuckburgh. Macmillan, London and New York, 1889. http://perseus.uchicago.edu/perseus-cgi/citequery3.pl?dbname=GreekTexts&query=Polyb.%2039.4.1&getid=1

***Polyb.*:** Polybius, *The Histories*, Vols. 1–6. Translated by William Roger Paton. Loeb Classical Library 128, 137–138, 159–161. Harvard University Press, Cambridge, MA, 1922–1927. http://penelope.uchicago.edu/Thayer/E/Roman/Texts/Polybius/home.html

***Prop.*:** Propertius, *Elegies*. Roman Erotic Elegy. Selections from Tibullus, Propertius, Ovid, and Sulpicia, translated, with notes and a glossary, by Jon Corelis. https://sites.google.com/site/romanelegybackup/

***Quint.Inst.*:** Quintilian, *Institutio Oratory*, Book 12. With an English translation by Harold Edgeworth Butler. Harvard University Press, Cambridge, MA; William Heinemann, London, 1922. http://penelope.uchicago.edu/Thayer/E/Roman/Texts/Quintilian/Institutio_Oratoria/home.html

***Sall.Cat.*:** Sallust, *The War with Catiline. The War with Jugurtha*. Translated by John C. Rolfe. Loeb Classical Library 116. Harvard University

Press, Cambridge, MA, 1921 (revised 1931). http://penelope.uchicago.edu/Thayer/E/Roman/Texts/Sallust/Bellum_Catilinae*.html

***Salv.De.Guber.Dei.*:** Salvian, *On the Government of God. The Fifth Century Polemic Done into English by Eva M. Sanford.* Columbia University Press, New York, 1930.

***Sen.*:** Seneca L. Annaeus, *Seneca, De Consolatione ad Helvium (Of Consolation to Helvia). Minor Dialogs Together with the Dialog "On Clemency."* Translated by Aubrey Stewart. Bohn's Classical Library Edition. G. Bell & Sons, London, 1900.

***Sen.Clem.*:** Seneca, *De Consolatione ad Helvium (Of Consolation to Helvia). Minor Dialogs Together with the Dialog "On Clemency."* Translated by Aubrey Stewart. Bohn's Classical Library Edition. G. Bell & Sons, London, 1900.

***Sen.De.Brev.*:** Seneca, L. Annaeus, *Seneca, De Brevitate Vitae (On the Shortness of Life).* Translated by John W. Basore. Loeb Classical Library 254. William Heinemann, London, 1932.

***Sen.Lucil.*:** Seneca, *Ad Lucilium. Epistulae Morales (Moral letters to Lucilius)*, Vols. 1–3. With an English translation by Richard M. Gummere. Loeb Classical Library 75–77. Harvard University Press, Cambridge, MA, 1917–1925.

***SHA*:** *Scriptores Historiae Augustae, or Historia Augusta, (Augustan History).* Translated by David Magie. Loeb Classical Library 139–140, 263. Harvard University Press, Cambridge, MA, 1921, 1924, 1932. http://penelope.uchicago.edu/Thayer/E/Roman/Texts/Historia_Augusta/home.html

***SHA.Hadr.*:** *Historia Augusta, Volume I: Hadrian. Aelius. Antoninus Pius. Marcus Aurelius. L. Verus. Avidius Cassius. Commodus. Pertinax. Didius Julianus. Septimius Severus. Pescennius Niger. Clodius Albinus.* Translated by David Magie. Loeb Classical Library 139. Harvard University Press, Cambridge, MA, 1921.

***SHA.Heliogab.*:** *Historia Augusta, Volume II: Caracalla. Geta. Opellius Macrinus. Diadumenianus. Elagabalus. Severus Alexander. The Two Maximini. The Three Gordians. Maximus and Balbinus.* Translated by David Magie. Loeb Classical Library 140. Harvard University Press, Cambridge, MA, 1924.

***Sil.Pun.*:** Silius Italicus, *Punica*, Vol. 1, Books 1–8, Vol. 2, Books 9–17. Translated by Duff, J.D. Loeb Classical Series Library 277 and 278. Harvard University Press, Cambridge, MA, 1934.

***Stat.Silvae.*:** Statius, Publius, *Silvae*, Book 1. Translated by A. S. Kline, 2012. https://www.poetryintranslation.com/PITBR/Latin/StatiusSilvaeBkI.php

***Strab.Geog.*:** Strabo, *Geographica* (*Geography*). Translated by Horace L. Jones. Loeb Classical Library 49/50. Harvard University Press, Cambridge, MA, 1917–1932. http://penelope.uchicago.edu/Thayer/E/Roman/Texts/Strabo/5C*.html

***Suet.*:** Suetonius, *De Vita Caesarum* (*The Lives of the Twelve Caesars*). Julius Caesar, Augustus, Tiberius, Caligula, Claudius, Nero, Galba, Otho, Vitellius, Vespasian, Titus, and Domitian. Translated by J. C. Rolfe. Loeb Classical Library 31. Harvard University Press, Cambridge, MA, 1913. http://penelope.uchicago.edu/Thayer/E/Roman/Texts/Suetonius/12Caesars/home.html

***Suet.Gram.Et.Rhet.*:** Suetonius, *De grammaticis et rhetoribus* (*Lives of Illustrious Men. Rhetoricians. Grammarians. Poets*). Terence, Virgil, Horace, Tibullus, Persius, and Lucan. *Lives of Pliny the Elder and Passienus Crispus*. Loeb Classical Library 38. Harvard University Press, Cambridge, MA, 1914. http://penelope.uchicago.edu/Thayer/E/Roman/Texts/Suetonius/home.html

***Tac.Agr.*:** Tacitus, *Agricola. Germania. Dialogue on Oratory*. Translated by M. Hutton and W. Peterson. Revised by R. M. Ogilvie, E. H. Warmington, and Michael Winterbottom. Loeb Classical Library 35. Harvard University Press, Cambridge, MA, 1914.

***Tac.Ann.*:** Tacitus, *Complete Works of Tacitus*. Translated by Alfred John Church and William Jackson Brodribb. Macmillan, London, 1876.

***Tac.Ger.*:** Tacitus, *The Germany and the Agricola of Tacitus*. The Oxford translation, revised with notes; with an introduction by Edward Brooks, Jr. David McKay, Philadelphia, 1897. http://www.gutenberg.org/files/7524/7524-h/7524-h.htm

***Tac.Hist.*:** Tacitus, *Histories*, Books 1–6. Translated by Clifford Moore. Loeb Classical Library 111, 249, 312. Harvard University Press, Cambridge, MA, 1925–1937. http://penelope.uchicago.edu/Thayer/E/Roman/Texts/Tacitus/home.html

***Tert.Apol.*:** Tertullian, *The Apology of Tertullian for the Christians*. Translated with introduction, analysis, and appendix containing the Letters of Pliny and Trajan respecting the Christians. By T. Herbert Bindley. Parker and Company, Oxford, 1890. http://www.tertullian.org/articles/bindley_apol/bindley_apol.htm

***Tert.Mart.*:** Tertullian, *Ad Martyras* (*An Address to the Martyrs*). Library of the Fathers 10. Translated by C. Dodgson, 1842, pp. 150–157.

***Tert.Perp.*:** Tertullian, *The Passion of the Holy Martyrs Perpetua and Felicitas. The Ante-Nicene Fathers: Translations of the Writings of the Fathers Down to A.D. 325*, Vol. 3. Edited by Alexander Roberts, Sir James Donaldson, and Arthur Cleveland Cox, 1885. Christian Literature Publishing Company, New York. http://tertullian.org/anf/index.htm

Theod.Hist.Ecc.: Theodoret, *Ecclesiastcial History. A History of the Church in Five Books. From A.D. 322 to the Death of Theodore of Mopsuestia A.D. 427*, Vol. 26. Samuel Bagster and Sons, London, UK, 1743 (1843).

Theophras.Caus.Pl.: Theophrastus, *Enquiry into Plants, and Minor Works on Odors and Weather Signs*. With an English translation by Sir Arthur Hort. William Heinemann, London; G. P. Putnam's Sons, New York, 1916.

Vell.Pat./Aug.: Paterculus, Velleius, *Compendium of Roman History. Res Gestae Divi Augusti*. Translated by Frederick W. Shipley. Loeb Classical Library 152, Books I and II. Harvard University Press, Cambridge, MA, 1924. http://penelope.uchicago.edu/Thayer/E/Roman/Texts/Velleius_Paterculus/home.html

Verg.: Vergil, *Bucolics, Aeneid, and Georgics of Vergil*. Edited by J. B. Greenough. Ginn & Co., Boston, 1900.

Vitr.de.Arch.: Vitruvius, *De Architectura* (*On Architecture*), Vol. 1, Books 1–5. Translated by Frank Granger. Loeb Classical Library 251. Harvard University Press, Cambridge, MA, 1931. http://penelope.uchicago.edu/Thayer/E/Roman/Texts/Vitruvius/home.html

Secondary Sources

Adcock, F. E., "Delenda Est Carthago," *Cambridge Historical Journal*, Vol. 8, No. 3 (1946), pp. 117–128.
Andrews, Evan, "10 Things You May Not Know about Roman Gladiators," *History.* March 4, 2014. https://www.history.com/news/10-things-you-may-not-know-about-roman-gladiators
Anonymous, *Spectacles of Blood: Roman Gladiators and Christian Martyrs. Primary Sources for Gladiatorial Games.* Bates College, Lewiston, ME, Fall 2001. http://abacus.bates.edu/~mimber/blood/gladiator.sources.htm#Cicero.
Anonymous, *The Tragedy of Caesar's Revenge.* Edited by F. S. Boas, 2010. Printed for the Malone Society by Horace Hart M. A., at the Oxford University Press, Oxford, 1911. http://www.gutenberg.org/files/30846/30846-h/30846-h.htm
Arnaud, Pascal, "Toi aussi, mon fils, tu mangeras ta part de notre poivoir—Brutus le Tyran?" *Latomus* T. 57, Fasc 1 (January–March 1998), pp. 61–71. Sociètè d'Études Latines de Bruxelles.
Ashley, O'rene Daille, "Et Tu Brute? Not Caesar's Last Words," *Today I Found Out.* April 30, 2013. http://www.todayifoundout.com/index.php/2013/04/et-tu-brute-not-caesars-famous-last-words
Barrett, Anthony A., *Caligula: The Abuse of Power. Roman Imperial Biographies.* Routledge, London and New York, 2015.
Barrett, Anthony A., *Caligula: The Corruption of Power.* Taylor and Francis e-Library, 2001.
Barrett, Anthony A., *Livia: First Lady of Imperial Rome.* Yale University Press, New Haven and London, 2002.

Barrett, Anthony A., "Tacitus, Livia and the Evil Stepmother," *Rheinisches Museum für Philologie* Neue Folge, 144. Bd., H. 2 (2001), pp. 171–175.

Barrett, Anthony A., Elaine Fantham, and John C. Yardley, *The Emperor Nero: A Guide to the Ancient Sources*. Princeton University Press, Princeton, NJ, 2016.

BBC, "Two: Caligula with Mary Beard." March 12, 2018. https://www.bbc.co.uk/programmes/b037w0qh

Beard, Mary, "Caligula," *BBC*. 2013 BBC Documentary, YouTube. July 29, 2013.

Beard, Mary, "10 Things You Thought You Knew about the Romans but Didn't," *A Don's Life*. August 30, 2007. https://www.the-tls.co.uk/10-things-you-thought-you-knew-about-the-romans-but-didnt/

Bertolazzi, Riccardo, "Depiction of Livia and Julia Domna by Cassius Dio," *Acta Antiqua Academiae Scientiarum Hungaricae*, Vol. 55, No. 1 (2015), pp. 413–432.

Bertrand, L., "Les Villes africaines," *Revue des Deux Mondes*, Vol. 5, No. 28 (1905), pp. 651–676. https://fr.wikisource.org/wiki/Les_Villes_africaines/03

Bissler, Joseph, *Caligula Unmasked: An Investigation of the Historiography of Rome's Most Notorious Emperor*. MA Thesis, Kent State, 2013. https://etd.ohiolink.edu/!etd.send_file?accession=kent1374749172&disposition=inline

Blissett, W., "Lucan's Caesar and the Elizabethan Villain," *Studies in Philology*, Vol. 53 (1956), pp. 553–575.

Brunet, Stephen, "Women with Swords: Female Gladiators in the Roman World," in *A Companion to Sport and Spectacle in Greek and Roman Antiquity*. Edited by Paul Christesen and Donald G. Kyle. Wiley-Blackwell, Chichester, 2014, pp. 478–491.

Butler, Stephanie, "Vomitoriums: Fact or Fiction?" *History*. November 20, 2012. https://www.history.com/news/vomitoriums-fact-or-fiction

Canter, H. V., "Conflagrations of Ancient Rome," *The Classical Journal*, Vol. 27, No. 4 (January 1932), pp. 270–288.

Cavendish, Richard, "The Great Fire of Rome," *History Today*, Vol. 64, No. 7 (June 2014). https://www.historytoday.com/archive/months-past/great-fire-rome

Champlin, Edward, *Nero*. Harvard University Press, Cambridge, MA and London, 2003.

Closs, Virginia M., *While Rome Burned: Fire, Leadership, and Urban Disaster in the Roman Cultural Imagination*. Dissertation, University of Pennsylvania, 2013.

Coleman, Kathleen. "*Missio* at Halicarnassus," *Harvard Studies in Classical Philology*, Vol. 100 (2000), pp. 487–500.

Cowles, Lauren E., "The Spectacle of Bloodshed in Roman Society," *Constructing the Past*, Vol. 12, No. 1, Article 10 (2011), pp. 1–6.

Cyrano, Monica Silveira, *Big Screen Rome*. Blackwell, Malden, MA, 2005.

Dando-Collins, Stephen, *The Great Fire of Rome: The Fall of the Emperor Nero and His City*. Da Capo Press (A Member of the Perseus Books Group), Cambridge, MA, 2010.

Davenport, C., and Shushma Malik, "Mythbusting Ancient Rome—The Truth about the Vomitorium," *The Conversation*. January 19, 2017. https://theconversation.com/mythbusting-ancient-rome-the-truth-about-the-vomitorium-71068

Davies, Dave, "From Gladiator Duels to Caesar's Last Words: The Myths of Ancient Rome," *Fresh Air, NPR*. November 30, 2015. https://www.npr.org/2015/11/30/457319066/from-gladiator-duels-to-caesars-last-words-the-myths-of-ancient-rome

Deatrick, Eugene P., "Salt, Soil, Savior," *The Biblical Archaeologist*, Vol. 25, No. 2 (May 1962), pp. 41–48.

Dove, Laurie L., "Did Romans Really Purge Their Bellies in Vomitoria?" *Howstuffworks*. https://history.howstuffworks.com/history-vs-myth/did-romans-purge-bellies-in-vomitoriums.htm

Draper, Robert, "Rethinking Nero," *National Geographic Magazine*. 2014. https://www.nationalgeographic.com/magazine/2014/09/emperor-nero/

Duke, T. T., "Women and Pygmies in the Roman Arena," *The Classical Journal*, Vol. 50, No. 5 (February 1955), pp. 223–224.

Durant, Will, "The Story of Civilization," *Los Angeles Times*. February 12, 1928, p. 54.

Echard, Laurence, *Roman History*, from the settlement of the empire by Augustus Caesar, to the removal of the imperial seat by Constantine the Great, Vol. 2. The fifth edition, corrected. By Laurence Echard printed for R. Bonwick, J. Tonson, W. Freeman, Tim. Goodwin, J. Walthoe, and six others in London, London, 1713.

Edwards, P., "6 Myths about the Ides of March, and Killing Caesar," *Vox*. March 15, 2017. https://www.vox.com/2015/3/15/8214921/ides-of-march-caesar-assassination

Fagan, Garrett G., "Gaius (Caligula) (AD 37–41)," *De Imperatoribus Romanis. An Online Encyclopedia of Roman Emperors*. Pennsylvania State University, 2004. https://www.roman-emperors.org/gaius.htm

Fagan, Garrett G., "The Genesis of the Roman Public Bath: Recent Approaches and Future Directions," *American Journal of Archaeology*, Vol. 105, No. 3 (July 2001), pp. 403–426.

Feldman, Cecelia, "Urban Water Supply in Roman Cities and Its Impact on the West," *The Middle Ground Journal*, Vol. 9 (Fall 2014), pp. 1–13.

Futrell, Alison. *Historical Sources in Translation: The Roman Games. Blackwell Sourcebooks in Ancient History*. Blackwell Publishing, Malden, MA, Oxford, UK, and Victoria, Australia, 2006.

Gainsford, Peter, "Caesar's Birth and Death," *Modern Myths about the Ancient World. Kiwi Hellenist.* September 29, 2017. http://kiwihellenist.blogspot.com/2017/09

Gainsford, Peter, "Salting the Earth," *Modern Myths about the Ancient World. Kiwi Hellenist.* December 12, 2016. http://kiwihellenist.blogspot.com/2016/12/salting-earth.html

Gainsford, Peter, "Vomiting Romans: Or Were the Romans Happy Chuckers?" *Modern Myths about the Ancient World. Kiwi Hellenist.* June 13, 2016. http://kiwihellenist.blogspot.com/2016/06/vomiting-romans-or-were-romans-happy.html

Gershenson, D. E., "*Kai su teknon*: Caesar's Last Words," *Shakespeare Quarterly*, Vol. 43, No. 2 (July 1992), pp. 218–219.

Gevirtz, Stanley, "Jericho and Schechem: A Religio-Literary Aspect of City Destruction," *Vetus Testamentum*, Vol. 13, Fasc. 1. (1963), pp. 52–62.

Gray-Fow, Michael, "The Wicked Stepmother in Roman Literature and History: An Evaluation," *Latomus*, Vol. 47, No. 4 (1988), pp. 741–757.

Grayson, Albert Kirk, *Assyrian Royal Inscriptions, Part 2: From Tiglath-pileser I to Ashur-nasir-apli II*. Otto Harrassowitz, Wiesbaden. 1976. http://www.geocities.ws/farfarer2001/inscriptions/adad_nirari_1.htm

Griffin, Miram T., *Nero: The End of a Dynasty*. Yale University Press, New Haven and London, 1984.

Gruen, Erich S., "Cato and Hellenism," in *Culture and National Identity in Republican Rome. Cornell Studies in Classical Philology*, Vol. 52. Cornell University Press, Ithaca, NY, 1992, pp. 52–83.

Gyles, Mary Francis, "Nero Fiddled While Rome Burned," *The Classical Journal*, Vol. 42, No. 4 (January 1947), pp. 211–217.

Hallwell, B. L., "The Fall of Carthage," *CAH*, Vol. 7 (1954), 466 ff.

Hansen, Roger D., "Waste and Waste Water in imperial Rome," *Journal of the American Water Resources*, Vol. 19, No. 2 (1983), pp. 263–269. http://www.waterhistory.org/histories/rome

Hare, Augustus, *Walks in Rome*, 2 vols. W. Ibister & Co., London, 1875, p. 479. https://www.gutenberg.org/files/39308/39308-h/39308-h.htm

Hartogs, Jörgen, "The Dangerous Streets of Ancient Rome," *History, Archaeology, Folklore and So On*. June 13, 2016. https://historyandsoon.wordpress.com/2017/01/13/the-dangerous-streets-of-ancient-rome/

Harvey, Brian, "Graffiti from Pompeii," *Pompeiana*. http://www.pompeiana.org/Resources/Ancient/Graffiti%20from%20Pompeii.htm

Hillard, Tom, "Livia Drusilla," *Groniek*, Vol. 198 (2013), pp. 5–22.

Hopkins, John N. N., "The Cloaca Maxima and the Monumental Manipulation of Water in Archaic Rome," *The Waters of Rome*, Vol. 4 (March 2007), pp. 1–15.

Hornblower, Simon, and Antony Spawforth, editors, *The Oxford Classical Dictionary: The Ultimate Reference Work on the Classical World*. 3rd ed. Oxford University Press, Oxford, 1999.

Huxley, Aldous, *Antic Hay*. Chatto and Windus, London, 1923, p. 252. https://archive.org/details/in.ernet.dli.2015.94072/page/n259

Jackson, Dana, "From History to the Stage: An Account of Shakespeare's Adaptation of Julius Caesar," *Shakespeare Online*. http://shakespeare-online.com/essays/fromhistorytostage.html

Jan, Ludwig von, *Macrobii Ambrosii Theodosii Opera Quae Supersunt* (*Macrobius: The Saturnalia*), 2 vols., Typis et Sumptibus G. Bassii, Quedlinburg and Leipzig, 1848–1852. http://penelope.uchicago.edu/Thayer/E/Roman/Texts/Macrobius/Saturnalia/home.html

Joshel, Sandra R., Margaret Malamud, and Donald T. McGuire, Jr., editors, *Imperial Projections: Ancient Rome in Modern Popular Culture*. Johns Hopkins University Press, Baltimore and London, 2001.

Justice, Faith L., "Busting Gladiator Myths." September 9, 2015. https://faithljustice.com/busting-gladiator-myths/

Justice, Faith L., "A Day at the Pompeii Arena." October 5, 2015. https://faithljustice.com/tag/gladiators/

Kimball, Sara E., and Jonathan Slocum, *Hittite Online. Lesson 1. The Proclamation of Anittas*. Linguistics Research Center, University of Texas at Austin. https://lrc.la.utexas.edu/eieol/hitol/10

Knapp, Robert, "Fame and Death: Gladiators," in *Invisible Romans*. Harvard University Press, Cambridge, MA, 2011, pp. 265–289.

Koloski-Ostrow, Ann Olga, "The Archaeology of Sanitation in Roman Italy: Toilets, Sewers, and Water Systems," in *Studies in the History of Greece and Rome*. Edited by Robin Osborne, James Rives, and Richard J. A. Talbert. The University of North Carolina Press, Chapel Hill, 2015.

Koloski-Ostrow, Ann Olga, "Talking Heads: What Toilets and Sewers Tell Us about Ancient Roman Sanitation," *The Conversation*. November

19, 2015. https://theconversation.com/talking-heads-what-toilets-and-sewers-tell-us-about-ancient-roman-sanitation-50045

Kyle, Donald G., *Spectacles of Death in Ancient Rome*. Routledge, New York, 1998.

L.C.J., "The 'Vomitorium,'" *The Windsor Star*, Windsor, Ontario, CA, Friday March 26, 1926, p. 1. https://www.newspapers.com/image/500565039/?terms=Vomitorium

Law, Emma, "What Goes in Must Come Out: The Truth behind Ancient Rome's Vomitoriums," *Culture Trip*. November 13, 2017. https://theculturetrip.com/europe/italy/articles/what-goes-in-must-come-out-the-truth-behind-ancient-romes-vomitoriums/

Lhomond, Charles François, *De viris illustribus Urbis Romae a Romulo ad Augustum: ad usum sextae scholae*. Apud Colas, Lutetiae Parisiorum, 1779.

Little, Charles E., "The Authenticity and Form of Cato's Saying 'Carthago Delenda Est,'" *The Classical Journal*, Vol. 29, No. 6 (March 1934), pp. 429–435.

Livingston, Michael, editor, *The Siege of Jerusalem*. 2004. https://d.lib.rochester.edu/teams/text/livingston-siege-of-jerusalem

Low-Chappell, Samuel, "Bravery in the Face of Death: Gladiatorial Games and Those Who Watched Them," *Hirundo*, Vol. 13 (2014–2015). https://www.mcgill.ca/classics/files/classics/2014-15-03.pdf

Malloch, J. V., "Gaius' Bridge at Baiae and Alexander-Imitatio," *The Classical Quarterly*, Vol. 51, No. 1 (2001), pp. 206–217.

Manas, Alfonso, "New Evidence of Female Gladiators: The Bronze Statuette at the Museum für Kunst und Gewerbe at Hamburg," *The International Journal of the History of Sport*, Vol. 28, No. 18 (2011), pp. 2726–2752.

Manning, Helen L., "Relation of Bad Cookery to Intemperance," *Chronicle*, Kansas City, Kansas, August 28, 1890, p. 7. https://www.newspapers.com/clip/33958677/the_chronicle/

Manu, Lakkur, "The Torch Bearer and the Tutor: Prevalent Attitudes towards the Roman Empire in Imperial Britain," *Classics*, Spring 2006. https://web.stanford.edu/group/journal/cgi-bin/wordpress/wp-content/uploads/2012/09/Lakkur_Hum_2006.pdf

Matyszak, Phillip, *Classical Compendium: A Miscellany of Curious Facts, Bizarre Beliefs & Scandalous Gossip from Ancient Greece and Rome*. Thames and Hudson Ltd., London, 2009.

McCullogh, Anna, "Female Gladiators in Imperial Rome: Literary Context and Fact," *Classical World*, Vol. 101, No. 2 (Winter 2008), pp. 197–209.

McKeown, J. C., *A Cabinet of Roman Curiosities: Strange Tales and Surprising Facts from the World's Greatest Empire*. Oxford University Press, Oxford, 2010.

McManus, Barbara, "Gladiatorial Games." http://www.vroma.org/~bmcmanus/arena.html

Miles, Richard, *Carthage Must Be Destroyed: The Rise and Fall of an Ancient Civilization*. Viking, Published by the Penguin Group, New York. 2010.

Mommsen, Theodor, *The History of Rome*, Vol. 3. Translated with the author's sanction and additions, by the Reverend William P. Dickson, D.D., with a preface by Dr. Leonhard Schmitz. Charles Scribner's Sons, New York, 1888.

Mouratidis, John, "Nero: The Artist, the Athlete and His Downfall," *Journal of Sport History*, Vol. 12, No. 1 (Spring 1985), pp. 5–20.

Mudd, Mary, *I. Livia, The Counterfeit Criminal*. Trafford Publishing, Victoria, BC, 2005.

Mumford, Lewis, *The City in History: Its Origins, Its Transformations, and Its Prospects*. A Harvest Book. Harcourt, Inc., San Diego, New York, and London, 1961, p. 224.

Murray, Steven, "Female Gladiators of the Ancient Roman World," *Journal of Combative Sport*, July 2003. https://ejmas.com/jcs/jcsart_murray_0703.htm

National Geographic, "July 19, 64 CE: Great Fire of Rome," Resource Library 1. *This Day in Geographic History*. n.d. https://www.nationalgeographic.org/thisday/jul19/great-fire-rome/

Noy, David, "Wicked Stepmothers in Roman Society and Imagination," *Journal of Family History*, 16 (1991), pp. 345–361.

O'Donovan, Gerard, "Mary Beard Takes on Caligula, the Emperor with the Worst Reputation in History," *The Telegraph*. July 26, 2013. https://www.telegraph.co.uk/culture/tvandradio/10199155/Mary-Beard-takes-on-Caligula-the-emperor-with-the-worst-reputation-in-history.html

O'Gorman, Ellen, "Cato the Elder and the Destruction of Carthage," *Helios*, 31 (2004), pp. 96–123.

Pappas, Stephanie, "Purging the Myth of the Vomitorium," *Scientific American*. August 28, 2016. https://www.scientificamerican.com/article/purging-the-myth-of-the-vomitorium/

PBS, "Gladiators," *The Roman Empire in the First Century*. https://www.pbs.org/empires/romans/empire/gladiators.html

PBS, "The Great Fire of Rome," *Secrets of the Dead.* June 4, 2014. https://www.pbs.org/wnet/secrets/great-fire-rome-interactive/1588

Pylat, M. Félix, "A Frenchman's Account of an English Christmas," *Western Mail.* Thursday, January 5, 1871. https://www.newspapers.com/image/488823265/?terms=The%2B%22Vomitorium%22

Radin, Alice P., "'Fictitious Facts': The Case of the Vomitorium," *APAClassics. American Philological Association*, January 8, 2003. https://web.archive.org/web/20030320192257/http://www.apaclassics.org/AnnualMeeting/03mtg/abstracts/radin.html

Ridley, R. T., "To Be Taken with a Pinch of Salt: Destruction of Carthage," *Classical Philology*, Vol. 81, No. 2 (April 1986), pp. 140–146.

Ruebel, James S., "Cato and Scipio Africanus," *The Classical World*, Vol. 71, No. 3 (November 1977), pp. 161–173.

Sahotsky, Brian, "Adventures in Architectural Symbolism: The Use and Misuse of Rebuilding Programs in Ancient Rome," *Places*, Vol. 21, No. 1 (29 May 2009), pp. 1–13. http://escholarship.org/uc/item/1kt276xg

Schram, Wilke, van Opstal, and Cees Passchier, *Roman Aqueducts.* www.romanaqueducts.info/index.html

Scobie, Alex, "Slums, Sanitation, and Mortality in the Roman World," *KLIO*, Vol. 68 (1986), pp. 399–433.

Shakespeare, William, *Henry VI, Part III* (1590). http://shakespeare.mit.edu/3henryvi/full.html

Stevens, Susan T., "A Legend of the Destruction of Carthage," *Classical Philology*, Vol. 83, No. 1 (January 1988), pp. 39–41.

Sullivan, Tom, "Imaginations of Ancient Rome in 19th Century Historical Novels," *Ancient History: Resources for Teachers. A Publication of the Macquarie Ancient History Association.* Edited by Dr. J. Leah Beness. Macquarie Ancient History Association, Macquarie University, Sydney, Vols. 41–44 (2015), pp. 93–126.

Thürlemann, Silvia, "Ceterum censeo Carthaginem esse delendam," *Gymnasium*, Vol. 81 (1974), pp. 79–95.

Vehling, Joseph Dommers, *Cookery and Dining in Imperial Rome: A Bibliography, Critical Review and Translation of Apicius de re coquinaria.* W. M. Hill, Chicago, 1934.

Vesley, Mark, "Gladiatorial Training for Girls in the *Collegia Iuvenum* of the Roman Empire," *Echos du Monde Classique: Classical Views*, Vol. XLII, n.s. 17, No. 1 (1998), pp. 85–93.

Visonà, Paolo, "Passing the Salt: On the Destruction of Carthage Again," *Classical Philology*, Vol. 83, No. 1 (January 1988), pp. 41–42.

Vogel-Weidemann, Ursula, "Carthago Delenda Est: Aita and Prophasis," *Acta Classica*, Vol. XXXII (1989), pp. 79–95.
Wald, Chelsea, "Ancient Rome's Terrorizing Toilets," *Discover Magazine* (July/August 2014). http://discovermagazine.com/2014/julyaug/4-archeological-crap-shoot
Wald, Chelsea, "The Secret History of Ancient Toilets," *Nature*. May 24, 2016.https://www.nature.com/news/the-secret-history-of-ancient-toilets-1.19960
Warmington, B. H., "The Destruction of Carthage: A Retractio," *Classical Philology*, Vol. 83, No. 4 (October 1988), pp. 308–310.
Warmington, B. H., *Nero: Reality and Legend. Ancient Culture and Society*. General Editor, M. I. Finley. W.W. Norton, New York, 1969.
Watson, P. A., *Ancient Stepmothers: Myth, Misogyny and Reality*. Mnemosyne, Suppl. 143. E. J. Brill, Leiden, 1995.
Winkler, Martin M., editor, *Gladiator: Film and History*. Blackwell, Malden, MA, 2005.
Woodman, A. J., "Tiberius and the Taste of Power: The Year 33 in Tacitus," *Classical Quarterly*, Vol. 56, No. 1 (2006), pp. 175–189.
Ziogas, I., "Famous Last Words: Caesar's Prophecy on the Ides of March," *Antichthon*, Vol. 50 (2016), pp. 134–153. https://www.cambridge.org/core/journals/antichthon/article/famous-last-words-caesars-prophecy-on-the-ides-of-march/7FF70D923E8416A20D303429C292AF5E/core-reader

Index

Apicius, 143, 146–147, 150, 152
Appian, 62–63, 70, 191–195
   Civil Wars, 62–63, 70, 191, 195–196
   Punica, 2, 6–7, 14, 16, 17, 23–24, 26, 30–31, 143, 146, 147, 150
Aqueducts, 109, 165, 166, 168, 171, 172, 174, 180, 182, 212. *See also* Hygiene/Health
Augustan History (SHA)
   Hadrian, 180
   Heliogabulus, 143, 147, 178
Augustus Gaius, Julius Caesar, 2, 18, 52, 59, 60, 73–89, 92–96
   Cinna, 87, 92–93, 96
   his death, 75, 86, 92
   Livia, 92–95
   modesty, 155, 157–159
Aurelius Victor, *De Caesaribus*, 31, 77, 101

Baiae
   bridge of Caligula, 98
   Sin City, 98
   Xerxes I, 98
Brutus, Decimus, 62, 65–68
Brutus, Marcus Junius, 49–50, 51–59, 61–63, 65–70
   Dante's *Inferno*, 62, 68

Caesar, Julius, 49–77. *See also Et tu, Brute*; Ides of March, warning
   Caesar's Revenge, 52, 57–58
   Calpurnia, 54, 56, 62, 64
   Julius Caesar (1599), xi, 50
   military, 65, 67
   Pharsalia, Lucan, 51, 53
   Roman Senate, 49, 50, 56, 62, 63, 65
   Shakespearean quotes, 51
Caligula (Gaius Julius Caesar Germanicus), 58, 76, 80, 88, 97–111, 112–119, 150, 171, 179, 182, 222, 225–227, 231
   Agrippina the Elder, 49
   appearance, 103, 116
   assassination, 104, 119
   bridge of Baiae, 98
   Chaerea, 103–104, 118–119
   Drusilla, 98, 107, 111, 118
   Gemellus (death), 108, 110
   Germanicus, 97, 111–114

Caligula (Gaius Julius Caesar Germanicus) *(continued)*
  humor, 1–7, 109–111, 116–117
  incest, 78, 97, 99, 100–101, 105, 107, 111, 117
  Incitatus, 97, 98, 116
  nickname, 97, 113
  Philo Judaeus of Alexandria, 99, 104–105, 110
  Vespasian, 179, 182–183
  virtues, 109–111
Carthage, Carthaginians
  Cato (fear of), 1, 2, 13, 15, 20, 21
  destruction of, 3, 5, 6, 7, 8
  Hamilcar, 14
  Hannibal, 1, 3, 13, 14, 18, 19, 22, 25, 52
  Hannibal is at the gates, 1, 22
  Hasdrubal, 5, 6, 16, 17, 23
  Hasdrubal's wife, 9, 17, 24
  Macrobius (curse), 8
  Nepos, Cornelius, 30, 219
  Plautus, Titus Maccius, 14–15
    Poenulus, 15
      and negative Carthaginian stereotypes, 14–15
  Punic War, First, 1
  Punic War, Second, 1
  Punic War, Third, 2, 9
  Scipio Africanus (the younger), 2, 3, 5–8, 16, 17, 24–26
  Scipio Nasica, 22, 30–31, 38
    defense of Carthage
  Varro, Marcus Terrentius, *De re rustica* on Mago of Carthage, 19–20
  war elephants, 1, 13
Carthage must be destroyed, 2, 21–22, 27–31, 37–38, 51
Casca, Servilius, assassination of Julius Caesar, 50, 55–56, 63, 69, 70
Cassius Longinus, assassination of Julius Caesar, 55–56, 59, 62–63, 66–70
Cato the Elder
  ambivalence to Greek culture, 40–41
  austerity/modesty, 39
  Greek culture, Philhellenes, 27–29, 33–35, 38–39
  Latin versus Greek, 40
  opposition to luxury, 39–40
  Plutarch on, 28–29
  Scipio family, 27, 29, 36–39
Christianity and Christians
  and alleged persecution, x, xii–xiii, 135, 190, 192, 199
  and the fire of 64 CE, 124, 132, 135, 138
  Pliny/Trajan, 207
  social status, 134
Cicero, Marcus Tullius
  Agrarian Law, 2
  Atticus, 1, 144, 157
  Deiot, 144, 157
  Duties, 191
  Friends, 40, 157
  Good and Evil, 40, 43–44, 46
  On Old Age, 29, 30, 38, 40, 154
  Tusculan Disputations, 29, 34, 40, 189, 191, 196
Cithera, 132
Claudius, Tiberius Augustus Caesar Germanicus
  death, 125, 139
  debauchery and gluttony, 146, 153, 155, 191
  emperor, 76, 114, 121, 137, 139, 171
  naumachia, 202
Conspirators. *See* Brutus, Decimus; Brutus, Marcus Junius; Casca, Servilius; Cassius Longinus; Decimus Junius Brutus Albinus

INDEX

Decimus Junius Brutus Albinus, 68
Dio Cassius, *Roman History*
   on Caesar, 52, 58, 63, 70
   on Caligula, 98, 100–102, 108–110, 116, 118
   on Claudius, 191
   on Livia, 75–76, 82–87, 92, 95
   on Nero, 123–124, 130
   on Vitellius, 147, 155, 191
Dio Chrysostom, *Discourses*
   on Nero, 123
Diodorus Siculus, *Bibliotheca Historica*
   on Carthage, 2
   on Cato, 3

Et tu, Brute, 49–51, 53, 56–57, 61, 63
   Acolastus, His After-witte, 52, 57
   Caesar Infectus, xi, 51
   Henry VI, Shakespeare, xi, 52, 56–57, 125
   Julius Caesar, Shakespeare, 50–54, 58
   as a warning, 58, 61

Feasting and dining
   Petronius, *Satyricon*
      purging for health, 144, 154
      Trimalchio's feast, 146, 157, 160–161
      Vitellius, 155
   vomitorium
      Apion, *On the Luxury of Apicius*, 146
      architectural feature, 145, 157
      banqueting, importance of, 144, 157–160
      Claudius, 155
      exotic food and overeating, 143, 146–147, 150–152, 154–156, 162–163
      Lucullus, 146
      modern sources on vomitorium, 144–145, 147–150
      modesty, frugality (contrast with debauchery, excess and luxury), 86–88, 139, 155–158, 203, 210
      overeating debauchery, and moral decline, 143, 146, 157
      Roman sources on feasting, 150–154
Fire of 64 CE, 121–124, 129–140. *See also* Christianity and Christians; Nero; Suetonius; Tacitus, Cornelius

Gladiatorial Games
   "bread and circuses," 190–191, 198
   Christians. *See* Christianity and Christians
   Commodus, 202
   dwarves, 202
   end of games, 190
   oath, 189, 192
   Pollice verso (thumbs up/down), 191, 193, 198, 201
   Spartacus, 189, 191, 193–196
   women gladiators, 202, 203, 208–210

Horace, Quintus Horatius Flaccus, 2, 10, 185
Hygiene/Health
   aqueducts, vii, x, 109, 115, 165–168, 171, 172, 174, 180
   bacteria, 177, 179
   chamber pot, 166
   sponge sticks, 166, 179
   toilets, 165–169, 178–180, 187
   urine collection, 179
   baths, vii, x, 104, 165, 166–169, 171, 173, 175–177
   health risks, 179

Hygiene/Health *(continued)*
  Celsus, 166, 177, 180
  Cloaca Maxima (Great Sewer and sewers), 166
    cleaning, 168, 178
    construction, 167, 172
    hygiene, 177
    open sewers, 177–178, 181–182
  Frontinus, 167, 174
  Galen, 167–168
  Pliny the Elder, 166–169, 171, 172, 178
  Pliny the Younger, 182
  social aspects of bathing, 185
  Strabo, 167, 172
  Vespasian, 179, 182
  Vitruvius, 173, 178

Ides of March, warning, xi, 1, 50, 51, 56, 61–62, 64–65

Josephus, Titus Flavius, *Antiquities of the Jews*, 52, 98–99, 105–107, 111, 119
Juvenal, *Satires*, 32, 99, 123, 128, 156, 167, 179, 189, 191–192, 198, 202–203, 209

Livia Drusilla (Augusta)
  alleged murders, 73–78, 80–84, 87–88
  herbals, *Liviana* fig, 86
  political influence, 52, 60, 85–87, 93, 95
  scandal, 79–80
  stepmother myth, vii, 60, 73–75, 77–83, 85, 88
  Tiberius, 74–77, 81, 82, 86
  virtuous wife, vii, 85–86, 88–96

Martial, *epigrams*, 31, 40, 168, 178–179, 184, 186

Nero
  Agrippina the Younger, 126
  alleged arsonist, 122, 133–134
  artistic endeavors, 123
  Christians. *See* Fire of 64 CE
  death and aftermath, 122, 141
  decadence/tyrannical murders, 125–127
  negative reputation xiii, xiv, 121–124, 127–128, 138
  fiddle myth, 124–125, 132–133
  Fire of 64 CE. *See* Fire of 64 CE
  leadership skills, 132, 134, 137
  popularity, vii, 122–123, 139–141

Pliny the Elder, *Natural History*, 4, 12–13, 28–30, 37, 134, 146, 166–169, 171–172, 201
Pliny the Younger
  Epistles, 134, 155–156, 159, 178, 182, 202, 207, 209
  Panegyricus, 123
Plutarch
  Caesar, 205–206
  Carthage, 29–30
  Cato the Elder, 28–31, 34–35, 37, 39–41, 44, 46–47, 51
  C. Gracchus, 2
  Crassus, 191, 193–196
  Parallel Lives, 51, 54
  Shakespeare, 51, 54–55, 58, 63, 70, 146
Polybius, *Histories*, 5, 14, 17–18, 24–25, 39, 44-45

Sallust, *The War with Catiline*, 2, 74, 81
Salting and plowing
  Assyrian and Hittite, 4, 11–12
  Biblical references, 4, 11
  curse, 2–4
  destruction (ritual) of cities, 9–11
  fertilizer, 4–5, 12–13

Medieval references, 12
modern sources, 11
Roman references, 5–8, 24
Seneca the Younger
   on Baths and Socializing, 186
   on *bestiarius*, 179
   on Caligula, 98–100, 103, 111, 116–117
   on Carthage, 2
   on Gladiators, 191, 197
   on heated pools, 183
   on Livia, 87, 89–90
   on Scipio's simple bathroom, 175–177, 184–185
   on stepmother, 78
   on vomitoria, 143–145, 150, 156, 162
Suetonius
   on feasting, 143
   on gluttony, 144
   Grammarians, on Crates of Mallos, 177–178
   source for Shakespeare, 52
   The Twelve Caesars
      on Augustus (Livia), 75–77, 79–81, 85–87, 92, 157
      on Caesar, 49, 58, 62–64, 69
      on Caligula, 97–101, 106–107, 109–112, 116, 179
      on Claudius, 146, 153, 155, 192
      on Domitian, 202
      on Galba, 52, 59
      on Nero, 123–128, 130, 132, 139, 141, 178
      on Vespasian, 128
      on Vitellius, 147, 153–155

Tacitus, Cornelius
   Agricola
      on gladiators, 189
      on women gladiators, 203, 209
   Annals
      on Caligula, 99, 102
      on Christians, 134, 198
      on Galba, 58–59
      on Livia, 73–86, 88, 94–95
      on Nero, 123–124, 126, 128–129, 132–134
   Germania, xi
      on Roman extravagance, 146
   Histories
      on extravagance, 155
Theodoret, 190
Theophrastus, 4

Varro, 19–20
Vergil, 12
Vitruvius, 173, 183

Zoilus, 31–32

About the Author

Monica M. Bontty, who received her PhD in Near Eastern Languages and Cultures from the University of California at Los Angeles, is professor of history at the University of Louisiana at Monroe and a respected authority on ancient history. She has edited a monograph on ancient Mediterranean oil lamps and has reviewed a number of books on Roman and Greek history in professional journals. She has presented numerous lectures and led discussions on Roman history and Rome's control of Egypt.

www.ingramcontent.com/pod-product-compliance
Lightning Source LLC
Chambersburg PA
CBHW070247230426
43664CB00014B/2425